OTHER A TO Z THE SCARECI

1. *The A to Z of Buddhism* by Charles
2. *The A to Z of Catholicism* by Willi
3. *The A to Z of Hinduism* by Bruce N
4. *The A to Z of Islam* by Ludwig W. Adamec, 2002. *Out of Print. See No. 123.*
5. *The A to Z of Slavery and Abolition* by Martin A. Klein, 2002.
6. *Terrorism: Assassins to Zealots* by Sean Kendall Anderson and Stephen Sloan, 2003.
7. *The A to Z of the Korean War* by Paul M. Edwards, 2005.
8. *The A to Z of the Cold War* by Joseph Smith and Simon Davis, 2005.
9. *The A to Z of the Vietnam War* by Edwin E. Moise, 2005.
10. *The A to Z of Science Fiction Literature* by Brian Stableford, 2005.
11. *The A to Z of the Holocaust* by Jack R. Fischel, 2005.
12. *The A to Z of Washington, D.C.* by Robert Benedetto, Jane Donovan, and Kathleen DuVall, 2005.
13. *The A to Z of Taoism* by Julian F. Pas, 2006.
14. *The A to Z of the Renaissance* by Charles G. Nauert, 2006.
15. *The A to Z of Shinto* by Stuart D. B. Picken, 2006.
16. *The A to Z of Byzantium* by John H. Rosser, 2006.
17. *The A to Z of the Civil War* by Terry L. Jones, 2006.
18. *The A to Z of the Friends (Quakers)* by Margery Post Abbott, Mary Ellen Chijioke, Pink Dandelion, and John William Oliver Jr., 2006.
19. *The A to Z of Feminism* by Janet K. Boles and Diane Long Hoeveler, 2006.
20. *The A to Z of New Religious Movements* by George D. Chryssides, 2006.
21. *The A to Z of Multinational Peacekeeping* by Terry M. Mays, 2006.
22. *The A to Z of Lutheranism* by Günther Gassmann with Duane H. Larson and Mark W. Oldenburg, 2007.
23. *The A to Z of the French Revolution* by Paul R. Hanson, 2007.
24. *The A to Z of the Persian Gulf War 1990–1991* by Clayton R. Newell, 2007.
25. *The A to Z of Revolutionary America* by Terry M. Mays, 2007.
26. *The A to Z of the Olympic Movement* by Bill Mallon with Ian Buchanan, 2007.
27. *The A to Z of the Discovery and Exploration of Australia* by Alan Day, 2009.
28. *The A to Z of the United Nations* by Jacques Fomerand, 2009.
29. *The A to Z of the "Dirty Wars"* by David Kohut, Olga Vilella, and Beatrice Julian, 2009.
30. *The A to Z of the Vikings* by Katherine Holman, 2009.
31. *The A to Z from the Great War to the Great Depression* by Neil A. Wynn, 2009.
32. *The A to Z of the Crusades* by Corliss K. Slack, 2009.
33. *The A to Z of New Age Movements* by Michael York, 2009.
34. *The A to Z of Unitarian Universalism* by Mark W. Harris, 2009.
35. *The A to Z of the Kurds* by Michael M. Gunter, 2009.
36. *The A to Z of Utopianism* by James M. Morris and Andrea L. Kross, 2009.
37. *The A to Z of the Civil War and Reconstruction* by William L. Richter, 2009.

38. *The A to Z of Jainism* by Kristi L. Wiley, 2009.
39. *The A to Z of the Inuit* by Pamela K. Stern, 2009.
40. *The A to Z of Early North America* by Cameron B. Wesson, 2009.
41. *The A to Z of the Enlightenment* by Harvey Chisick, 2009.
42. *The A to Z Methodism* by Charles Yrigoyen Jr. and Susan E. Warrick, 2009.
43. *The A to Z of the Seventh-day Adventists* by Gary Land, 2009.
44. *The A to Z of Sufism* by John Renard, 2009.
45. *The A to Z of Sikhism* by William Hewat McLeod, 2009.
46. *The A to Z Fantasy Literature* by Brian Stableford, 2009.
47. *The A to Z of the Discovery and Exploration of the Pacific Islands* by Max Quanchi and John Robson, 2009.
48. *The A to Z of Australian and New Zealand Cinema* by Albert Moran and Errol Vieth, 2009.
49. *The A to Z of African-American Television* by Kathleen Fearn-Banks, 2009.
50. *The A to Z of American Radio Soap Operas* by Jim Cox, 2009.
51. *The A to Z of the Old South* by William L. Richter, 2009.
52. *The A to Z of the Discovery and Exploration of the Northwest Passage* by Alan Day, 2009.
53. *The A to Z of the Druzes* by Samy S. Swayd, 2009.
54. *The A to Z of the Welfare State* by Bent Greve, 2009.
55. *The A to Z of the War of 1812* by Robert Malcomson, 2009.
56. *The A to Z of Feminist Philosophy* by Catherine Villanueva Gardner, 2009.
57. *The A to Z of the Early American Republic* by Richard Buel Jr., 2009.
58. *The A to Z of the Russo-Japanese War* by Rotem Kowner, 2009.
59. *The A to Z of Anglicanism* by Colin Buchanan, 2009.
60. *The A to Z of Scandinavian Literature and Theater* by Jan Sjåvik, 2009.
61. *The A to Z of the Peoples of the Southeast Asian Massif* by Jean Michaud, 2009.
62. *The A to Z of Judaism* by Norman Solomon, 2009.
63. *The A to Z of the Berbers (Imazighen)* by Hsain Ilahiane, 2009.
64. *The A to Z of British Radio* by Seán Street, 2009.
65. *The A to Z of The Salvation Army* by Major John G. Merritt, 2009.
66. *The A to Z of the Arab-Israeli Conflict* by P. R. Kumaraswamy, 2009.
67. *The A to Z of the Jacksonian Era and Manifest Destiny* by Terry Corps, 2009.
68. *The A to Z of Socialism* by Peter Lamb and James C. Docherty, 2009.
69. *The A to Z of Marxism* by David Walker and Daniel Gray, 2009.
70. *The A to Z of the Bahá'í Faith* by Hugh C. Adamson, 2009.
71. *The A to Z of Postmodernist Literature and Theater* by Fran Mason, 2009.
72. *The A to Z of Australian Radio and Television* by Albert Moran and Chris Keating, 2009.
73. *The A to Z of the Lesbian Liberation Movement: Still the Rage* by JoAnne Myers, 2009.
74. *The A to Z of the United States–Mexican War* by Edward R. Moseley and Paul C. Clark, 2009.
75. *The A to Z of World War I* by Ian V. Hogg, 2009.
76. *The A to Z of World War II: The War Against Japan* by Ann Sharp Wells, 2009.
77. *The A to Z of Witchcraft* by Michael D. Bailey, 2009.

78. *The A to Z of British Intelligence* by Nigel West, 2009.
79. *The A to Z of United States Intelligence* by Michael A. Turner, 2009.
80. *The A to Z of the League of Nations* by Anique H. M. van Ginneken, 2009.
81. *The A to Z of Israeli Intelligence* by Ephraim Kahana, 2009.
82. *The A to Z of the European Union* by Joaquín Roy and Aimee Kanner, 2009.
83. *The A to Z of the Chinese Cultural Revolution* by Guo Jian, Yongyi Song, and Yuan Zhou, 2009.
84. *The A to Z of African American Cinema* by S. Torriano Berry and Venise T. Berry, 2009.
85. *The A to Z of Japanese Business* by Stuart D. B. Picken, 2009.
86. *The A to Z of the Reagan–Bush Era* by Richard S. Conley, 2009.
87. *The A to Z of Human Rights and Humanitarian Organizations* by Robert F. Gorman and Edward S. Mihalkanin, 2009.
88. *The A to Z of French Cinema* by Dayna Oscherwitz and MaryEllen Higgins, 2009.
89. *The A to Z of the Puritans* by Charles Pastoor and Galen K. Johnson, 2009.
90. *The A to Z of Nuclear, Biological and Chemical Warfare* by Benjamin C. Garrett and John Hart, 2009.
91. *The A to Z of the Green Movement* by Miranda Schreurs and Elim Papadakis, 2009.
92. *The A to Z of the Kennedy–Johnson Era* by Richard Dean Burns and Joseph M. Siracusa, 2009.
93. *The A to Z of Renaissance Art* by Lilian H. Zirpolo, 2009.
94. *The A to Z of the Broadway Musical* by William A. Everett and Paul R. Laird, 2009.
95. *The A to Z of the Northern Ireland Conflict* by Gordon Gillespie, 2009.
96. *The A to Z of the Fashion Industry* by Francesca Sterlacci and Joanne Arbuckle, 2009.
97. *The A to Z of American Theater: Modernism* by James Fisher and Felicia Hardison Londré, 2009.
98. *The A to Z of Civil Wars in Africa* by Guy Arnold, 2009.
99. *The A to Z of the Nixon–Ford Era* by Mitchell K. Hall, 2009.
100. *The A to Z of Horror Cinema* by Peter Hutchings, 2009.
101. *The A to Z of Westerns in Cinema* by Paul Varner, 2009.
102. *The A to Z of Zionism* by Rafael Medoff and Chaim I. Waxman, 2009.
103. *The A to Z of the Roosevelt–Truman Era* by Neil A. Wynn, 2009.
104. *The A to Z of Jehovah's Witnesses* by George D. Chryssides, 2009.
105. *The A to Z of Native American Movements* by Todd Leahy and Raymond Wilson, 2009.
106. *The A to Z of the Shakers* by Stephen J. Paterwic, 2009.
107. *The A to Z of the Coptic Church* by Gawdat Gabra, 2009.
108. *The A to Z of Architecture* by Allison Lee Palmer, 2009.
109. *The A to Z of Italian Cinema* by Gino Moliterno, 2009.
110. *The A to Z of Mormonism* by Davis Bitton and Thomas G. Alexander, 2009.
111. *The A to Z of African American Theater* by Anthony D. Hill with Douglas Q. Barnett, 2009.

112. *The A to Z of NATO and Other International Security Organizations* by Marco Rimanelli, 2009.
113. *The A to Z of the Eisenhower Era* by Burton I. Kaufman and Diane Kaufman, 2009.
114. *The A to Z of Sexspionage* by Nigel West, 2009.
115. *The A to Z of Environmentalism* by Peter Dauvergne, 2009.
116. *The A to Z of the Petroleum Industry* by M. S. Vassiliou, 2009.
117. *The A to Z of Journalism* by Ross Eaman, 2009.
118. *The A to Z of the Gilded Age* by T. Adams Upchurch, 2009.
119. *The A to Z of the Progressive Era* by Catherine Cocks, Peter C. Holloran, and Alan Lessoff, 2009.
120. *The A to Z of Middle Eastern Intelligence* by Ephraim Kahana and Muhammad Suwaed, 2009.
121. *The A to Z of the Baptists* William H. Brackney, 2009.
122. *The A to Z of Homosexuality* by Brent L. Pickett, 2009.
123. *The A to Z of Islam, Second Edition* by Ludwig W. Adamec, 2009.
124. *The A to Z of Buddhism* by Carl Olson, 2009.
125. *The A to Z of United States–Russian/Soviet Relations* by Norman E. Saul, 2010.
126. *The A to Z of United States–Africa Relations* by Robert Anthony Waters Jr., 2010.
127. *The A to Z of United States–China Relations* by Robert Sutter, 2010.
128. *The A to Z of U.S. Diplomacy since the Cold War* by Tom Lansford, 2010.
129. *The A to Z of United States–Japan Relations* by John Van Sant, Peter Mauch, and Yoneyuki Sugita, 2010.
130. *The A to Z of United States–Latin American Relations* by Joseph Smith, 2010.
131. *The A to Z of United States–Middle East Relations* by Peter L. Hahn, 2010.
132. *The A to Z of United States–Southeast Asia Relations* by Donald E. Weatherbee, 2010.
133. *The A to Z of U.S. Diplomacy from the Civil War to World War I* by Kenneth J. Blume, 2010.
134. *The A to Z of International Law* by Boleslaw A. Boczek, 2010.
135. *The A to Z of the Gypsies (Romanies)* by Donald Kenrick, 2010.
136. *The A to Z of the Tamils* by Vijaya Ramaswamy, 2010.
137. *The A to Z of Women in Sub-Saharan Africa* by Kathleen Sheldon, 2010.
138. *The A to Z of Ancient and Medieval Nubia* by Richard A. Lobban Jr., 2010.
139. *The A to Z of Ancient Israel* by Niels Peter Lemche, 2010.
140. *The A to Z of Ancient Mesoamerica* by Joel W. Palka, 2010.
141. *The A to Z of Ancient Southeast Asia* by John N. Miksic, 2010.
142. *The A to Z of the Hittites* by Charles Burney, 2010.
143. *The A to Z of Medieval Russia* by Lawrence N. Langer, 2010.
144. *The A to Z of the Napoleonic Era* by George F. Nafziger, 2010.
145. *The A to Z of Ancient Egypt* by Morris L. Bierbrier, 2010.
146. *The A to Z of Ancient India* by Kumkum Roy, 2010.
147. *The A to Z of Ancient South America* by Martin Giesso, 2010.

148. *The A to Z of Medieval China* by Victor Cunrui Xiong, 2010.
149. *The A to Z of Medieval India* by Iqtidar Alam Khan, 2010.
150. *The A to Z of Mesopotamia* by Gwendolyn Leick, 2010.
151. *The A to Z of the Mongol World Empire* by Paul D. Buell, 2010.
152. *The A to Z of the Ottoman Empire* by Selcuk Aksin Somel, 2010.
153. *The A to Z of Pre-Colonial Africa* by Robert O. Collins, 2010.
154. *The A to Z of Aesthetics* by Dabney Townsend, 2010.
155. *The A to Z of Descartes and Cartesian Philosophy* by Roger Ariew, Dennis Des Chene, Douglas M. Jesseph, Tad M. Schmaltz, and Theo Verbeek, 2010.
156. *The A to Z of Heidegger's Philosophy* by Alfred Denker, 2010.
157. *The A to Z of Kierkegaard's Philosophy* by Julia Watkin, 2010.
158. *The A to Z of Ancient Greek Philosophy* by Anthony Preus, 2010.
159. *The A to Z of Bertrand Russell's Philosophy* by Rosalind Carey and John Ongley, 2010.
160. *The A to Z of Epistemology* by Ralph Baergen, 2010.
161. *The A to Z of Ethics* by Harry J. Gensler and Earl W. Spurgin, 2010.
162. *The A to Z of Existentialism* by Stephen Michelman, 2010.
163. *The A to Z of Hegelian Philosophy* by John W. Burbidge, 2010.
164. *The A to Z of the Holiness Movement* by William Kostlevy, 2010.
165. *The A to Z of Hume's Philosophy* by Kenneth R. Merrill, 2010.
166. *The A to Z of Husserl's Philosophy* by John J. Drummond, 2010.
167. *The A to Z of Kant and Kantianism* by Helmut Holzhey and Vilem Mudroch, 2010.
168. *The A to Z of Leibniz's Philosophy* by Stuart Brown and N. J. Fox, 2010.
169. *The A to Z of Logic* by Harry J. Gensler, 2010.
170. *The A to Z of Medieval Philosophy and Theology* by Stephen F. Brown and Juan Carlos Flores, 2010.
171. *The A to Z of Nietzscheanism* by Carol Diethe, 2010.
172. *The A to Z of the Non-Aligned Movement and Third World* by Guy Arnold, 2010.
173. *The A to Z of Shamanism* by Graham Harvey and Robert J. Wallis, 2010.
174. *The A to Z of Organized Labor* by James C. Docherty, 2010.
175. *The A to Z of the Orthodox Church* by Michael Prokurat, Michael D. Peterson, and Alexander Golitzin, 2010.
176. *The A to Z of Prophets in Islam and Judaism* by Scott B. Noegel and Brannon M. Wheeler, 2010.
177. *The A to Z of Schopenhauer's Philosophy* by David E. Cartwright, 2010.
178. *The A to Z of Wittgenstein's Philosophy* by Duncan Richter, 2010.
179. *The A to Z of Hong Kong Cinema* by Lisa Odham Stokes, 2010.
180. *The A to Z of Japanese Traditional Theatre* by Samuel L. Leiter, 2010.
181. *The A to Z of Lesbian Literature* by Meredith Miller, 2010.
182. *The A to Z of Chinese Theater* by Tan Ye, 2010.
183. *The A to Z of German Cinema* by Robert C. Reimer and Carol J. Reimer, 2010.
184. *The A to Z of German Theater* by William Grange, 2010.

185. *The A to Z of Irish Cinema* by Roderick Flynn and Patrick Brereton, 2010.
186. *The A to Z of Modern Chinese Literature* by Li-hua Ying, 2010.
187. *The A to Z of Modern Japanese Literature and Theater* by J. Scott Miller, 2010.
188. *The A to Z of Old-Time Radio* by Robert C. Reinehr and Jon D. Swartz, 2010.
189. *The A to Z of Polish Cinema* by Marek Haltof, 2010.
190. *The A to Z of Postwar German Literature* by William Grange, 2010.
191. *The A to Z of Russian and Soviet Cinema* by Peter Rollberg, 2010.
192. *The A to Z of Russian Theater* by Laurence Senelick, 2010.
193. *The A to Z of Sacred Music* by Joseph P. Swain, 2010.
194. *The A to Z of Animation and Cartoons* by Nichola Dobson, 2010.
195. *The A to Z of Afghan Wars, Revolutions, and Insurgencies* by Ludwig W. Adamec, 2010.
196. *The A to Z of Ancient Egyptian Warfare* by Robert G. Morkot, 2010.
197. *The A to Z of the British and Irish Civil Wars 1637–1660* by Martyn Bennett, 2010.
198. *The A to Z of the Chinese Civil War* by Edwin Pak-wah Leung, 2010.
199. *The A to Z of Ancient Greek Warfare* by Iain Spence, 2010.
200. *The A to Z of the Anglo–Boer War* by Fransjohan Pretorius, 2010.
201. *The A to Z of the Crimean War* by Guy Arnold, 2010.
202. *The A to Z of the Zulu Wars* by John Laband, 2010.
203. *The A to Z of the Wars of the French Revolution* by Steven T. Ross, 2010.
204. *The A to Z of the Hong Kong SAR and the Macao SAR* by Ming K. Chan and Shiu-hing Lo, 2010.
205. *The A to Z of Australia* by James C. Docherty, 2010.
206. *The A to Z of Burma (Myanmar)* by Donald M. Seekins, 2010.
207. *The A to Z of the Gulf Arab States* by Malcolm C. Peck, 2010.
208. *The A to Z of India* by Surjit Mansingh, 2010.
209. *The A to Z of Iran* by John H. Lorentz, 2010.
210. *The A to Z of Israel* by Bernard Reich and David H. Goldberg, 2010.
211. *The A to Z of Laos* by Martin Stuart-Fox, 2010.
212. *The A to Z of Malaysia* by Ooi Keat Gin, 2010.
213. *The A to Z of Modern China (1800–1949)* by James Z. Gao, 2010.
214. *The A to Z of the Philippines* by Artemio R. Guillermo and May Kyi Win, 2010.
215. *The A to Z of Taiwan (Republic of China)* by John F. Copper, 2010.
216. *The A to Z of the People's Republic of China* by Lawrence R. Sullivan, 2010.
217. *The A to Z of Vietnam* by Bruce M. Lockhart and William J. Duiker, 2010.
218. *The A to Z of Bosnia and Herzegovina* by Ante Cuvalo, 2010.
219. *The A to Z of Modern Greece* by Dimitris Keridis, 2010.
220. *The A to Z of Austria* by Paula Sutter Fichtner, 2010.
221. *The A to Z of Belarus* by Vitali Silitski and Jan Zaprudnik, 2010.
222. *The A to Z of Belgium* by Robert Stallaerts, 2010.
223. *The A to Z of Bulgaria* by Raymond Detrez, 2010.

224. *The A to Z of Contemporary Germany* by Derek Lewis with Ulrike Zitzlsperger, 2010.
225. *The A to Z of the Contemporary United Kingdom* by Kenneth J. Panton and Keith A. Cowlard, 2010.
226. *The A to Z of Denmark* by Alastair H. Thomas, 2010.
227. *The A to Z of France* by Gino Raymond, 2010.
228. *The A to Z of Georgia* by Alexander Mikaberidze, 2010.
229. *The A to Z of Iceland* by Gudmundur Halfdanarson, 2010.
230. *The A to Z of Latvia* by Andrejs Plakans, 2010.
231. *The A to Z of Modern Italy* by Mark F. Gilbert and K. Robert Nilsson, 2010.
232. *The A to Z of Moldova* by Andrei Brezianu and Vlad Spânu, 2010.
233. *The A to Z of the Netherlands* by Joop W. Koopmans and Arend H. Huussen Jr., 2010.
234. *The A to Z of Norway* by Jan Sjåvik, 2010.
235. *The A to Z of the Republic of Macedonia* by Dimitar Bechev, 2010.
236. *The A to Z of Slovakia* by Stanislav J. Kirschbaum, 2010.
237. *The A to Z of Slovenia* by Leopoldina Plut-Pregelj and Carole Rogel, 2010.
238. *The A to Z of Spain* by Angel Smith, 2010.
239. *The A to Z of Sweden* by Irene Scobbie, 2010.
240. *The A to Z of Turkey* by Metin Heper and Nur Bilge Criss, 2010.
241. *The A to Z of Ukraine* by Zenon E. Kohut, Bohdan Y. Nebesio, and Myroslav Yurkevich, 2010.
242. *The A to Z of Mexico* by Marvin Alisky, 2010.
243. *The A to Z of U.S. Diplomacy from World War I through World War II* by Martin Folly and Niall Palmer, 2010.
244. *The A to Z of Spanish Cinema* by Alberto Mira, 2010.
245. *The A to Z of the Reformation and Counter-Reformation* by Michael Mullett, 2010.

The A to Z of Lesbian Literature

Meredith Miller

The A to Z Guide Series, No. 181

The Scarecrow Press, Inc.
Lanham, Maryland • Toronto • Plymouth, UK
2010

Published by Scarecrow Press, Inc.
A wholly owned subsidiary of
The Rowman & Littlefield Publishing Group, Inc.
4501 Forbes Boulevard, Suite 200, Lanham, Maryland 20706
http://www.scarecrowpress.com

Estover Road, Plymouth PL6 7PY, United Kingdom

Copyright ©2006 by Meredith Miller

All rights reserved. No part of this book may be reproduced in any form or by any electronic or mechanical means, including information storage and retrieval systems, without written permission from the publisher, except by a reviewer who may quote passages in a review.

British Library Cataloguing in Publication Information Available

Library of Congress Cataloging-in-Publication Data

The hardback version of this book was cataloged by the Library of Congress as follows:

Miller, Meredith, 1965–
 Historical dictionary of lesbian literature / Meredith Miller.
   p. cm. — (Historical dictionaries of literature and the arts ; no. 8)
 Includes bibliographical references.
 1. Lesbians' writings—Bio-bibliography—Dictionaries. 2. Lesbian authors—Biography—Dictionaries. 3. Lesbianism—Dictionaries. I. Title. II. Series.
PN491.3.M55 2006
809'.89206643—dc22   2005020658

ISBN 978-0-8108-7609-5 (pbk. : alk. paper)

∞™ The paper used in this publication meets the minimum requirements of American National Standard for Information Sciences—Permanence of Paper for Printed Library Materials, ANSI/NISO Z39.48-1992.
Printed in the United States of America

For Maia Pollio, the cleverest woman I know

Contents

Editor's Foreword *Jon Woronoff*	xv
Preface	xvii
Acknowledgments	xix
Acronyms and Abbreviations	xxi
Chronology	xxiii
Introduction	xxxi
THE DICTIONARY	1
Bibliography	221
About the Author	239

Editor's Foreword

Most of the categories appearing in this series on literature and the arts have grown relatively undisturbed out of a long tradition, but this is hardly the case for lesbian literature. Although there have been early examples in ancient times, it has only been over the past century or so (and more particularly in the past few decades) that the genre has experienced explosive growth, resulting in an amazing profusion of works. In the past, lesbian literature has been hidden, repressed, suppressed, banned, and even burned. Thus the history of the literature can be understood only in the broader context of the movement of lesbian liberation, as well as the various literary trends and periods in which it emerged, from classical to postmodernist. *The A to Z of Lesbian Literature* therefore has to delve into the past to uncover earlier works and also scrutinize those publications that are both openly and guardedly lesbian in nature. The main focus then becomes the authors of works of lesbian literature and the often restrictive context in which these works were created.

This latest historical dictionary was written by Meredith Miller, a Lesbian Avenger more than a decade ago and a student of women's literature before that. After studying in the United States, she moved to Great Britain to work toward her Ph.D. and eventually to teach. At present, she teaches English literature and creative writing at the College of St. Mark and St. John in Plymouth, England. Her *Feminism and the Lesbian Paperback in Postwar America* is soon to be published.

Jon Woronoff
Series Editor

Preface

To take on a task with the title *The A to Z of Lesbian Literature* is to confront, at once, one's own inadequacy. In a world where identities are both infinitely powerful and infinitely unstable, it seems arrogant to presume to define such a category. Nevertheless ideas of what it means to be lesbian, and therefore what it means for a woman to master her own sexuality within narrative, have evolved within particular strands of literature over the past few hundred years. My research in other areas has taught me that a category thought of as lesbian literature informed the identifications, and the material, political and sexual lives of many thousands of women. Therefore the category is as relevant as it is indefinable. I have done my humble best to give an idea of the development of the lesbian in literature, and of the cultural influences which informed that development. My hope is that this work will aid further, more in-depth study.

This dictionary has been created with the instability of the lesbian identity in mind. The list of its entries is not restricted by any strict notions of what a lesbian might be. Rather, it is hoped that the entries, taken together, will provide an idea of the factors that have influenced the development of the lesbian identity as an interaction between readers and writers of all kinds of literature—poetic, fictional, pornographic and scientific. A number of the most important critical and theoretical concepts that inform lesbian literary theory are also included. Thus, the dictionary could be used as a starting point for both historical and theoretical explorations of lesbian literature. I have focused primarily on English-language literature. French literary works and German.scientific works have had such an impact cross-culturally that many are included here. A strong tradition of South Asian lesbian literature exists and continues to grow, in English and in indigenous languages. I have done my best to give some idea of the scope of this literature and provide a starting point for future study. Likewise many lesbians in the Americas live and work in both English and Spanish and I have tried to provide an idea of the bilingual literature of the Latina lesbian. Occasionally, I have included entries on women writing in the Arabic world, Sub-Saharan Africa and East Asia. Usually this is where these works have been influential in English translations, but I also hope they give some sense of the gaps in my own knowledge and the inadequacy of an Anglo-centric picture of lesbian literature. I hope they will point toward the exciting work that is emerging globally and lead English-speaking readers to further research.

Acknowledgments

I would like to thank the Lesbian Herstory Archives, Brooklyn, New York, for inspiration and practical assistance over the past seven years of research on this and other projects. Both Shamira Meghani and Diana Wallace have shared their expert knowledge, their friendship and their libraries with me. Paulina Palmer and Alan Sinfield have been supportive beyond anything I deserve over the past four years. If not for Vincent Quinn's kind remembrance I would not have written this dictionary. Finally, my friends and students at The College of St. Mark and St. John have made life unexpectedly bearable, and even (for an academic) fun, while I finished this book.

Acronyms and Abbreviations

BBC British Broadcasting Corporation
B.C.E. Before Christian Era
C.E. Christian Era
D.O.B. Daughters of Bilitis
LGBTQ Lesbian, Gay, Bisexual, Transgendered, Queer
NAACP National Association for the Advancement of Colored People
NOW National Organization for Women (USA)
SM Sado-Masochism

Chronology

c. 630 B.C.E. Birth of the poet Sappho on the Island of Lesbos. Her poems are popular and well respected for the next several centuries.

380 C.E. Gregory of Nazianzus orders the burning of Sappho's work.

c. 550 The Sanskrit language book known as the *Kama Sutra* is compiled from a number of older sources. In it, women are classified according to economic, sexual and social relationships, including those that are independent of men.

1001 The Arabic language poet Walladah bint Al-Mustakfi is born in what is now Spain. Her poetry argues for the equality of women and celebrates her passion for a female lover.

1073 Pope Gregory VII orders the second burning of Sappho's work.

1098 Birth of the philosopher, composer, poet and mystic Hildegard of Bingen in Germany. Her medical works contain what may be the first description of the female orgasm. Hildegard wields such influence that when her "special companion," a woman named Ricardis, is assigned to a separate convent, she writes to the Pope in anger, and is taken seriously.

1248 Angela of Folignio is born in Umbria (now Italy). After the deaths of her husband and children (for which she prayed to God) she founds an all female independent community and begins recording her visions through a confessor. At this period, a number of all female lay communities (whose members are often referred to as beguines) exists throughout France and Italy.

1405 Christine de Pizan writes *The Book of the City of Ladies*.

1516 Ludovico Ariosto's *Orlando Furioso* first appears in print in Venice.

1611 Thomas Middleton and Thomas Dekker's popular play *The Roaring Girl* fictionalizes the life of the cross-dressing pick-pocket Mary Frith.

1620 The Pamphlet *Hic Mulier* (The Male Woman) is published in London. It decries the fashionable practice of cross-dressing and the breakdown of traditional gender roles.

1648 Juana Asbaje (Later Sor Juan De La Cruz) is born on a rural plantation in Mexico. As an adult she writes a number of philosophical and mathematical treatises, secular plays and romantic poems celebrating her love for Maria Luisa, condesa de Paredes, wife of the Spanish colonial viceroy.

1732 William King publishes a long humorous poem entitled *The Toast*. The poem uses lesbian as an adjective in its first (1732) edition and as a noun in a later (1736) printing.

1748–1749 John Cleland's *Fanny Hill* first published. The novel contains explicit descriptions of lesbian sex, as well as a contented (if unsympathetic) bisexual woman character.

1760 The French philosopher and fiction writer Denis Diderot finishes his novel *La Religieuse (The Nun)*, a pornographic fantasy about a young nun who is corrupted by a lesbian abbess. This is the first full-length novel with a sustained lesbian theme.

1780 Eleanor Butler and Sarah Ponsonby (known as the Ladies of Llangollen) declare their love for each other and elope from Ireland to Wales where their scholarly and secluded lifestyle, recorded in their journals, is much admired by romantic writers.

1788 Mary Wollstonecraft publishes *Mary: A Fiction*, which gives a fictional account of one of Wollstonecraft's own romantic friendships.

1791 Olympe de Gouges publishes the feminist manifesto "A Declaration of The Rights of Women and Female Citizens," challenging, among other things, the institution of marriage.

1792 Mary Wollstonecraft publishes *A Vindication of the Rights of Woman*.

1793 Olympe de Gouges is executed in Paris.

1796 Denis Diderot's *La Religieuse* (*The Nun*) first published.

1797 Mary Wollstonecraft dies of complications after the birth of her daughter, the novelist Mary Godwin (later Shelley).

c. 1800 Birth of the Chinese poet WuTsao whose tremendously popular work often celebrates her love for various female courtesans.

1847 Charlotte Brontë publishes *Jane Eyre*. Some call the novel seditious. It describes a woman's sexual desire in forceful and active language.

1848 First women's rights convention held in Seneca Falls, New York. The "Declaration of Sentiments" (a feminist manifesto) is signed there by many noted abolitionists and feminists.

1851 The abolitionist and feminist Sojourner Truth delivers her famous "Ain't I a Woman" speech at an antislavery convention in Acron, Ohio. The speech deconstructs culturally accepted norms of femininity.

1862 Christina Rossetti publishes the poem "Goblin Market," an allegory that depicts the salvation of a "fallen" woman through a sensuous lesbian encounter. The poem is not read as lesbian until the 20th century.

1870 Adolphe Belot publishes *Mademoiselle Giraud, ma femme*, the first novel about female same-sex desire in which the influence of sexology can be clearly traced.

1880 Emile Zola publishes the novel *Nana*. This contains the first depiction of a modern, recognizably lesbian subculture.

1886 Henry James publishes his novel *The Bostonians*, which depicts the struggle between a young man and an older feminist for the affections of a young girl.

1895 Sigmund Freud and Josef Breuer publish *Studies on Hysteria* in Germany.

1897 Magnus Hirschfeld founds the Scientific Humanitarian Committee. The Committee eventually publishes 23 volumes of the journal *Yearbook for Sexual Science*. Havelock Ellis begins publication of *Studies* *in the Psychology of Sex*, which introduces the idea of sexual inversion to the public. The book is prosecuted for obscenity in the United Kingdom.

1900 Colette first publishes *Claudine à l'école* (*Claudine at School*).

1903 The American-French poet Renée Vivien (Pauline Tarn) translates surviving fragments of Sappho's poetry into modern French. Vivien models her life on Sappho's, thus creating a template for the modernist lesbian identity.

1904 At an event sponsored by the Scientific Humanitarian Committee in Berlin, Anna Rüling delivers a speech entitled, "What Interest Does the Women's Movement Have in Solving the Homosexual Problem?"

1906 The Eulenberg scandal breaks in Germany, revealing the homosexual activity of several ranking government officials. This leads to a suppression of lesbian and gay publishing, which does not revive until the era of the Weimar Republic.

1910 The first works of Sigmund Freud are translated into English. Gertrude Stein and Alice B. Toklas establish a house together in Paris, which becomes one of the focal points for the modernist movement.

1915 The English transgender journal *Urania* begins publishing. The journal includes lesbianism in its broad positive vision of the breakdown of gender roles in modern society. *Urania* remains in publication, privately circulated, until 1940.

1916 Angelina Weld Grimké's antiracist, feminist play *Rachel* is performed in Washington, D.C.

1919 Magnus Hirschfeld founds the Institute for Sexual Science in Berlin. Lesbian Sylvia Beach opens the bookshop Shakespeare and Company in Paris. The shop becomes a gathering place for modernist writers.

1920 Sholem Asch's Yiddish-language play *The God of Vengeance*, which features a lesbian character, is prosecuted for vice in New York City.

1920s Throughout this decade, in the progressive atmosphere of the Weimar Republic, at least five national lesbian magazines are in print in Germany.

1924   Radclyffe Hall wins the French *Prix Femina, étranger* for her novel *The Unlit Lamp*.

1925   Helene Deutsch publishes *The Psychology of Women's Sexual Functions*, the first psychoanalytic work devoted entirely to women.

1928   Ma Rainey records "Prove It On Me," the most famous of many lesbian Blues songs of the 1920s and 1930s. Publication of *Ladies Almanack* by Djuna Barnes, *The Well of Loneliness* by Radclyffe Hall and *Orlando* by Virginia Woolf. The publishers of *The Well of Loneliness* are prosecuted for obscenity in the United Kingdom. This results in the novel being banned there.

1929   Publishers of *The Well of Loneliness* are prosecuted in the United States. Here the prosecution is unsuccessful and the book remains in print for decades.

1933   A group of Nazi youth destroy virtually all of the contents of the archives of the Insitute for Sexual Science in Berlin. Photos of this event are frequently reproduced generically as "Nazi's burning books." Countless historical and literary documents relating to lesbian sexuality are destroyed. Christa Winsloe publishes *The Child Manuela*, a novel based on the script of the earlier all-female film production *Mädchen in Uniform*, a lesbian school romance. The journalist Lorena Hickok resigns her position as a White House correspondent with the Associated Press because she feels that her relationship with Eleanor Roosevelt impairs her objectivity.

1934   Lillian Hellman's play *The Children's Hour* is first performed on Broadway.

1936   Djuna Barnes first publishes the novel *Nightwood*.

1939   Publication of Daphne Du Maurier's *Rebecca*. The tremendous success of this novel, with its specter of lesbian desire, initiates a formula for the mass market romance. *Diana: A Strange Autobiography*, the first of the classic "lesbian pulp" paperbacks is published in the United States.

1939–1942   The American feminist Betty Friedan studies at Smith College with the Marxist-feminist lesbian, Dorothy Wolff-Douglas, who is a clear but unacknowledged influence on the development of her political consciousness.

1942 Ismat Chugtai publishes her short story "Lihaaf" ("The Quilt"), which details both lesbian and gay male relationships. She is prosecuted for obscenity by the British Raj.

1947 "Lisa Ben" (Edythe Ede) self publishes the first issue of the lesbian paper *Vice Versa*. Nine issues in all are published in 1947 and 1948.

1948 The ban on Radclyffe Hall's *The Well of Loneliness* in the United Kingdom is lifted and the novel enters lending libraries for the first time, making it available to a wide range of readers.

1950 Mattachine Society and the antiracist homophile organization, Knights of the Clock are founded in California.

1952 December: The Committee for the Investigation of Current Pornographic Materials holds hearings in Washington, D.C. Lesbian pulp fiction, among other literature, is held up to public scrutiny and defended by publishers.

1953 Patricia Highsmith publishes the lesbian novel *The Price of Salt* under the pseudonym Claire Morgan.

1955 The American lesbian organization Daughters of Bilitis is founded and begins establishing a number of lesbian lending libraries at its branches throughout the 1950s and 1960s.

1956 Jeannette Foster publishes the groundbreaking study *Sex Variant Women in Literature*. The Daughters of Bilitis begin publishing *The Ladder*. Publication continues, under changing editorial styles until the 1970s.

1957 Ann Bannon publishes her first novel, *Odd Girl Out*, with Fawcett Publications. Fawcett quickly becomes a center for "lesbian pulp" publishing. Under the editorship of Fiona Nevler in the early 1960s Bannon and Valerie Taylor are able to publish lesbian novels without being held to formulaic unhappy endings.

1959 Lorainne Hansberry becomes the first black American to win the Drama Critics Circle Award for *A Raisin in the Sun*.

1963 Adrienne Rich publishes *Snapshots of a Daughter-in-Law*.

c. 1964 Mattachine Society organizes a regular lesbian and gay picket of the White House in Washington, D.C. Jane Rule publishes *Desert of* *the Heart*, a landmark lesbian romance in which the characters have an uncomplicated happy ending.

1966 Maureen Duffy first publishes the novel *Microcosm*, which fictionalizes London lesbian subculture.

1969 Gay Women's Liberation Group founded in California. Isabel Miller publishes *A Place for Us* (later *Patience and Sarah*). Monique Wittig publishes *Les Guérillières*, an epic about a war between amazon and patriarchal warriors.

1968 Bisexual writer Kate Millet publishes the groundbreaking literary study *Sexual Politics*, which gives a feminist reading of canonical male authors.

1970 A Woman's Place, the first Women's Book Store in the United States, is founded in Oakland, California. Radicalesbians publish "The Woman-Identified-Woman Manifesto." Feminist lesbian Shulamith Firestone publishes the radical feminist classic *The Dialectic of Sex*. The Gay Liberation Front begins organizing in New York and London.

1971 Isabel Miller wins the first American Library Association Award for Gay and Lesbian Literature for *Patience and Sarah* (first published in 1969). *The Lesbian Tide*, possibly the first U.S. magazine to use the word lesbian in its title, begins private publication. Judy Grahn first publishes *Edward the Dyke and Other Poems*.

1973 The Boston Women's Health Book Collective begins publishing the self-help book *Our Bodies, Ourselves*, which revolutionizes American women's relationship to health care. Barbara Grier and Donna MacBride found Naiad Press, which gradually becomes the largest and most successful lesbian press in the world.

1974 "Combahee River Collective Statement" first published. The statement articulates a lesbian-centered, antiracist black feminism. Valerie Taylor and others organize the Lesbian Writer's Conference in Chicago.

1975 Joanna Russ' novel *The Female Man* popularizes lesbian science fiction.

1981 Philosopher and activist Angela Y. Davis publishes *Women, Race and Class*. Gloria Anzaldúa and Cherrie Moraga publish the edited collection *This Bridge Called My Back: Writings by Radical Women of Color*.

1984 Barbara Wilson first publishes *Murder in the Collective*, which inaugurates the lesbian crime fiction genre.

1987 Barbara Smith, Patricia Bell Scott and Gloria T. Hull publish the influential black feminist anthology *All the Women Are White, All the Blacks Are Men, But Some of Us Are Brave*. Gloria Anzaldúa publishes *Borderlands/La Frontera*, positing a new model of identity based on blending and liminality.

1988 The American organization Lambda Literary Foundation institutes awards for Lesbian and Gay Writing. Helena Whitbread edits and publishes the sexually explicit diaries of the early 19th-century English lesbian landowner Anne Lister, thus demonstrating that a conscious lesbian identity is older than had been previously assumed.

1989 Lesléa Newman publishes the children's book *Heather Has Two Mommies*, about a child who has two lesbian parents.

1990 Sakhi, India's first openly lesbian collective, makes a public statement in the Bombay-based Gay magazine *Bombay Dost*. Sakhi founds the Jami Project lesbian archives in Delhi. Publication of Judith Butler's *Gender Trouble: Feminism and the Subversion of Identity* marks a new set of questions about womanhood, feminism, gender and sexuality and heralds the height of the Lesbian Studies movement in academia.

1992 Novelist Sarah Schulman and others form the Lesbian Avengers and publish "The Dyke Manifesto." Dorothy Allison publishes *Bastard Out of Carolina*. Death of the poet and essayist Audre Lorde.

1993 Leslie Feinberg first publishes the influential novel *Stone Butch Blues*, articulating a transgender lesbian identity.

1994 Anchee Min first publishes *Red Azalea: Life and Love in China*.

1998 Pat Califia first publishes *Macho Sluts*, which vastly influences lesbian pornography. The English novelist Sarah Waters achieves large-scale publishing success for her first novel *Tipping the Velvet*. Lesbian fiction becomes a globally marketable commodity.

2003 Death of the writer and theorist Monique Wittig.

2004 May: Death of the writer and theorist Gloria Anzaldúa.

Introduction

WHAT IS A LESBIAN ANYWAY?

Throughout the early 1970s, a debate around lesbian sexuality and lesbian rights was raging within the feminist movement. In the United States, "mainstream" feminist organizations publicly debated the relationship between lesbianism and feminism. In 1970, the American group National Organization for Women (NOW) defeated a resolution for the support of equal rights for lesbian women. Betty Friedan—author of *The Feminine Mystique* (1963), the book that is said to have inspired the second wave of feminism—was one of the resolution's chief opponents. By 1971 the NOW convention passed a resolution in support of lesbian and bisexual women. Again in 1973, the debate flared up, and Friedan expressed the fear that "anti-male" lesbians sought to dominate the women's movement. Finally, in 1977 Friedan supported a lesbian rights resolution at the NOW annual convention.[1] Lesbians would seem to be, by definition, *women* who love women, and yet many feminists have not appeared to include lesbians in the category, "woman," which they sought to champion.

Behind this argument was a fundamental question. What is the relationship between the category "lesbian" and the category "woman"? Feminism purported to represent "women," to make the oppression of women visible and to fight for the liberation of women. The most significant criticisms of white, middle-class American feminism have pointed out the blindness that feminist arguments embody regarding race. "All" women often meant all white women, and implicitly all heterosexual, white, middle-class women. Thus the feminist movement galvanized a huge fight for the right to legalized abortion while in the same nation at the same time black and Native American women were being sterilized without their own consent in the thousands.[2] What did feminists mean when they used the term "women" to describe the category they represented? What does lesbian mean and how does it relate to the category women? What is the real relationship between the feminist movement and the increasing visibility of lesbians in culture?

These questions are relevant here because the development of feminism and the development of the lesbian identity have progressed hand in hand in Western culture. The struggle for sexual autonomy and the struggle for sexual determination are common to lesbians and feminists. More importantly here, the creation of a space in culture (most significantly and enduringly in literature) where women can articulate agency and reject the passive requisite of femininity might be said to be the primary aim of feminism. The gains made by feminism in this respect have directly enabled the visibility of the lesbian identity. Likewise, many of the women most instrumental in pushing for feminist change have loved each other. Mary Wollstonecraft, often thought of as the Enlightenment "mother" of English-language feminism, spent a large part of one of her most significant works (*Mary: A Fiction*, 1788) describing her romantic attachment to another young woman.

Categories of masculine and feminine have traditionally been correlated with active and passive desires, respectively. The feminine position has been described, and often policed, as one of passivity. From at least the late 16th century, one can see a clear tradition in English-language writing by women, whereby arguments are made for the expression of active desires in women. Lesbianism, by its very nature, implies an active female sexuality. If the "heterosexual contract," as Monique Wittig has called it, stipulates that the male is the active and the female the passive sexual partner, then at least one member of a lesbian couple has stepped out of her prescribed role, by asserting agency. Therefore both lesbians and feminists challenge the culturally accepted definition of "woman." Hence popular misconceptions that conflate the two categories. This is also the origin of Monique Wittig's argument that, if woman is merely a culturally constructed position of passivity, then lesbians are not women. The subject of this dictionary is therefore unstable. We can never quite know what lesbian means. We can know that, since the advent of modernity, it has been a challenge, sometimes a revolutionary challenge, to existing structures of power when women declare their love for one another. This idea of the lesbian arises when culture begins to ask itself questions about the nature of sexual power.

Thus the same era that gave rise to early debates that might be called feminist (the 17th century) gives us the first idea of a figure we might call lesbian in the modern sense.

The term lesbian entered the English language from the Greek and owes its prominence to the classical bent of many European scholars. Neoclassicism in the early modern period gave rise to the use of the word lesbian to describe women who had romantic and sexual attachments to other women. The term did not necessarily mean, as it does today, that these women would live together, independently of men. Prior to the use of lesbian, the ancient Latin and Greek word tribade described women who had sex with each other. The *Concise Oxford Dictionary* describes tribade as deriving both from the Greek for "lewd woman" and from the verb *trib*, to rub. Thus tribadism, as a verb, clearly marks a male language, which cannot imagine sex in the absence of the penis. Lesbian came into use as an allusion to the Greek language poet Sappho, whose few surviving fragments of work speak of her love for women and her life in a female community. Thus, this term focuses on romantic classical allusion and the idea of woman-centered community, rather than on imagined sexual acts.

It is tempting to think of lesbian, as it is tempting to think of all identity categories, as stable and clearly limited. As popularly conceived, lesbians are women who have no feelings for men, who feel sexual desire for women and who live independently of patriarchal control. A lesbian is a lesbian because she is born that way, and remains so for all of her life. Yet this definition fits very few of the women whose literature is significant to the development of that very lesbian identity. What of a woman like Virginia Woolf, whose only real passion may have been for other women, but who lived with a husband she loved and may never have enjoyed physical sex of any kind? What of Sor Juan De La Cruz, a nun whose poetry speaks of her love for another woman, but whose primary struggle in life was between the secular and the spiritual, rather than between any of the sexual identity categories we might place her in today? What of the many medieval women mystics, who often lived in all female communities with particular attachments to female companions, and who often bravely fought for freedom from heterosexual marriage, but whose primary articulated sexual desire was for the dead body of Christ? The category lesbian, as it is popularly defined today, cannot contain any of these women or their desires. Yet all of them are instrumental in the development of that very category and all of them belong to a history of resistance to heterosexual structures of power. The contemporary category lesbian, embodying both ideas of women's sexual desire for each other, and their economic and social independence from men, has been tremendously challenging and useful. It has provided a focus for the liberation struggles of hundreds of thousands of women, and even a bridge, in some cases, for organizing across boundaries of class, race, religion and ethnicity. Lesbian activists, working from this position, have often pushed the feminist movement forward.

Feminism as a challenge to gender inequality, is a challenge to those very same structures of heterosexual power. Prescribed male and female roles, ideas of masculine and feminine normality, all exist as props to a power structure that privileges men and upper-class, white women. Black men, as well as black and white women, suffer from the imposition of sex and gender norms. These structures are far more complex than popular conceptions of separate liberation movements might make them. Therefore challenges to feminism from lesbians and other black and working-class women are challenges that broaden and redefine the movement itself, giving a more realistic picture of what feminism might actually be.

The category lesbian is a fairly recent invention. Sappho, whose life and place of birth give rise to the term, would not have understood it as many of us understand it today. Though individual women have perhaps always loved each other, and though they may have often congregated and communicated in subcultural groups, sexual identities are historically contingent. They change with time and women who love other women fit into their cultures in ever changing ways. This introduction will discuss the history of theories of lesbian identity in more depth below. First, however, we might think about what the category "lesbian literature" might mean.

WHAT IS LESBIAN LITERATURE?

Possibly the first attempts to catalog and interpret literature dealing with homosexuality, in both men and women, were made in Germany from about 1900. The Jewish gay sexologist Magnus Hirschfeld published a journal, *Jahrbuch fur sexuelle Zwischenstufen* from 1900. In the

Jahrbuch, Hirschfeld regularly listed all recently published works with lesbian, gay or transgender themes. The American Jeannette Foster, who drew on Hirschfeld's work, might be thought of as the first great scholar of a specifically lesbian literature. She published her most important work, *Sex Variant Women in Literature,* in 1956. It is significant that Foster was an independent researcher. The acknowledgments of the famous "Kinsey Report," *Sexual Behavior in the Human Female* (1953), credit Foster as the librarian on Kinsey's project for four years. Though she worked as a librarian at what would become The Kinsey Institute, and elsewhere, no library or academic institution funded Foster's work. She worked for 40 years to collect and compile information on virtually every Western European and North American source for the depiction of female gender deviance or same-sex desire in literature. *Sex Variant Women in Literature* does not use the term lesbian to describe the category of literature it discusses. Indeed, it cannot be said to delineate any single category of literature at all. Foster uses the term "sex variance," which she borrows from the sexologist George Henry. Henry worked with a group of researchers in New York City for several decades in the mid-20th century. He used the term sex variance to describe any characteristics or behaviors that deviate from masculine and feminine heterosexual norms. Thus, what we would now term transgender movement is included along with bisexual and lesbian identities and behaviors. Foster uses this framework of Henry's to create a special reading practice in her study of the history of women's sexuality in literature.[3]

The term sex variance gives Foster a greater latitude than the term lesbian would. It also solves obvious historical and literary difficulties. Anything strictly defined as lesbian literature could only go as far back as the early 18th century, at best, and would be confined to very specific social and cultural areas. Literature that had been tremendously significant to lesbians, but was written by men like Charles Baudelaire and Pierre Louÿs, could not be included. The development of what would become the lesbian identity in literature evolved through texts like Sarah Scott's *Millenium Hall* and Emile Zola's *Nana*, which, in various ways, might not fit the definition of lesbian literature. Foster focuses on representation, rather than on the identities of authors. This enables her to trace the development of women's desire in literature and to include nearly all of the literature that may have been important to women readers seeking to understand dissident sexual identities.[4] In that sense, her study focuses on readers, rather than on the authors of texts.

Beginning in the 1960s and moving into academia in the 1980s and 1990s with the expansion of women's studies and gay and lesbian studies, a number of anthologies and critical works focused on the lesbian identity. This identity was put to a variety of ideological uses and in the process much valuable literature was recovered and republished. Our understanding of women writers such as Aphra Behn, Sarah Scott and Emily Dickinson was expanded or radically changed by the Lesbian Studies movement. Numerous anthologies of contemporary writing sought to define ever more specific identity positions within the overall category lesbian.

Terry Castle's recent volume, *The Literature of Lesbianism: A Historical Anthology from Ariosto to Stonewall* is dedicated to Jeanette Foster. Castle, like Foster, chooses items for inclusion on the basis of representation of love between women, rather than on author identity. Using a methodology based on the historical philosophy of Michel Foucault, she focuses on what she calls the "lesbian topos" in Western literature. Castle traces the development of *the idea* of the lesbian in Western culture. Thus, like Foster, she looks at male and female authors, and at both positive and negative portrayals of women who desired other women.

Jeannette Foster, like many scholars of homosexual literature and culture, begins with classical Greece. The influence of classical studies on studies of sexuality in the West has been tremendous. From 19th-century sexologists to post-modern historians like Michel Foucault, the classical Greek world has functioned as a kind of originary moment for lesbian and gay identities as we have come to understand them. At the same time, orientalist studies have affected fanciful Western notions of sexual deviance and excess. In the literature translated by orientalist scholars, Western writers have found rich expressions of male homoeroticism. Travel accounts and political histories have also fed fantasies about the all-female environments that existed in Arab countries and their colonies. These have influenced decadent European literature for centuries.

From the classical world Foster moves to medieval ballads, which she says are probably influenced by tales translated from the Arabic. These are humorous tales of cross-dressing and gender confusion, rather than tales of active female desire. Foster cites a ballad called *Huon of Bordeaux* (c. 1220) as the earliest of these. In a world dominated, defined and segregated by ideas of gender, in which the maintenance of both masculinity and femininity, and the distinction between male and female bodies is one of the primary organizing principles of culture, it is natural that anxieties around gender confusion would often be expressed. Tales in which women dress as men in order to escape danger or attain freedom are common from the Middle Ages through the early modern period in Europe and from the classical period in South Asia. In many of these tales another women falls for the woman in her male disguise. In some cases the attraction is physically expressed and occasionally it persists even after the revelation of true identity. In any case these stories differ from modern lesbian stories in that they express a slippage and confusion regarding gender, rather than an active assertion of essential identity or romantic choice. Nevertheless, they allow for the exploration of same-sex desires that must have existed at the time, and they represent a significant development in the history of expressions of same-sex desire in literature.

Both Foster and Terry Castle focus on a long Italian narrative poem first published by Ludovico Ariosto in 1516. Castle uses this poem, *Orlando Furioso*, as the starting point for tracing the evolution of the idea of the lesbian in modern literature. *Orlando Furioso* contains an inset narrative that tells a tale of cross-dressing gender confusion similar to the ones contained in earlier ballads like *Huon of Bordeaux*. The poem itself, however, had a widespread influence on the development of modern narrative in Europe. It is therefore significant that it contains a story of what might very broadly be called a lesbian encounter. It will be evident that transgender and lesbian movement are conflated when one views *Orlando Furioso* as part of a lesbian tradition in literature. This is a common critical move with a long history that will be discussed further below.

The early modern period, which we might see as beginning after Ariosto and continuing until roughly 1800, saw an increase in tales of cross-dressing, gender confusion and gender transgression. Anyone familiar with the plays of Shakespeare will be able to think of several examples of cross-dressing narratives at this period. Throughout the 17th century, these and similar stories were very common on the British stage. A group of pamphlets that historians and literary critics often refer to as embodying the *"querelle des femmes"* shows the first evidence of what we might think of as modern gender anxieties. Questions of female masculinity, male femininity, women's sexual agency, the right to public expression for women and the sexual exploitation of women were all debated in this furious exchange of pamphlet literature in the late 16th and early 17th centuries. These concerns make the debate recognizably modern, though it is often framed through Christian philosophical notions of the chain of being and women's place within it, which are less common (though still extant) in the 21st century. These pamphlets show clear evidence of a conscious resistance to accepted norms of gender and sexual behavior (they often speak out *against* this gender deviance, thus inadvertently giving us evidence of its existence), and are thus significantly different to the accidental gender farces of earlier literature.

By the early 18th century modern pornography had recognizably emerged. John Cleland's *Fanny Hill*, first published in 1748-1749 but written at least a decade earlier, displays a prurient interest in lesbian sexual activity and a clear framework for imagining sexual encounters between women. The novel is structured around ideas of virtue and romance, but these are used as a vehicle for the presentation of a variety of sexual scenarios. On the whole, Cleland, like other 18th century pornographers, celebrates a phallic sexuality that makes the presence of the male necessary for the ultimate satisfaction of women. Yet the eponymous character's first real sexual encounter is with a woman, and she has this to say about it:

> What pleasure she had found I will not say; but this I know, that the first sparks of kindling nature, the first ideas of pollution, were caught by me that night; and that the acquaintance and communication with the bad of our sex is often as fatal to innocence as all the seductions of the other. (Cleland, 28)

Here, Cleland is representing woman's active desire, and the idea that two women's desire for each other could be as strong as their desire for men. Significantly, Phoebe, the character who seduces Fanny, is a happily bisexual woman and lives, like her madam, in a socially independent female household. Their business, of course, depends on the patronage of men. At this same period a medical literature began to emerge in Europe that was concerned with the physical nature of women's sexual pleasure and the anatomy of women apart from their reproductive function. Some anatomists begin to investigate the clitoris, possibly as a response to the widely known existence of sexual relationships between women and the desire to understand how sex might occur in the absence of the phallus.[5]

Poetry that celebrated a highly romanticized idea of friendship between women also flowered in the 17th and 18th centuries. Aphra Behn and Katherine Fowler Philips are good examples of this. This literature, created by literary circles of domestically educated, wealthy women who were widely read and often widely respected, created a space for female agency to express itself. The travel letters of Lady Wortley Montague famously describe women through an active and appreciative female gaze, significantly complicated by a discourse of race that exoticizes the women she describes.

The combination of explicit descriptions of sex between women, evolving expressions of an active female gaze and a discourse of romantic friendship between women in literature created a lesbian space that might exist separately from the transgender movement. Still, the connection between active female desire and the transgression of the bounds of acceptable feminine passivity remained. Figures such as the English writer and actress Charlotte Charke are transgender women who are still claimed (uneasily) as part of a lesbian tradition. As today, lesbians and transgender women were conflated in the popular imaginary, whether or not the individuals in question inhabited both categories.

By the late 18th century the diaries and journals of women like the famous Ladies of Llangollen show evidence of a subcultural group of wealthy women who chose to live independently of men. Sarah Scott's utopian novel *Millenium Hall* (1762) describes a world where redemption might be achieved through such partnerships. The literature of this period makes it clear that lesbianism as we know it was not yet as fully imagined, and therefore was not as threatening as it would later become. Though it is difficult to conceptualize, we must realize that the lesbian identity is a convergence of a number of historical, economic and social developments, and that only a few of these had been reached at this point. The combination of independent and active sexuality with financial self-determination was achieved by only a very few, very privileged women in the 18th century.

The 18th century also saw the emergence of a decadent literature dominated by French and British male authors, which took lesbianism as a central theme. Mandy Merck has argued that a male-dominated discourse of art (she is speaking of art cinema) in a world where women are commonly objects of visual and imaginative consumption, will naturally focus on the lesbian.[6] Like later 19th-century decadent literature, pamphlets and poems produced in the 18th century present prurient descriptions of lesbian vice within a moral framework that simultaneously condemns it. Denis Diderot's *La Religieuse* (*The Nun*, 1760) is possibly the first fully fledged example of the decadent literature of lesbianism that would proliferate in France over the next 150 years.

It is clear that myths of the sexual repression and ignorance of the 19th century give a distorted picture of a reading public that in reality had access to a variety of images of lesbian sex and female same-sex romantic partnerships. This reading public was a much smaller segment of society than it is today and was disproportionately male. Still, a growing female readership clearly had access to ideas of lesbian "vice." Both Jeanette Foster, in *Sex Variant Women in Literature*, and Lillian Faderman, in *Surpassing the Love of Men*, discuss a sensational court case involving two mistresses of a girl's school who were accused of lesbianism in Edinburgh in 1811. Miss Woods and Miss Pirie sued their accuser for libel. One of the questions surrounding this case is whether and how lesbian sexual activity could be popularly imagined (the women were actually accused of tribadism). A young witness at the trial, a student at the school, provided quite specific detail of fully genital sexual encounters. During the case itself and in the nearly two centuries since, there have been persistent questions about whether this young girl might have invented such details, and about whether the two school mistresses might have had the sexual knowledge, ability and desire required to engage in such acts. The popular idea that lesbian sex was not imaginable at this period is belied both by this trial and by the existence of such widely (if privately) circulated texts as *Fanny Hill* and *La Religieuse*. It is significant, however, that these questions about visibility and the lesbian imaginary persist. A variety of theoretical arguments that might explain them will be discussed below.

The diaries and letters of the early 19th-century landowner Anne Lister, first published in 1988, speak of an active and self-aware subculture of upper-class English women who pursued romantic and sexual relationships with each other. Lister describes both romance and sex in detail. She also documents her life as the transgender figure of a country squire. The publication of Lister's writings pushed back the historical date at which scholars are willing to imagine something like a contemporary lesbian identity. It is significant, however, that this identity existed in carefully guarded, upper-class subcultural groups. Economics are a central and often overlooked factor in the possibility for lesbian expression in culture.

Mid-19th-century literature, at least in the middle- and high-brow arenas, was clearly more sexually conservative than 18th-century literature. A kind of conservative backlash was fed by Europe's developing idea of itself as the moral center of a Christian empire. Still, penny dreadfuls and popular ballads, as well as a thriving pornography industry, kept sexual inquiry alive, and found a willing audience. Until the end of the century, English fiction of the middle and upper classes was dominated by the 19th-century realist project, spearheaded by Jane Austen in direct response to the decadence and frivolity of Gothic literature. Within this fiction, however, the tradition of female romantic friendship continued and developed. Charlotte Brontë's *Jane Eyre* and *Villette* both describe intense romantic friendships between young women. Nineteenth-century women's poetry began a tradition of passionate expressions of love and desire between women. Christina Rossetti in England and Emily Dickinson in the United States are two examples here. The two English women writing together as Michael Field embodied a lesbian identity in both life and work. Evidence suggests that they were aware of this to some degree at least, that is, that they viewed their relationship as something more contentious than romantic friendship. In the 1860s, sensation fiction in Great Britain began to anxiously explore questions of female sexual identity and agency, though it rarely, if ever, suggested lesbianism directly.

In France, decadent literature continued to explore female gender transgression and same-sex desire. In 1835 both Théophile Gautier's *Mademoiselle de Maupin* and Honoré de Balzac's *The Girl with the Golden Eyes* were published. By the 1880s both Guy de Maupassant and Emile Zola were creating recognizably modern lesbian characters. These women lived independent lives, transgressed the boundaries of feminine passivity, loved each other physically and emotionally, and often cross-dressed. The cross-dressing bisexual French novelist George

Sand is perhaps the historical embodiment of such characters. The significance of this trend and its widespread influence can be guessed by the number of times in English fiction of the same period that a character's dissipation and questionable morality is signified by his or her reading of "French novels." At the same time a tradition of French decadent poetry, exemplified by Paul Verlaine and Charles Baudelaire and imitated by the English poet Algernon Charles Swinburne, focused on the lesbian figure as a symbol for sumptuous excess, decadent fascination and sometimes horror.

Throughout the later 19th century a powerful and highly influential feminist movement gained visibility and avenues for the expression of women's concerns and desires were opened. Connections between feminism, threats to heterosexual marriage and gender deviance can be seen in such novels as Anthony Trollope's *He Knew He Was Right* (1868–1869) and Henry James' *The Bostonians* (1886). Jeannette Foster identifies what she calls "the masculine protest" in novels of the later 19th century. She describes this as "the deliberate adoption of male attire and outlook" as a "rebellion against the feminine role" (Foster, 91). At the same time, the scientific discourse of sexology, which emerged in the 1860s and 1870s, began the classification of human subjects according to the degree of deviance from norms of gender and sexual desire. Sexology drew heavily on existing literature, often quoting examples from fiction and poetry. In turn the language and ideas provided by sexology facilitated a lesbian characterization within the novel that persists into the 21st century. The conjunction of feminist protest, the conventions established by decadent literature and the identitarian framework provided by the discourse of sexology together form the tools with which a modern lesbian identity in literature was formed.

At the turn of the 20th century numerous women stepped into decadent novelistic and poetic traditions, equipped with these tools. The American-French poet Renée Vivien translated the poet Sappho into modern French and patterned her own life after her, thus creating a model for lesbian identity and community that would persist at least into the 1980s. A group of poets and prose writers connected with Vivien and her lover Natalie Clifford Barney carried this tradition into the 20th century. Among these can be counted the novelists Colette, Gertrude Stein, Djuna Barnes and Radclyffe Hall. These writers were all significant figures in the modernist movement of the early 20th century.

Both modernism in Europe and the Harlem Renaissance (then called the New Negro Movement) in the United States were focal points for new explorations of sexuality and sexual identities. Each movement contained a high proportion of lesbian, gay, bisexual and transgender writers, visual artists and musicians among what are considered to be its most significant figures. Bonnie Kime Scott, in *The Gender of Modernism*, argues that the traditional view of modernist literature as concerned with innovations in form and narration is male-centered and misleading. An analysis that foregrounds women writers within the movement will show that questions of gender and sexuality mark modernist texts at least as much as narrative experimentation. Thus Radclyffe Hall's *The Well of Loneliness*, which makes no such innovations, can be set alongside Djuna Barnes *Nightwood* or Rosamund Lehmann's *The Weather in the Streets*, which do, because all three novels push the boundaries of what can be expressed about women's bodies and desires in fiction. The black American poet Angelina Weld Grimké, though contemporary with these figures, made very different interventions in the expression of women's desires and identities. At least two of her plays center around women who refuse to marry or reproduce, as a means of resisting racial/sexual oppression. Grimké made highly influential antiracist feminist statements with her plays, and influenced the New Negro Movement. Her large body of lesbian love poetry, however, remained unpublished.

Hazel Carby and other scholars have examined expressions of dissident gender and sexual identities in women's blues lyrics of the Harlem Renaissance era. It is here, rather than in fictional works, that the majority of scholars see influential lesbian interventions into American culture made by Harlem Renaissance women. Nevertheless, Nella Larsen and Alice Dunbar Nelson are significant figures in the development of the contemporary lesbian identity in literature, as the scholarship of Gloria T. Hull has made clear.

Again, feminism is significant in this period for its assertion of women's active desire and right to free sexual expression. Rosamund Lehmann's bold descriptions of both bisexuality and an unmarried woman's abortion were contentious when first published in the 1920s and 1930s. Representations of both same-sex desire and the availability of birth control were enabled by a feminist movement that talked about women's sexual bodies in new and public ways. Though tainted by its sometime association with eugenics, the feminist birth control movement asserted the right of women to control their own sexuality. Birth control activist Marie Stopes' wildly popular *Married Love* posited a new model of sexual desire based on the cycles experienced by women's bodies. This cannot, realistically, be historically separated from the development of lesbian expressions of active female desire. Figures such as Virginia Woolf demonstrate the connections between early 20th century feminism and the expression of gender transgression and same-sex desire in women's literature. Once this space for the expression of active desire was created within the culture, and the conditions for female economic independence had spread to the middle-classes, the conditions for the emergence of the lesbian identity we know today were met.

A great deal of scholarship points to the relationship between the work done by women during the two World Wars and the attainment of greater freedoms for women. It could certainly be argued that the economic conditions of modernity were affecting rapid changes in, and anxieties about, the roles of women from at least the 1860s. Nevertheless, 20th century wars were about production and thus they accelerated the economic changes already in motion. Radlyffe Hall's *The Well of Loneliness* contains a rousing narrative digression on the way in which World War I enabled women to find a new agency and autonomy, and the irrevocable nature of this change. Many American lesbians described the same set of feelings regarding the work they did during World War II. In addition, war propaganda that celebrated the strength of women workers on both sides of both wars, departed radically from the view of women as passively feminine.[7]

A similarly dominant historical view sees the postwar period of the 1950s in the United States as a period of backlash and oppression. The fierce competition between men and women, Americans of color and white Americans for jobs did indeed undermine many of the gains made by people of color and other women during the war. However, women's discontent with domestic work, paid (in the case of many women of color) and unpaid (in the case of middle-class women) did not go away. A profound and powerful dissatisfaction was expressed by women in the United States throughout the 1950s. At the same time urban lesbian and gay subcultures that had begun to emerge in the 1930s, functioning much as they did until the 1980s, grew and gained visibility in this period. This was true, with a great deal of local variation, throughout Europe and the Americas. Both feminist and lesbian literature continued to develop in the postwar period. The publication of Simone de Beauvoir's *Le Deuxième Sexe* (*The Second Sex*) in 1949 was a major turning point and had immediate affect in both the United States and Britain, where it was in print by 1953. De Beauvoir was the first theorist to posit the cultural construction of woman, though her lengthy section on lesbianism relies heavily on the categories and ideas of deviance set up by sexology.

In the United States the most important development in postwar lesbian literature was the mass-market publication of literally hundreds of lesbian paperbacks (most often referred to as "lesbian pulp novels," though many of them were not novels at all). From scientific studies to literary anthologies to accounts of the lesbian subcultural world that resemble travel literature to romance novels, publishers of paperback original fiction found the figure of the lesbian highly profitable. This literature is significant for a number of reasons. First and foremost it disseminated ideas of lesbian identity and subculture in unprecedented volume. Second, the best of lesbian pulp literature articulates the concerns of an emerging feminist movement while even the worst of it highlighted the anxieties around women's work, consumption and sexuality that dominated the period.

The concerns raised within the work of paperback writers like Ann Bannon and Valerie Taylor form the substance of the popular feminist movement that emerged in the 1960s. Alongside the struggle for lesbian representation, which continued within mainstream feminism after 1977, an emerging and consciously lesbian feminism articulated a specific analysis of the relation between sexism and homophobia. A number of powerful manifestos, including "The Woman-Identified-Woman-Manifesto" and the "Combahee River Collective Statement," exemplify the complex and radical understanding of class, race and gender that marked this movement. Lesbianism is seen, in these works, as the root (radical) for overall social change (revolution). This idea was influential even among heterosexual feminists, some of whom chose to live for a time as "political lesbians." Certain literary works, such as Marge Piercy's *Woman at the Edge of Time* (1978) are documents of this era, during which gender dissidence and same-sex desire were championed by otherwise heterosexual feminist writers. Since the control of women's sexuality is seen as the lynchpin of so many structures of social power—the family, the marketplace, the media—the unleashing of women's sexual power could upset the whole applecart.

Counteracting the silencing of women in these same arenas—the family, the media, the marketplace—was a major focus of lesbian feminist activism. Lesbian feminist literature of the 1970s is marked by ideas of silence, voice and the power of language. The ability to express the victimization of lesbians and other women in language, spoken or written, had been historically denied and was asserted by lesbian feminists through independent publishing projects, literary collectives and public readings. An understanding of how the structure of language itself denied representation to lesbians and other women and of the relationship between linguistic expression and the experience of reality itself informed the writing and publishing efforts of lesbian feminists like Audre Lorde, Judy Grahn and Joan Nestle. This focus on the radical nature of expression and representation eventually formed a basis for the first organized academic interventions in lesbian literary studies.

By the 1980s in Western Europe and the Americas, certain classes of women became the subjects of a new relationship to work, media and consumption. Capitalism proved itself flexible enough to contain expressions of women's active sexual desire, mostly, as in previous decades, through consumption. A publishing industry, a sex industry and a number of professional sectors now absorbed women as active agents of various needs and desires. Sexism remained, but the popularity of feminism waned. Still a strong core of lesbian feminists continued to write and publish, and to extend and deepen queries about the nature and functions of the lesbian identity.

During this period numerous anthologies reflected the engagement of the lesbian feminist movement with its former limitations. Independent publishing projects supported lesbians of color in the global north and south, working-class white lesbians, bisexual women and lesbians whose sexual desires and practices had been rejected by an earlier mainstream feminism with a less sophisticated understanding of sex and power. Important landmarks of these interventions were *All the Women Are White, All the Blacks Are Men, But Some of Us Are Brave*, edited by Barbara Smith, Patricia Bell Scott and Gloria T. Hull in 1981, and anthologies edited by Cherrie Moraga and Gloria Anzaldúa, both *This Bridge Called My Back* (Moraga and Anzaldúa) and *Haciendo*

Caras/Making Face, Making Soul (Anzaldúa). These anthologies not only collected a wealth of poetic and fictional works, but also theoretically challenged the construction of women's sexual identities from a number of positions in terms of class, race, ethnicity and ideas of nationhood. Also significant were the works of theorists and pornographers like Pat (now Patrick) Califia, who overturned ideas of what feminist sexual power might be. Similar questions were reflected in the popular works of lesbian fiction writers like Ellen Galford, Jeanette Winterson and Jackie Kay, all of whom challenge the idea of fixed and stable lesbian identities through their novels. This trend carried with it fictional and self-reflexive (sometimes, as in Winterson's case, overly self-conscious) narrative style that is often labelled postmodern, though it does not differ significantly from modernist experiments made by writers like Virginia Woolf and Djuna Barnes. These interrogations of the nature and stability of the lesbian identity reflect the development of the academic discipline of lesbian studies during the same era.

THEORY FOR READING LESBIAN LITERATURE

From the earliest sexological studies of lesbian desires and behaviors, literature has formed an important source of information, and arena for reflection, on the nature of lesbianism. The 19th-century sexologists Havelock Ellis and Magnus Hirschfeld depended on literary examples for their elucidations of the nature of female same-sex desire. At the same time they understood the importance of literature as an organ for human inquiry and understanding. Thus Magnus Hirschfeld regularly published literary reviews of publications dealing with same-sex desire and transgender movement and Ellis was persuaded to write the preface for Radclyffe Hall's *The Well of Loneliness* in 1928. Almost three decades later, the American sexologist George Henry wrote the preface for Jeannette Foster's groundbreaking study *Sex Variant Women in Literature*. Here Henry asserts that "sexual variance shows itself in so many different ways that all types of imaginative writings have to be studied if we are to understand human motivations and behavior" (Foster, 6). Thus, a medical justification was argued for a literature that might otherwise have been considered obscene. This trend, conflating erotic and medical literature, is continuous from the 18th through the 20th centuries. Midwifery texts were read as pornography in the 18th century and Sigmund Freud worries, in his famous "Dora" case, that some doctors will read his writing for their own "delectation." Likewise literature that served primarily erotic functions often masked itself as medical or scientific, as in the case of many pulp paperbacks in the 1950s and 1960s.

In the late 19th and early 20th centuries, literature that describes and expresses female same-sex desire found in medical science a set of discourses which enable this expression. Djuna Barnes' *Nightwood* would not be what it is without psychoanalysis, any more than *The Well of Loneliness* would be what it is without sexology. The American postwar lesbian organization Daughters of Bilitis stated as two of its goals both the dissemination of lesbian literature and the understanding of and cooperation with social and medical science. So, the earliest theories of the lesbian subject that inform literature and literary readings come out of medical science.

It is evident from a look at literary studies and lesbian anthologies like Jeannette Foster's and Terry Castle's that a conflation between female same-sex desire and female to male transgender movement has persisted for centuries. Early examples used by both Foster and Castle focus on transgender movement first and same-sex desire only as a consequence of this. This same conflation is reflected in sexological science, which produced the first modern theories of the lesbian subject. Beginning in Germany in the 1860s and continuing well into the 20th century in Western Europe and the United States, and until the present day in China, sexological studies find and document "masculine" characteristics in women who desire other women. In some cases, as in the work of Havelock Ellis, characterizations of lesbian and bisexual women as transgender rest on the idea that ideal masculine and feminine norms do exist and that these women deviate from them. Often these theories are supported by physical examinations and documentations, which, like similar psychological investigations, assume ideal male and female bodies. Thus infinite variations in human morphology and behavior are compared to a mythical norm. Though it cannot possibly exist, this mythical norm remains the standard by which the bodies and behaviors of men and women are measured to produce ideas of deviance.

Other sexologists have questioned ideas of masculine and feminine as polar opposites. To quote again from George Henry's preface to Jeannette Foster:

The sex variant has always been with us and probably always will be. He [sic] has been thus classified, partly because of the arbitrary designations *male* and *female*. As I have shown in *All the Sexes*, there are any number of possible gradations of human behavior—from that of a theoretical masculine to that of a theoretical feminine being.[8] (Foster, 5)

Sexology and the literature of lesbianism, which draws upon sexological inquiry, see masculinity and femininity as biological states. Whether, like Havelock Ellis, they uphold ideas of an ideal masculinity and femininity or, like George Henry, they seek to promote a new, less dualistic understanding of human sexual biology, sexological thinkers continue to see gender and sexuality as a matter of the body.

Psychoanalysis, in its early development, was more dependent on sexology than is commonly acknowledged. Sigmund Freud cites sexological research in essays like "Some Psychical Consequences of the Anatomical Distinction between the Sexes," and in one letter refers the mother of a young homosexual man to the work of Havelock Ellis. From 1910, when the first of Freud's essays were translated into English, his work had a tremendous influence on the writing of lesbian, bisexual and transgendered women in English. James Strachey, Freud's patient and chosen English translator was associated with the sexually dissident writers of the Bloomsbury Group. The Strachey translations were published by the press (Hogarth) founded by Virginia and Leonard Woolf. Radclyffe Hall and Una Troubridge record in their journals and letters that they read Freud aloud to each other. Djuna Barnes created long stream-of-consciousness ramblings for her homosexual characters that resemble Freud's famous talking cure, and incorporate ideas of the Oedipal conflict.

Freud built upon and complicated sexological ideas of gender variance and same-sex desire by developing the concepts of aim and object choice. Through his particular and universalizing myth of the child's development within the family, he articulated a number of ways in which the development of the human sense of self involves desires for and identifications with both the male and female parent. In a clearly preferred scenario the child will ultimately identify with the parent of the same sex and desire the gendred other. However these are separate actions and might "go wrong" in any number of ways. Therefore one's aim might be either masculine or feminine, that is one might desire *to be* either masculine or feminine. At the same time one's object choice—preferred object of desire—might be of either the same, the opposite or both sexes. Sexological ideas of masculine and feminine bodies become psychoanalytic ideas of masculine and feminine psyches. Still, same-sex desire is married in many cases to masculine and feminine identifications, aim to object choice. It is famously asserted that Freud claimed that all humans are born bisexual. This is strictly true, but not in the sense in which that term is commonly used. For Freud a newborn girl has the capacity to desire union with either her mother or her father, but a clearly preferred "normal" development scenario has her relinquish desire for the mother in favor of desire for the father.

The work of Sigmund Freud affected lesbian literature in two important ways. First, the idea of the so-called "talking cure" popularized the notion that subconscious truths and desires lay beneath the surface of all dialogue and that an unrestricted flow of language might reveal them. Freud's idea of conscious and subconscious selves, or layers of the psyche, and the notion of free and unfettered narrative flow informed modernist experiments in narrative style. Virginia Woolf, H.D. (Hilda Doolittle), Gertrude Stein, Rosamund Lehmann and Djuna Barnes all transformed the talking-cure into their literary investigations of the sexual self. Secondly, ideas of aim and object-choice and of the fluid nature of the psychic sexual self have been incorporated into literary characterization of lesbians since the day they first appeared. Woolf's theoretical ideas about masculine, feminine and androgynous minds, Barnes' damaged inverts scarred by loss, and pulp characterizations of lesbian survivors of rape, abuse and domineering mothers and fathers all are enabled by the ideas of psychoanalysis. Even where writers like Woolf consciously distance themselves from Freud's narrative of sexual development, evidence of the influence of his method appears in their work.

Medical theories, including psychoanalysis, share an idea of masculinity and femininity as somehow essential. Whether gender falls into two categories, or exists as a continuum along which an infinite number of human variables fall, it is psychically or biologically an attribute of the individual. On the other hand, an important branch of lesbian feminist theory sees gender as socially constructed. Gender is a hierarchal social system, rather than a quality attributable to individuals. Gender, according to materialist feminists, is a system created to differentiate one class of humans from another, in order to oppress them. Thus ideas of masculinity and femininity are mythic and the associations they have with bodily morphology are merely arbitrary.

Materialist feminisms have their basis in the work of Fredrich Engels, specifically his *The Origins of the Family, Private Property and the State* (1884). Here Engels argues that women were the first oppressed class. In order for men to consolidate private property and pass it on through privately controlled families, they must first control the sexuality of "their" women, in order to ensure the patrimony of their children. Therefore, through the social contract of marriage and through an array of formal and informal social rules, a woman's sexuality was made the private property of the men in her family—first her father, who then effectively bartered her to her husband. Heterosexuality then is a system of power, rather than a biologically preferred state. French feminists have recognized the exploitative nature of the marriage contract since the 18th century. In 1791 Olympe deGouges proposed an entirely new and radically fairer marriage contract. Her work, focusing on the relation of female subjects to the Enlightenment idea of the social contract, engendered a French feminist tradition that continued into the late 20th century lesbian-feminist writings of Monique Wittig.

A strong socialist feminism, kept alive throughout the 19th and 20th centuries, saw the oppression of women as part of the maintenance of power by European, male global elites. In 1949 Simone de Beauvoir articulated a decidedly materialist, but more specifically single-issue, feminism in *The Second Sex*. This work had a tremendous influence on lesbians and other feminists after World War II. Here, de Beauvoir famously claimed that one is not born, but rather is made into a woman. She therefore popularized the idea that femininity, as separate from biological sex, was a socially constructed set of imperatives and prohibitions to which women were held in order to keep them in a subordinate social, political and economic position. It was only a small step from here to the realization that heterosexuality, depending as it does on essentialist notions of masculinity and femininity, is also a social construct that supports gender hierarchy. Interestingly, though she was the acknowledged site of origin for many of the most important and radical ideas of postwar lesbian feminism, her own chapter on lesbianism depends heavily on sexology and paints a troubled portrait. An understanding of the relationship between the economic and the sexual oppression of women characterizes both lesbian and other feminist writings for at least three decades after the war. Popular lesbian paperbacks of the 1950s and early 1960s nearly always associate the journey towards lesbianism with forays into paid labor and economic independence. Lesbian feminist writings of the 1970s more explicitly decry the relegation of women to unpaid and alienating labor in the family home and the culture at large.

The French feminist Monique Wittig marries an interrogation of the gendered nature of language to a strongly materialist view of sex and gender. Thus Wittig radically synthesizes symbolic and materialist approaches to the lesbian figure. Femininity, for Wittig, is a position within language and a position within material culture. Gender, as it appears within language, marks a position of subordination within culture. Wittig argues against the naturalization of categories of male and female, masculine and feminine, whether by misogynists or radical feminists:

> By doing this, by admitting that there is a "natural" division between women and men, we naturalize history, we assume that "men" and "women" have always existed and will always exist. Not only do we naturalize history, but also consequently we naturalize the social phenomena which express our oppression, making change impossible. (Wittig, 11)

At the same time she makes explicit and explains the historical conflation of lesbian and female transgender identities. Her materialist analysis allows us to see that femininity is a construct designed to keep women in a passive position as sexual objects. Therefore any move toward sexual agency is also a move out of the position of femininity. "The category of sex is the product of heterosexual society that sees half the population as sexual beings [beings marked by sex/gender]" (Wittig, 7). Wittig then sees the lesbian as the radical category in a materialist feminist view of sex and gender. As a sexual agent in a woman's body she obviates and thus overthrows artificial constructions of femininity. "What a materialist analysis does by reasoning, a lesbian society accomplishes practically . . ." (Wittig, 9).

Wittig's influential essays, collected in the straight mind, were first published in the 1980s. At the same period (beginning in 1976), the works of the French historian and philosopher Michel Foucault began to have a tremendous impact on the developing field of lesbian and gay studies. At heart, Foucault's theories are also materialist. He was concerned with the way in which human identity was the product, or the point of intersection, of any number of interlocking social discourses of power. Much attention is paid to a particular statement of Foucault's, made in his *History of Sexuality: Volume One*. Here he asserts, citing the development of sexology, that it was not until the latter 19th century that the homosexual became "a species." Foucault does not mean, by this, that there were no people who lived in same-sex romantic and sexual relationships before this period, nor even that subcultures built around these behaviors did not exist. Rather, he argues, much like Wittig, that sexual identities only become highly visible and widely recognized throughout a culture when they are implicated in social relations of power. Throughout his works, Foucault documents an increasing concern with individual identities and bodies as constituents of the social order, arising with industrial capitalism and the growth of modern cities. In *History of Sexuality: Volume One*, he counts both the discipline of sexology and the medical "hysterisization of women's bodies" as forces that marked a change in the meanings of sexual identities and relations of power in the 19th century. Medical and scientific taxonomies that arose during this period inspire Foucault's use of the word "species" in this context.

The work of Michel Foucault unleashed sexual identities from notions of essentialism and influenced a number of lesbian theorists, such as Sue-Ellen Case and Judith Butler, who questioned historically recognized categories of female sexual identities. Both Butler and Case argue for a view of gender and sexuality as performative. Gender and sex, for these theorists, are a collection of learned behaviors and affects. Lesbian, gay and transgender practices can subvert traditional notions of gender and are thus both codes by which individuals can communicate with each other and open challenges to heterosexual structures of power. Butler and other so-called postmodern theorists after Foucault have looked again at the relationship between the psyche, the body and social institutions and discourses as they meet in the figure of the lesbian. Butler's work builds upon both psychoanalysis, via Freud and Jacques Lacan, and the interventions in social history made by Foucault. She looks at the unstable and shifting relationships between psychic and material structures in the creation of the lesbian subjectivity. She also creates an unstable space between individual subjects and the larger symbolic structures that organize their lives by allowing for imperfect individual reiterations of various identity categories. That is to say, individual women may reflect social ideas of womanhood imperfectly, thus challenging and mutating these very ideas.

These postmodern theories of lesbian subjectivity are similar in many ways to postcolonial interventions that question the stability of identity categories. The work of Gloria Anzaldúa is of tremendous significance here. Anzaldúa refuses to view any identity category as exhaustive and uses her own position as an individual living between national borders, ethnic identities, class boundaries and ideological positions to highlight the contingent nature of each of these identity positions vis à vis the others. Following the Mexican philosopher Jose Vascocelos, she argues, in *Borderlands/La Frontera*, for an embrace of the state of living between, a *mestiza* (blended) consciousness:

> As a *mestiza* I have no country, my homeland cast me out; yet all countries are mine because I am every woman's sister or potential lover. (As a lesbian I have no race, my own people disclaim me; but I am all races because there is the queer of me in all races.) I am cultureless because, as a feminist, I challenge the collective cultural/religious male-derived beliefs of Indo-Hispanics and Anglos; yet I am cultured because I am participating in the creation of a new culture . . . (Anzaldúa, pp. 80–81)

Anzaldúa writes in the way that many American Latinas speak, in a mixture of Spanish and English. Often she does not provide a parallel taxonomy for the monolingual reader. Thus her *mestiza* text itself can make us feel the inadequacy of monolithic identifications. Unless we embrace a blend of languages we cannot understand everything she writes. Her interventions in debates around the lesbian identity in theory, poetry, fiction and through a dedicated career in independent publishing of other lesbians and feminists of color have had far-reaching effect. She is a significant figure in a longer history of lesbian feminist writers who foreground an understanding of the lesbian identity as existing at the intersection of a number of positions of race, class, nation and language. Poetry and fiction writers such as Jackie Kay have created work that embodies the radical literary potential of such an understanding.

This brief sketch of the history of theories of the lesbian subject gives some sense of the tools that have been available to lesbian readers and critics over the past two centuries. As an identity position that both creates and embodies anxieties around sexed and gendered structures of power, the lesbian always arises at critical moments in the history of literature and generates a tremendous amount of theorizing. Likewise in a world where women are the prime objects of visual, and the prime subjects of material, consumption, the lesbian is a tremendously lucrative position. Lesbians are put on display for the titillation of both men and women, and they are a growing concern of target marketers seeking new opportunities for creating consumption. Therefore the lesbian continues to be highly visible in culture and theory. Some lesbian writers are now finding mainstream publishing success with openly lesbian novels in a global literature industry. The theoretical positions outlined above are more important than ever as the lesbian identity continues to operate in the global marketplace.

WHY DO LESBIANS READ?

From the earliest publications of Magnus Hirschfeld's *Jahrbuch fur sexuelle Zwischenstufen* in 1899, lesbians have talked about reading as an important part of their process of identification. Lesbian novels were listed in the *Jahrbuch*, and publicly discussed as important material by members of the Scientific Humanitarian Committee, which Hirschfeld founded. American lesbian pulp fiction of the postwar era has been referred to by Joan Nestle as "lesbian survival literature," the category under which it is housed in the Lesbian Herstory Archives in Brooklyn, New York. Oral histories from Great Britain, the United States and Australia repeatedly describe a process by which young women experience same-sex desires, yet do not have a language to describe or communicate about them. Trips to the library or corner drugstore in search of dictionary definitions and fictional representations provided the necessary explications. It is in literature, as much as in bars or schools, that women describe, again and again, the process of developing a lesbian identity. These stories are often told in a way that makes the young person essentially lesbian but without the knowledge to understand herself, until she finds the literature that gives her that knowledge. It could also be argued, in a Foucauldian sense, that the lesbian identity exists in the literature and is built around an interaction between that literature and a set of desires that did not previously define the individual's identity. That is to say, that literature is one forum where, between writers and readers, the lesbian identity was created.

Narrative is a human instinct. It is the way in which we make sense of the disordered events and impressions that make up our world. In order to create and understand identity positions and their functions we tell stories about them and we read and listen to those stories. The novelistic form known to critics as the *bildungsroman* (the novel of education, *bildung* in German refers both literally to building and to the process of education) is a prime embodiment of this process of creating identity through narrative. In the *bildungsroman* a typically young hero leaves a closed, often provincial setting, and proceeds through the world overcoming obstacles to eventually find a place in the social structure and a personal identity. The so-called "coming out novel" is the specifically homosexual form of the *bildungsroman*. As such, it highlights the way in which narrativizing in literature has been a major vehicle for the production of what we know as lesbian identity. For women who love each other, literature has been both a revolutionary and an oppressive tool. For a literature formed by ideas of romance and sensual revelation, the lesbian figure has been a rich mine of ideas and sensations for centuries.

NOTES

1. See Joanne Myers, *Historical Dictionary of the Lesbian Liberation Movement: Still the Rage* for a detailed discussion of the history of lesbian feminist debate in the 1970s.

2. For a specific in-depth study of a government sponsored program of eugenic extermination practiced on Native Americans see Nancy Gallagher, *Breeding Better Vermonters*. For a more comprehensive study of eugenic sterilization programs in Britain and North America see Stephen Trombley, *The Right to Reproduce: A History of Coercive Sterilization*.

3. See George Henry, *Sex Variants: A Study of Homosexual Patterns*.

4. For an articulation of the idea of "sexual dissidence" see Jonathan Dollimore, *Sexual Dissidence: Augustine to Wild, Freud to Foucault*.

5. See Bernadette Brooten, *Love between Women: Early Christian Responses to Female Homoeroticism*.

6. See Mandy Merck "Lianna and the Lesbians of Art Cinema" in *Perversions*.
7. See Maureen Honey, *Creating Rosie the Riveter: Class, Gender and Propaganda During World War II* and Michael Renov, *Hollywood's Wartime Women: Representation and Ideology* for specifically American discussions of work and the representation of gender during World War II.
8. See also George Henry, *All the Sexes: A Study of Masculinity and Femininity* and *Sex Variants: A Study of Homosexual Patterns, Volumes I and II*.

WORKS CITED

Anzaldúa, Gloria. *Borderlands/La Frontera*. San Francisco: Spinster/Aunt Lute Press, 1987.
—— (ed.). *Haciendo Caras/Making Face, Making Soul: Creative and Critical Perspectives by Feminists of Color*. San Francisco: Spinster/Aunt Lute Press, 1990.
——, and Cherrie Moraga (eds.). *This Bridge Called My Back*. Watertown, Mass.: Persephone Press, 1981.
Balzac, Honoré de. *The Girl with the Golden Eyes*. New York: Caroll and Graf, 1998.
Barnes, Djuna. *Nightwood*. London: Faber and Faber, 1996.
De Beauvoir, Simone. *The Second Sex*. London: Vintage, 1997.
Brontë, Charlotte. *Jane Eyre*. New York: W. W. Norton, 1971.
——. *Villette*. London: Wordsworth, 1993.
Brooten, Bernadette. *Love between Women: Early Christian Responses to Female Homoeroticism*. Chicago: University of Chicago Press, 1998.
Carby, Hazel. "It Jus Be Dat Way Sometime: The Sexual Politics of Women's Blues." In Sue Fisher and Alexandra Todd (eds.), *Gender and Discourse: The Power of Talk*. Norwood, N.J.: Abley Press, 1988.
Castle, Terry. *The Literature of Lesbianism: A Historical Anthology from Ariosto to Stonewall*. New York: Columbia University Press, 2003.
Cleland, John. *Fanny Hill, or Memoirs of a Woman of Pleasure*. London: Penguin, 1994.
Combahee River Collective. "A Black Feminist Statement." In Patrica Bell, Gloria T. Hull and Barbara Smith (eds.), *All the Women Are White, All the Blacks are Men, But Some of Us Are Brave*. Old Westbury, N.Y.: Feminist Press, 1982 (pp. 13–22).
Diderot, Denis. *The Nun*. Harmondsworth: Penguin, 1977.

Dollimore Jonathan. *Sexual Dissidence: Augustine to Wild, Freud to Foucault*. Oxford: Clarendon, 1991.
Engels, Friedrich. *The Origins of the Family, Private Property and the State*. London: Penguin, 1986.
Faderman, Lillian. *Surpassing the Love of Men: Romantic Friendship and Love between Women from the Renaissance to the Present*. London: The Women's Press, 1985.
Foster, Jeannette. *Sex Variant Women in Literature*. Tallahassee, Fla.: Naiad, 1985.
Foucault, Michel. *The History of Sexuality, Volume One: The Will to Knowledge*. (Robert Hurley, trans.) London: Penguin, 1979.
Friedan, Betty. *The Feminine Mystique*. New York: W.W. Norton, 1963.
Freud, Sigmund. "Some Psychical Consequences of the Anatomical Distinction between the Sexes." In *The Standard Edition of the Complete Psychological Works of Sigmund Freud, Volume XIX*. London: Hogarth Press, 1961 (essay originally published in German in 1925).
Gallagher, Nancy. *Breeding Better Vermonters*. Hanover, N.H.: University Press of New England, 1999.
Gautier, Théophile. *Mademoiselle de Maupin*. (Joanna Richardson, trans.) Harmondsworth, England: Penguin, 1981.
Hall, Radclyffe. *The Well of Loneliness*. London: Virago, 1997.
Henry, George. *All the Sexes: A Study of Masculinity and Femininity*. New York: Rinehart and Company, 1955.
———. *Sex Variance: A Study of Homosexual Patterns, Volumes I and II*. New York: Paul B. Hoeber, 1941.
Hirschfeld, Magnus (ed.). *Jahrbuch für sexuelle Zwischenstufen*. Berlin, 1899–1921. (Some originals and facsimiles are held in the British Library, Euston, London.)
Honey, Maureen. *Creating Rosie the Riveter: Class, Gender and Propaganda during World War II*. Amherst, Mass.: University of Massachusetts Press, 1984.
James, Henry. *The Bostonians*. London: Penguin, 2000.
Kinsey, Alfred, et al. *Sexual Behavior in the Human Female*. Philadelphia: W. B. Saunders, 1953.
Lehmann, Rosamund. *The Weather in the Streets*. London: Virago, 1994.
Merck, Mandy. *Perversions*. London: Virago, 1993.
Myers, JoAnne. *The Historical Dictionary of the Lesbian Liberation Movement: Still the Rage*. Lanham, Md: Scarecrow Press, 2003.
Piercy, Marge. *Woman at the Edge of Time*. London: The Women's Press, 1993.
Radicalesbians. "The Woman-Identified-Woman Manifesto." Pittsburgh, Pa.: Know Inc., 1970 (held in the Special Collections at Duke University Library, Durham, North Carolina).

Renov, Michael. *Hollywood's Wartime Women: Representation and Ideology.* Ann Arbor, Mich.: U.M.I. Research Press, 1988.
Scott, Bonnie Kime. *The Gender of Modernism.* Bloomington: Indiana University Press, 1990.
Scott, Sarah. *A Description of Millenium Hall and the Country Adjacent . . .* London: Virago, 1986.
Stopes, Marie. *Married Love.* London: Victor Golancz, 1995.
Trollope, Anthony. *He Knew He Was Right.* Oxford: Oxford University Press, 1998.
Trombley, Stephen. *The Right to Reproduce: A History of Coercive Sterilization.* London: Wiedenfield and Nicolson, 1988.
Wittig, Monique. *The Straight Mind and Other Essays.* Boston: Beacon Press, 1992.
Zola, Emile. *Nana.* Oxford: Oxford University Press, 1992.

The Dictionary

– A –

ABJECTION. The concept of abjection is derived from **psychoanalysis**. The most influential developments in the theory of abjection have been made by the psychoanalyst and philosopher Julia Kristeva, in her *Powers of Horror* (1980). Abjection refers to the idea that in order to remain psychically whole each human subject must reject that which would engulf or destroy it. Death, decay, feces and menstrual blood are all material components of the abject. We can never entirely separate ourselves from the abject. We all reject and continually produce these things. We are all moving toward death and decay, yet the definition of being is the rejection of death. Kristeva draws on both **Sigmund Freud** and **Jacques Lacan** in arguing that the first thing a child abjects is its mother's body. Therefore the maternal, the feminine and the material in general are all linked in the theory of abjection.

The lesbian theorist **Judith Butler** has developed Kristeva's theory of abjection in relation to gender in her *Bodies That Matter* (1993). She argues that opposite poles of gendered masculinity and femininity can be maintained only through the abjection of genderless, transgender or intersex individuals. "The construction of gender," she says, operates "by exclusionary means."

ACADEMY OF WOMEN. This name was sometimes given to a group of wealthy lesbian, bisexual and transgender women writers, artists and intellectuals who congregated in Paris from 1900 to the late 1930s. This group was also sometimes referred to as "The Amazons." This salon was first focused on the poet **Renée Vivien** and, after Vivien's illness and death, around the writer **Natalie Clifford Barney**.

Rachilde, Colette, Gertrude Stein, Lucie Delarue-Mardrus and **Radclyffe Hall** were all members of, or visitors to, this group at various times. Hall's *The Well of Loneliness* presents a fictionalized description of this salon, and of Barney's garden, with its Greek temple motif, where they would often gather. *See also* AMAZON.

ACKER, KATHY (1945–1997). The American poet, performance artist and novelist Kathy Acker was born and raised in New York, and lived for lengthy periods in both London and California. Trained first as a poet, Acker maintained a fascination with the power of language throughout her life. She claimed the beat writer William Boroughs as an early major influence, and was later interested in the work of **Monique Wittig**. Acker is often described as a **postmodernist**. Her narrators and characters speak in many-layered voices and illustrate unstable and troubling identities. *The Childlike Life of the Black Tarantula by the Black Tarantula* (1978) is a good example. Written in the first person, it includes biographical details of Acker's own life but also factual historical information on the lives of a number of 19th-century women convicted of murder. This blending of characters, free play with fact and extensive borrowing of material led to at least one legal action against Acker by another writer. Her intent, however, was not to plagiarize, but to throw into question the nature of accepted truth, the origin of speech and the integrity of human identity. Often, Acker used these techniques to highlight the invisibility of the female voice and the instability of gender. An epigraph to a section of her *Don Quixote* (1986) reads, "Being dead, Don Quixote could no longer speak. Being born into and part of a male world, she had no speech of her own. All she could do was read male texts that weren't her own."

Blood and Guts in High School (1984) is a biographical novel that first earned her a devoted following, among which were many lesbians. Other works include: *Portrait of an Eve* (1992), *Pussy, King of Pirates* (1993), and *My Mother: Demonology* (1993). She also wrote an opera entitled *Birth of a Poet*, the screenplay for the film *Variety*, directed by Bette Gordon, and collected some of her critical writings in *Bodies of Work: Essays* (1996). At the time of her death from cancer in 1997, she was working on *Eurydice in the Underworld*.

ACKLAND, VALENTINE (1906–1969). The English journalist and poet Valentine Ackland was a public **cross-dresser** by the time she reached adulthood in the 1920s. Her life partner was the writer **Sylvia Townsend Warner**. Together the two women published a book of verse entitled *Whether a Dove or a Seagull* in 1934. Both women were committed leftists, and in response to the rise of fascism in Europe, Ackland joined the communist party in the 1930s. She worked as assistant to a British medical unit serving the leftist cause in the Spanish Civil War. In 1949 Ackland wrote a short biography, *For Sylvia: An Honest Account*. This work was finally published in 1985. The papers of Ackland and Warner are housed in a dedicated room in the Dorset County Museum in Dorchester, England.

AIDOO, AMA ATA (1942–). The Ghanaian poet, playwright and novelist Ama Ata Aidoo has attempted to define **feminism** and women's writing in specifically African ways. Teaching in Ghana, Kenya and the United States she has spoken out against the "brain drain," which draws valuable African intellectuals into the West and against the objectification of African women by white Western feminists. Her essay "Literature, Feminism and the African Woman Today" (1996) describes this objectification, defines a relationship between African feminism and African literature and literary criticism, and also acknowledges homophobia as a component of gender oppression. Aidoo is especially significant here for her 1977 novel *Our Sister Killjoy: Or Reflections From a Black-Eyed Squint*. In an innovative mixture of prose and poetry this novel tells the story of a Ghanaian scholarship student who spends a year abroad in Germany and England. The female protagonist has two relationships, one with a black man and one with a white woman, each of whom objectify her in different ways. The lesbian desire of the protagonist's white German friend is portrayed as the desire to possess an exotic **other** rather than as a product of the character's identity.

AIM. The concept of masculine or feminine aim, as it derives from 19th-century sexual psychology, refers to an individual's drive toward gender identification. Does one want to dress, live, work, love, in a masculine or a feminine manner? The distinction between masculine and feminine aim is often read as the distinction between activity and passivity, respectively. As developed through Freudian **psychoanalysis**, the concept of aim, and its distinction from **object-choice**, allows a more complicated view of sexual identity. From the 1870s, the science of **sexology** often confused the desire for a person of the same sex with the desire to be a person of the "opposite" gender. This confusion has an even longer tradition in literature. The distinction between aim and object-choice eventually allowed the distinction between transgender and lesbian identities. Within **Sigmund Freud**'s case studies, as for example his "Psychogenesis of a Case of Homosexuality in a Woman," there remains an apparent confusion between aim and object-choice. Freud notes that the bisexual object of his patient's desire is romantically active and a feminist, suggesting that these "masculine" aims explain her same-sex desires.

ALLEGORY. Allegory refers to the literary and dramatic practice of substituting one set of events or persons for another in an extended metaphor. Objects, people or actions in an allegorical narrative stand in for other objects, people or actions, or for concepts, ideas or states of being. For example, in medieval European morality plays characters called "sin" and "virtue" battled over characters called "the soul." This is a felicitous example because allegorical narratives tend to invite and to be associated with ideas of morality.

In many eras when lesbian love, sex and sentiment were unacceptable in certain areas of literature, lesbian writers used allegory as a means of communicating about their dissident desires, practices and feelings. Both the historical past and the future are fertile sites for the creation of allegory. The lesbian writer **Mary Renault** told tales of ancient Greek male love as a way of communicating about modern same-sex desires and gay and lesbian identities. Likewise lesbian **science fiction** writers throughout the 20th century used allegorical devices to talk about same-sex desires. Speaking of lesbian and gay 19th-century poetry and fiction, Graham Robb says that allegory "could create another world in which whole dramas were acted out and even brought to satisfactory conclusions." In any era when lesbian writers felt wary of overt expression, allegory became an important tool.

ALLEN, PAULA GUNN (1939–). The American poet, novelist and academic Paula Gunn Allen was born into a family of mixed, Pueblo,

Lakota, Lebanese and Scottish ancestry. She was raised in Pueblo culture and draws on it for much of her work. Allen began her academic career in a study of the influence of oral tradition on Native American literature. Her first book was *Blind Lion Poems* (1974). She published *A Cannon between My Knees* in 1981, and *The Woman Who Owned the Shadows* in 1983. In 1986 she developed her own brand of mystical spirituality based on the woman-centered religion, myths and traditions of Pueblo and other Native American peoples in *The Sacred Hoop: Recovering the Feminine in American Indian Tradition*. In the introduction to this work Allen comes out as a lesbian. *The Sacred Hoop* was influential in the women's spirituality movement burgeoning in the 1980s and 1990s and is an important example of American **cultural feminism**. In 1991 Allen followed with *Grandmothers of the Light: A Medicine Woman's Sourcebook*. She has also written a number of children's books and collected four decades of her poetry in the volume *Life Is a Fatal Disease: Collected Poems 1962–1995*.

ALLISON, DOROTHY (1949–). The American poet, performance artist and novelist Dorothy Allison was born and raised in a working-class family in South Carolina. Her Southern, white, working-class lesbian identity defines her work. Allison first published a chapbook of poems, *The Women Who Hate Me*, with Long Haul Press in 1983. These poems express the alienation experienced by a southern working-class lesbian, even at the height of **second-wave feminism**'s popularity. In many ways this work lies in the tradition of confessional poetry exemplified by poets such as Ann Sexton and Sylvia Plath. Much of it functions as autobiography and this creates its impact. *The Women Who Hate Me* discusses lesbian sex, sexual abuse, same-sex domestic violence, rural and urban poverty. All of this hinges on the insight and integrity of the central first person character who narrates the poems.

In 1992 Allison achieved widespread recognition for the novel *Bastard Out of Carolina*. This semiautobiographical work, which tells of the violent sexual abuse of a lesbian child by her stepfather, communicated trauma in a way that no novel had for decades. It also communicated all of Allison's political convictions through the straightforward narration of the truth of one life. This is the self-confessed key to Allison's work and her message. "I try to live as naked as I can," she has said. *Bastard* gained Allison a devoted readership and audience for her performance work. Angelica Houston produced a television adaptation of the novel.

Allison has collected two volumes of her performance pieces, *Two or Three Things I Know for Sure* and *Skin: Talking about Sex, Class and Literature* (both 1995). *Skin* added the American Library Association's award to Allison's other distinctions. She published a second novel, *Cavedweller*, in 1998, and a collection of stories entitled *Trash* in 2002. Allison has founded the Independent Spirit Award for an individual who contributes to the ongoing work of small presses in the United States. She is a committed anti**censorship** feminist and member of PEN international.

AMAZON. The word amazon first appeared in English in the medieval period, deriving from references to Classical Greek and Latin literature. The myth of the amazons in Classical Greece and Rome referred to a race of independent warriors, living in a women-only or female-dominated society who lived in what is now northern Turkey. Interestingly there is now evidence at two archeological sites in Turkey of an early agricultural, Goddess-worshipping culture in which women held a great deal of power. Could the myth be based on the memory of these people? In any event, these archeological sources inspired Riane Eisler's *The Chalice and the Blade* (1988), a significant, though heterosexually biased, example of **cultural feminist** spirituality.

The most significant example of the amazon in late classical literature is surely Virgil's *Aeniad*. Queen Califia and her woman-only band of warriors present a group of powerful, active and independent women in a remarkably positive light. **Early modern** literature drew extensively on classical examples of amazon warriors. These were sometimes presented as exciting and sometimes as threatening. In both classical Greece and Rome and in early modern England, the myth of a fierce, matriarchal society seems to have been placed at the borders of empire. European colonists imagined amazons in South America. If patriarchal empire defined itself as the epitome of civilization and justified its dominance of other peoples through creating them as barbaric, then matriarchy, as opposed to imperial patriarchy, seems to have functioned as one sign of this barbarism. Kathryn

Schwarz's *Tough Love: Amazon Encounters in the English Renaissance* (2000) gives an overview of the amazon topos in early modern English literature and presents a theory about the gender anxieties that give rise to the use of the amazon in culture.

The history of lesbian literature includes a thread of texts that play on the idea of the amazon. **Natalie Clifford Barney** was known as "the amazon" and the circle of lesbian writers and artists who surrounded her were sometimes referred to as The Amazons. Charlotte Perkins Gillman's *Herland* (1915) presented a female only society whose members could reproduce by parthenogenesis. **Monique Wittig**'s **lesbian feminist** classic *Les Guérillières* (1973) is the epic story of a conflict between amazon and patriarchal warriors. **Marion Zimmer Bradley**'s *Darkover Series* of fantasy novels includes a community of amazons among its array of cultural groups.

ANDERSON, MARGARET (1886–1973). The American editor and writer Margaret Anderson is of literary significance for her founding and editing of the modernist journal *The Little Review*. During her early adult life in New York she was a member of a group of bisexual, lesbian and heterosexual feminist activists that included **Emma Goldman**. Long term collaborators and partners were Jane Heap and later Georgette Leblanc.

Anderson founded *The Little Review* in Chicago in 1914 where it was published until 1916. During its 15 year life the journal was based in San Francisco (during 1916), Chicago again (1916–1917), New York (1917–1926) and Paris (1926–1929). Anderson serialized James Joyce's *Ulysses* in 1918 and was brought up on obscenity charges. Both Anderson and Jane Heap were found guilty and fined. During the life of the journal Anderson began an extensive correspondence with the modernist poet Ezra Pound, which has survived. During the 1920s she also contributed reviews to the modernist journal *The Dial*. She published a *Little Review Anthology* in 1953.

Anderson's autobiography was published in three volumes throughout her lifetime: *My Thirty Years War* in 1930, *The Fiery Mountains* in 1953 and *The Strange Necessity* in 1962. She wrote a work of fiction, *Forbidden Fires*, which wasn't published until 23 years after her death. Many of her papers are held in the Michael Currer-Briggs Collection in London.

ANTHOLOGIES. Anthologies have been a particularly important tool in the **lesbian-feminist** movement. Collections of writings by lesbian women allow authors and editors to express a collective lesbian-feminist voice and identity that works against the phallic notion of the lone individual subject (and the lone individual creative artist). Since the **pulp** productions of the 1950s, countless anthologies of lesbian fiction have been produced, covering any variety of historical periods, cultural positions and identity categories.

Historically based anthologies like Lillian Faderman's landmark *Chloe Plus Olivia: An Anthology of Lesbian Literature from the Seventeenth Century to the Present* (1994) solidify the idea of lesbian identity by creating a sense of historical progress and continuity. Terry Castle's *The Literature of Lesbianism: A Historical Anthology from Ariosto to Stonewall* (2003) follows current scholarship by questioning this notion of a continuous lesbian identity. Instead Castle traces the history of what she calls "the lesbian topos" in Western literature over the past five centuries.

In response to the racial, class, age, ability, gender and national bias of mid-20th-century feminism, anthologies have asserted a number of increasingly specific identity positions and sought to articulate both specific and diverse experiences of lesbianism and bisexuality from these positions. Two examples that challenge universalizing collections like *Bushfire: Stories of Lesbian Desire* (Karen Barber, ed., 1991) are: *The Very Inside: An Anthology of Writing by Asian and Pacific Islander Lesbian and Bisexual Women* edited by Sharon Lim-Hing (1994) and *Does Your Mama Know?: An Anthology of Black Lesbian Coming-Out Stories* edited by Catherine E. McKinley and DeLaney L. Joyce (1997). The language used in the titles here is illuminating. It indicates a particular position in terms of power and identity through both spatial metaphor ("The Very Inside") and a celebration of particular dialect and idiom ("Does Your Mama Know?").

Any number of generic categories have produced specifically lesbian anthologies, from the obvious love poetry and erotica to **science fiction** and detective fiction. *Dark Angels: Lesbian Vampire Stories*, edited by Pam Keesey (1995) is but one such production. A more complete list of lesbian literary anthologies is provided at the back of this dictionary.

ANZALDÚA, GLORIA (1942–2004). The poet, short story writer and academic Gloria Anzaldúa was born in the borderlands of the United

States and Mexico into a farm-working family. She received a master's degree from the University of Texas and was completing a doctorate at the time of her death. She began her career teaching the children of migrant workers and began academic work as a lecturer at San Francisco State University in 1979.

Anzaldúa is best remembered for her influential interventions in postcolonial theory. She redefined ideas of identity and nationalism in ways that have had a far-reaching effect on a generation of **lesbian**, **feminist** and post**colonial** theorists. Anzaldúa refused to prioritize any of the many identity categories into which she was placed, and made this refusal into an argument for destabilizing the identities that form targets for violent oppression, alienate individuals and divide cultural groups. At the same time she would fearlessly and productively challenge perpetrators of racism, homophobia and classism. In her writings and interviews she describes her teaching methods. She consciously and carefully broke through the barriers that kept her students from challenging each other, while encouraging them to respect each others' positions.

In *Borderlands/La Frontera* (1987), Anzaldúa builds on the work of Mexican philosopher Jose Vascocelos to develop her most well-known articulation of **hybridity**. She argues for a *"mestiza* consciousness" that would exist outside of/between/simultaneously within multiple identity positions, radically disrupting them. Like most of Anzaldúa's poetry and prose, *La Frontera* is written in a Spanish/English mixture that does not always bother to translate from one to the other. Thus, she welds form and content in challenging the unified consciousness of her readers. She explains her editorial method for the anthology *Haciendo Caras/Making Face, Making Soul: Creative and Critical Perspectives by Feminists of Color* (1990) as

> another way of organizing experience, one that reflects our lives and the way our minds work. As the perspective and focus shift, as topics shift, the listener/reader is forced into participating in the making of meaning—she is forced to connect the dots, to connect the fragments.

For these reasons many academics find her writings a powerful teaching tool.

Anzaldúa promoted the notion of "new tribalism" as an antidote to the worst dangers and excesses of nationalism. New tribalism, as she saw it, would allow peoples to name their oppression in groups without seeing those categories as exhaustive or limiting and without playing into the hands of capitalist nation-building enterprises. Her ideas on nationalism can be categorized with those of Edward Said and Gayatri Spivak. Anzaldúa's lesbian identity formed one of the flashpoints of her cultural critique. She was a committed **lesbian-feminist**, but would never allow this to form an exhaustive definition of who she was. Throughout her life, in spite of increasing world popularity, she demonstrated her political commitment by publishing consistently with Aunt Lute Press, which describes itself as a not-for-profit, multicultural women's press.

Anzaldúa's first gained widespread attention along with Cherrie Moraga for *This Bridge Called My Back: Writings by Radical Women of Color* (1981). Other publications include Interviews/Entrevistas (edited by Analouise Keating), which include interviews from as far back as 1982, and *This Bridge We Call Home: Radical Visions for Transformation*, edited with AnaLouise Keating (2002). She has also written several bilingual children's books. She won the National Endowment for the Arts Award for fiction, as well as a Lambda Literary Foundation award.

ARABIC LITERATURE. The vast majority of criticism that exists on homosexuality in Arabic literature, both classical and modern, focuses on male same-sex desire. There is, however, considerable evidence of female same-sex desire and transgender movement since the classical period. This doesn't seem so much to have been censored as it has been ignored. There are a number of Arabic words for female same-sex practices. These include *sihaq*, which, like the English **tribadism**, focus on the idea of sexual activity in the absence of a penis. The net result is the same—lack of visibility. Most English-language sources on female same-sex love in Arabic literature seem to rely on a single article by As'ad Abukhalil, "A Note on the Study of Homosexuality in Arab/Islamic Civilization."

Stephen O. Murray argues that female same-sex activity was ignored in both Classical Greek and Arabic culture unless either or both of the women violated gender norms by assuming a masculinized identity or performing sex acts that were considered the province of men. Paul Sprachman reports that Persian literature paints lesbianism as decidedly unexciting. In Europe the case was very different. Not only did male erotic writers and pornographers present lesbianism as titillating from at least the 18th century, they also often associated it with romanticized Eastern tales of the all-female environments of the harem or baths. The letters of **Lady Wortley Montague**, first published in the 18th century, were one point of origin for these fantasies. **Jeannette Foster** also identifies an older (16th century) text called *La Fleur Lascive Orientale*, which may have contributed to **cross-dressing** and **transgender** fantasy tales in Europe. By the 19th century when Richard Burton made his influential and highly personalized translation of the *Thousand and One Nights*, he claimed in a note that harems were "hotbeds" of lesbianism.

The one poet who receives any attention is **Walladah Bint Al-Mustakfi**, who lived in Andalusia in the 11th century. Al-Mustakfi was part of a strong female tradition of lyric poetry in Arabic. Within the discipline of women's studies those of her poems with lesbian content are sometimes ignored, as they have often been by male scholars of Arabic literature.

Currently, there is an active movement among Arabic lesbian, gay, bisexual and transgendered people. This is giving rise to an emerging literature. At least one Internet listserv specifically for Arabic lesbians, called *Iman* (faith), exists.

ARIOSTO, LUDOVICO (1474–1533). The Italian language poet Ludovico Ariosto was born in what is now the province of Emelia-Romana. He is celebrated as an innovator in both the use of imaginative language and narrative structure. Ariosto is significant here for his long poem *Orlando Furioso*. The poem, covering Europe's war with the Saracens, was begun in 1505 and first appeared in print in Venice in 1516. One of its tangential episodes describes the confusion caused by the **cross-dressing** woman Bradamante. A women, Fiordispina, falls in love with her, thinking that she is her brother. Both **Jeannette Foster** and Terry Castle focus on this as an important moment in the history of sexually dissident women in literature. Foster, however, records the earlier medieval *Huon of Bordeaux* as the first of these romances of cross-dressing confusion. This narrative motif remained popular until the **nineteenth century**.

AUTOBIOGRAPHY. *See* LIFE-WRITING.

AWARDS. Literary awards serve an important function in creating recognition, support and infrastructure for particular areas of literature.

Gradually as the 20th century went forward, lesbians and other women sought to create such supports for women's, and specifically lesbian, writing through the establishment of a variety of specific literary prizes. An early prize that is significant to the history of lesbian literature is the French *Prix Femina*. The prize isn't exclusive to lesbian literature but is perhaps the first woman-centered literary prize. In place since 1904, it is decided each year by an all-female jury. **Radclyffe Hall** one the *Femina* prize for foreign language literature for *The Unlit Lamp* in 1924. Both **Françoise Mallet-Joris** and **Marguerite Yourçenar** have also won it. Another important French prize is given yearly by the Académie Goncourt. Both **Colette** and Françoise Mallet-Joris have held lifetime chairs at the academy.

In the United States, Barbara Gittings initiated the first award for lesbian and gay writing through the American Library Association. Gittings wanted to promote the availability of lesbian and gay literature in libraries so that no adolescent would have to experience the dearth of information she found in libraries as a young woman. The first recipient was **Isabel Miller** in 1971. The original award has now grown into several Stonewall Awards. The Lambda Literary Foundation has been granting awards for lesbian and gay literature since 1988. The lesbian writer **Dorothy Allison** has founded the Independent Spirit Award, for dedication to the work of small presses. Allison has done this because small presses are often the places where those on the margins of political, economic and cultural activity (including lesbians) can find a place for their work.

In Great Britain no large scale lesbian literary award exists. The Orange Prize for women's fiction was established by members of the publishing industry in 1992. Lesbians remain underrepresented in its list of winners.

– B –

BALZAC, HONORÉ DE (1799–1850). The French novelist Honoré de Balzac began his literary career writing what would now be called pulp fiction. He turned to more "serious" or high-culture work in the 1830s, and is best known for the interconnected series of novels known collectively as the *Comedie Humaine*. Significant here are three works. *Seraphitus-Seraphita* (1834) has an androgynous heroine. The novel details her love affairs with both a man and a woman. Neither affair is consummated, but this is in some ways Balzac's kindest portrait of a sexually dissident woman. The eponymous antiheroine of *La Cousine Bette* (1846) displays an evil-tinged infatuation with another woman. It is *The Girl with the Golden Eyes* (1835), however, which is most remarked upon by scholars who study the image of the lesbian in literature. Another evil lesbian figure, this time entirely overt, is here called Margarita. She has seduced and corrupted (and eventually murders) the hero's object of desire, young Paquita. This novel is important in the history of French **decadent literature**, both poetry and prose, in which the image of excessive, often lesbian, feminine desire, figures strongly.

BANNON, ANN (1932–). The novelist born Ann Weldy is the most celebrated of American "lesbian **pulp**" writers of the 1950s and 1960s. She eventually earned a Ph.D. in linguistics and has taught for many years in California. During the 1950s and early 1960s, however, she lived with a husband and children in the suburbs of New York City, occasionally traveling into Manhattan to visit the urban lesbian subculture in which most of her novels were set. Bannon was one of the lucky writers to work under the editorship of Fiona Nevler at Fawcett Publications, a major pulp house then based in Connecticut. Bannon is famous for a group of novels referred to as the *Beebo Brinker Series*. These novels trace several characters through various permutations of relationships with each other. They began with *Odd Girl Out* (1957), which was an immediate publishing success. Barbara Grier has reported that this was the best-selling paperback original of 1957. The novel traces a love triangle between two women and one man. Man and woman eventually marry, but later novels return to describe the failure of the character Beth's marriage and her eventual journey to New York in search of her woman lover. *I Am a Woman* (1959) introduced the butch heroine Beebo Brinker. *Woman in the Shadows* (1959) details Beebo's emotional breakdown and is in many ways the most abject and negative, but also the most interesting novel of the series. *Journey to a Woman* (1959) returns to the character Beth and details the resolution of her lesbian identity. The final novel, *Beebo Brinker* (1962), circles back to a time before *Odd Girl Out* to detail Beebo's early life and her arrival in Greenwich Village. An offshoot of this series, *The Marriage* (1960) details the marriage of convenience that takes place between two characters, Jack and Laura, from the *Beebo Brinker Series*.

Naiad Press reprinted all of Bannon's novels apart from *The Marriage* in the 1980s. In 2001 Cleis Press again re-released them at a time when the mass-market lesbian paperback had finally achieved recognition as a significant generic category in the study of the history of lesbian fiction. Ann Bannon has been interviewed repeatedly about her life and her writings. *Gay Community News* published an interview with her in 1970 and the documentary films *Before Stonewall* (1984) and *Forbidden Love* (1992) also feature Bannon.

BARNES, DJUNA (1892–1982). The American writer Djuna Barnes was born into an intellectual family in rural New York. She studied visual art in New York City then embarked on a career as a playwright, illustrator and journalist before moving to Paris in 1921. Her first book of poems, *The Book of Repulsive Women*, was published in New York in 1915. The theme of a woman-centered **abjection**, which is begun here, continues throughout her work and makes it important both historically and theoretically. Among Barnes's earliest literary works were plays performed by the now famous Provincetown Players in 1919 and 1920. Throughout her literary career Barnes continued to produce illustrations, which appeared alongside her journalistic work and as an integral part of some of her book projects.

From 1921 to 1939 Barnes lived in Paris where she was employed as a journalistic correspondent by several magazines, including *McCall's*, *Vanity Fair*, *Charm* and *New Yorker*. Much of this work consisted of interviews with the social, artistic and literary figures then comprising the bohemian Paris with which America was so fascinated. The interviews that Barnes conducted and wrote during these years were later published as *I Could Never Be Lonely without a Husband, Interviews*. It was also during these years that Barnes produced her most important literary works. *A Book* (1923) combines the genres of poetry, memoir and fiction. *Ladies Almanack* (1928) is a loving satire based on the circle of women known variously as The Amazons or the **Academy of Women**, which included the most important lesbian literary figures residing in Paris between the wars. This book was first privately printed, but is now widely available. In the same year (1928) Barnes produced *Ryder*, a kind of autobiography disguised as allegory. *Ryder* focuses its ideas of family, descent and inheritance on the connections between female figures.

In 1936 Barnes produced what might be called her most important work, *Nightwood*, which in part fictionalizes Barnes' relationship with a woman named Thelma Wood. Though the novel itself is clearly a conscious exploration of sexual **inversion** (all three of its central characters are sexually dissident), Barnes was annoyed to be categorized as a lesbian by her readers in the 1960s and 1970s. In later life she refused any ascription of sexual identity, saying that she was simply a person who had loved Thelma Wood. Sadly, one reason why *Nightwood* is more widely read and more highly regarded than other of Barnes' works is that her friend T. S. Eliot praised the work highly and wrote two separate introductions to early editions. Still the novel is deeply significant in its own right. Its surrealist style is a landmark in literary modernism, fusing poetically phrased psychological monologues with Gothic description and narrative structure to produce a kind of unconscious map of the modern sexual city. *Nightwood* is significant in the history of lesbian literature in that it moves beyond the desire of contemporary works to produce portraits of lesbianism as either "good" or "bad." It is a story of specifically lesbian desire and loss, which created a new space for the lesbian character in literature. At the same time the influence of both **psychoanalysis** and **sexology** can be read in the book's characters, as can evidence of the lesbian subculture of Paris between the wars.

Barnes moved back to New York City in 1939 and remained there for the rest of her life. Her last significant work was a verse play called *The Antiphon* (1958). Before her death she sold her papers to the University of Maryland, where they remain.

BARNEY, NATALIE CLIFFORD (1876–1972). Natalie Barney is perhaps better known as a social figure portrayed in the writings of other lesbians than she is for her own work. Early in her adult life she was the lover of the poet **Renée Vivien**. Together the two women traveled extensively and studied classical Greek language and literature. After Vivien's death, Barney carried forward her ideal of a modern lesbian life patterned on the classical example of **Sappho**. While writing highly popular memoirs and less recognized poetry, she held a salon at her Paris home, where her garden contained a faux Greek temple. She had highly visible love affairs with the writers **Elisabeth de Gramont** and **Lucie Delarue-Mardrus**.

Barney published *Quelque portraits: sonnets des femmes* in 1900 and *Five Short Greek Dialogues* in 1901. Collections of her autobiographical writings include *Pensées d'un Amazon* (1920) and *Nouvelles pensées d'un Amazon* (1939). Easily recognized character portraits of her are found in **Liane de Pougy**'s *Idylle Sapphique* (1901), which details the two women's love affair, **Colette**'s *Claudine s'en va* (1903), **Radclyffe Hall**'s *The Well of Loneliness* (1928) and **Djuna Barnes**' *Ladies Almanack* (1928).

BAUDELAIRE, CHARLES (1821–1867). The decadent French poet Charles Baudelaire is significant here for his portrayals of excessive lesbian figures. Baudelaire traveled in the French colonies as a young man, absorbing both an **orientalist** aesthetic and a cynical attitude toward bourgeois French social culture. In 1857 he published *Les fleurs du mal*, which was quickly prosecuted for obscenity. The section entitled "Les femmes damnées" associates the lesbian figure with horror and excess. Like the other figures of horror in Baudelaire's work, however, lesbians are clearly a source of **abject** pleasure here. Terry Castle reproduces Richard Howard's translation of the first narrative section of "Les femmes damnées," in which two characters called Delphine and Hyppolyta experience orgiastic lesbian pleasures. Hippolyta's postcoital address to Delphine exemplifies the Gothic nature of Baudelaire's lesbians: "Delphine / I am grateful to you, I have no regrets, / yet I am troubled and my nerves are tense, as if a dreadful feast had fouled the night . . ." Like other decadent writers, Baudelaire uses extravagant language and imagery to produce lesbian characters who are almost vampiric in the devouring excess of their sexual nature. According to **Jeannette Foster**, Baudelaire's publisher announced a forthcoming work called *Les lesbiennes* in 1846. The work never appeared, though the advertisement attests to the marketable nature of the lesbian figure at this period.

Baudelaire's character portraits had a far-reaching influence on lesbian literature. Imitators such as **Algernon Charles Swinburne** and **Aleister Crowley** spread this particular development of the lesbian character into English, while novelists like **Honoré de Balzac** translated it into prose. The poet **Renée Vivien** was influenced profoundly by both Baudelaire's poetic style and his development of a vocabulary of lesbian imagery and desire, yet she reworked his picture of the lesbian into something much more affirmative.

BEACH, SYLVIA (1887–1962). The American expatriate Sylvia Beach is highly significant to the development of modernist literature in English, largely as a patron and social figure. With her partner **Adrienne Monnier**, she founded the English-language bookshop Shakespeare and Company in Paris in 1919. The shop was given financial support by the wealthy lesbian modernist writer and critic, **Bryher**. Beach's most lasting contribution to literature is her publication of James Joyce's novel *Ulysses*. She organized the typesetting and printing of the novel in 1922, when no other publisher (including Leonard and **Virginia Woolf**'s Hogarth Press) would touch the book.

In 1956 Beach wrote a memoir entitled *Shakespeare and Company*, which is of biographical interest to anyone studying the modernist movement. Among other figures depicted in the book are **Gertrude Stein** and **Alice B. Toklas**, whom she gives a very unfriendly treatment. About her own relationship with Monnier, Beach is curiously silent, though not quite closeted, in her memoir.

BEDFORD, SYBILLE (1911–). Sybille Bedford was born in Germany but lived most of her life in England, where she is highly respected as a journalist and fiction writer. Her journalistic work has included coverage of the trial of the staff of the Auschwitz concentration camp, the trial of Lee Harvey Oswald, the assassin Jack Ruby and the censorship trial of *Lady Chatterly's Lover* at the Old Bailey in London in 1959. Her first novel was *The Legacy* (1956). She is perhaps most significant here for the two linked novels *A Favourite of the Gods* and *A Compass Error* (1963), which detail the lives of a mother and daughter respectively. *A Compass Error* focuses on the coming of age and concurrent "coming out" of its protagonist, Flavia.

BELLEAR, LISA (1961–). The aboriginal poet, activist and academic Lisa Bellear has raised the profile of indigenous poetry in Australia, in both popular and academic arenas. She is an active public speaker and teacher, and has published a volume of poems entitled *Dreaming in Urban Areas* (1996).

BEN, LISA (1921–). Lisa Ben (an anagram for lesbian) is the pseudonym under which Edythe Ede self-published the lesbian magazine *Vice Versa* from her secretarial desk in California in 1947 and 1948. The magazine's title played on ideas of both vice and **inversion** and most of its contents were produced by Ede herself, who distributed the magazine by hand and urged the women who read it to pass it on to others. In various articles Ede talks about psychiatry and notions of the third sex, thus giving insight into how one lesbian saw herself through a variety of medical and psychological discourses at this period. In addition Ede argued that women could live and work independently, thus connecting economic autonomy with the possibility for lesbian identification. After a change of employment forced Ede to stop producing *Vice Versa* she began rewriting satirical lesbian versions of popular folksongs, which she performed in bars. Once *The Ladder* began publication she wrote for it, still using the Lisa Ben pseudonym. *The Ladder* produced a recording of her folksongs in 1960. An interview with Ede is included in Eric Marcus' *Making History: The Struggle for Gay and Lesbian Rights: 1945–1990* (1992).

BEHN, APHRA (1640–1689). The bisexual writer Aphra Behn has served as a model for women writers for four centuries. In her extended essay *A Room of One's Own* (1929), **Virginia Woolf** calls for all women to lay flowers at the grave of Aphra Behn because, Woolf claims, she was the first woman to earn a living by her pen. Behn was a staunch royalist and spent time working for the crown as a spy in Amsterdam, living in prison and traveling to the colony of Surinam. She wrote 18 plays for the London stage, including *The Rover* (1677) and *The Feigned Courtesan* (1679). In the 1680s she pioneered a longer prose narrative form that would become the English novel. The epistolary *Love Letters between a Nobleman and His Sister* (1687) and the famous *Oroonoko, or, The Royal Slave* (1688, based on her experiences in Surinam) are good examples here. There is a convincing argument for Behn as the first real English novelist.

It is in her poetry that Behn expresses both an active female sexuality and a number of specifically lesbian desires. Poems of particular interest in these regards are "The Disappointment," "The Dream" and "To the Fair Clarinda."

BERMAN, SABINA (1956–). There are all too few English translations of the work of the Mexican-Jewish playwright and poet Sabina Berman. Her autobiographical novel *Bubbeh* has been translated by Andrea Labinger (1998) and the play *Happy New Century Dr. Freud*, which critiques the psychoanalyst's handling of the famous "Dora case," has been performed in English. Berman has been a tremendous influence on lesbian writing in Spanish, and an object of study for English-language scholars working on Central American writing. Adam Versenyi has translated some of her dramatic works, published in the volume *The Theatre of Sabina Berman:* The Agony of the Ecstasy *and Other Plays* (2002).

BETHAM, MARY MATILDA (1776–1852). Mary Matilda Betham was a clergyman's daughter who moved to London in 1800, where she proceeded to make her own living as a poet and portrait painter. She was compared to Sappho by Coleridge, who admired her work. The full implications of this comparison are unclear. Coleridge, as we know from his own work, was familiar with the lesbian figure and its classical associations, yet Sappho was often invoked merely as the most accomplished of women poets. In any case, Betham was an imposing woman who never married.

Betham's first published work was *Elegies and Other Small Poems* (1797). She was in many ways an early feminist scholar. In 1804 she produced an exhaustive study entitled *Biographical Dictionary of the Celebrated Women of Every Age*. In 1816, she published a long romantic poem, *The Lay of Marie*, which fictionalized the life of the 12th-century poet Marie de France.

BIBLICAL PERIOD. This term generally refers to the historical period covered by the Jewish Torah or Christian Old Testament (roughly from 2500 to 500 B.C.E.). Overall the literature from this period, which most contemporary scholars read as lesbian, displays the conflation of gender deviance and same-sex **object-choice**. That is to say that if women love women it is because they are in the position of men, either through accident or intentional disguise. The myth of the **amazon**, which evolved late in this period, represents a certain set of anxieties about the position of women in society and its possible reversals. Codes of laws established in the Mediterranean World at this period for the most part solidify the relegation of women to the power of fathers and husbands and the privatization of wealth that is passed down through the male line.

Though much concerned with male sodomy and love between men, the Old Testament has virtually nothing to say about sexual love between women. One significant description of female same-sex love occurs in "The Book of Ruth." This book tells the story of a young wife who clings to her husband's mother after his death. Ruth follows her mother-in-law Naomi to Israel where as a result of her dutiful love she is eventually rewarded with marriage to the king, Boaz. Despite this heterosexual ending many women have read the Ruth story as lesbian, because of its moving descriptions of the love of one woman for another. It has been an important influence on 19th- and 20th-century lesbian literature. Another notable Old Testament book is Esther, which tells the story of a Jewish queen's heroic, antiracist act of speech, made in spite of her husband's rule of female silence. An important figure in this story is the dead Vashti, first queen of Ahausuerus. When her drunken husband requested that she display her naked body for the pleasure of himself and his banqueting friends, Vashti refused and was beheaded. She became an important metaphorical figure for 19th-century feminists.

South Asian sacred stories being collected and canonized at this same historical period present many **transgender** figures. Most of these stories focus on deviant or miraculous forms of procreation or on female-to-male warrior figures. *See also* CLASSICAL GREECE AND ROME.

BILDUNGSROMAN. The German term *bildungsroman* is used by literary critics to describe a particular novelistic structure in which a central character leaves an isolated or provincial setting, has various experiences of the world and eventually finds her or his place in the social order. A sense of identity is the goal of the *bildungsroman*, whose protagonist often begins the novel as an adolescent and ends it as an adult. Both **Charlotte Brontë**'s *Jane Eyre* and Charles Dickens' *David Copperfield* are classed as *bildungsromane*. This novelistic genre is significant in the literature of sexuality because of its concern with identity and the struggle of young individuals to negotiate a place within the social order. **Radclyffe Hall**'s *The Well of Loneliness* can be seen as a *bildungsroman*, as can **Bryher**'s novels from the 1920s and many of those pulp novels best loved by lesbians. In the later 20th century the specifically lesbian, gay and transgender form of the **coming-out** novel developed out of the *bildungsroman*.

BIOMYTHOGRAPHY. *See* LIFE-WRITING.

BISHOP, ELIZABETH (1911–1979). The poet Elizabeth Bishop was born in Massachusetts, but spent much of her early life in Nova Scotia. Her independent wealth allowed her both to remain unmarried and to travel extensively. She was close to both Robert Lowell and **Marianne Moore**, and the latter poet was something of a mentor to her in early life. Bishop lived in Brazil for 18 years with her female partner Lota de Macedo Soares. After Soares' suicide she returned to the United States where she took up a residency at Harvard in 1969.

Bishop produced a small but very highly regarded body of work. Her first collection was *North and South* (1946). *A Cold Spring* (1955) and *Questions of Travel* (1965) followed. *Geography III* (1976) was her final collection. It is fair to say that her reputation has grown since her death.

BLACK FEMINISM. In some sense it is illogical to separate black feminism from the "general" category, since both the **first** and **second waves** of feminism in the 19th and 20th centuries were often led by antiracist black feminists. On the other hand, as the contributions of black feminists have been so often ignored it is important to highlight them in one entry. As always in the feminist movement, many of the most significant contributions were made by sexually dissident women. In the United States, the 19th-century feminist abolitionist Sojourner Truth had an enormous impact on both the feminist and abolitionist movements. One of her speeches, made at an antislavery convention in Acron, Ohio, in 1851, is still generating theoretical insight and debate today. In this speech Truth argues that ideals of femininity are unstable and misleading. She illustrates this point with the example of her own life, during which she was granted none of the concessions normally given to the "weaker sex" and yet survived and prospered intellectually and spiritually. Truth then makes a powerful theological argument for the equality of women.

Throughout the late 19th and early 20th centuries, black feminist activists and educators such as Anna Julia Cooper (1858–1963) and Nannie Helen Burroughs (1883–1961) kept a strong tradition of black feminist activism and intellectual inquiry alive. Living in communities constantly threatened by racial violence, material deprivation and genocide, black feminists have necessarily developed more subtle and complex understandings of gender and power than many women who had the privilege of isolating gender as the single and unified cause of their oppression. The journalist and antilynching activist Ida B. Wells, working in the early 20th century ought to be included in the tradition of Southern activism exemplified by Cooper and Burroughs. At the same period literary figures such as **Angelina Weld Grimké** and the suffragist poet **Alice Dunbar Nelson** exemplify the strong relationship between gender politics, antiracist activism and sexual dissidence.

The second wave of feminism was influenced by contemporary antiracist work perhaps less than the first wave, but still very significantly, especially for black women. Much popular discourse discussed the sexism experienced by women in the civil rights movement and the racism, which debilitated the feminist movement. Debates around gender and power ensued. As ever, the sense of a threatened community of both men and women made such discussions more difficult, but ultimately more fruitful. The National Black Feminist Organization was founded in 1973 and the influential Boston-based group the **Combahee River Collective** in 1974. The Combahee River Collective named itself after the scene of a civil war battle led by the abolitionist revolutionary Harriet Tubman. Black feminists were often responded to as a threat both within the wider black activist community and within the white-dominated feminist movement. Apart from the "Combahee River Collective Statement," some landmarks of black feminist publishing have been Angela Davis' *Women, Race and Class* and the collection edited by **Gloria Anzaldúa** and **Cherríe Moraga** entitled *This Bridge Called My Back: Writings by Radical Women of Color* (both 1981) and *All The Women Are White, All the Blacks Are Men, But Some of Us Are Brave* (1987). In 1990, Patricia Hill Collins shifted academic discussions of race and gender with her *Black Feminist Thought: Knowledge, Consciousness and the Politics of Empowerment*. Collins' work focuses on the formation of individual subjectivities within regimes of identity-based power. Representations of black feminism both popular and radical have been significantly advanced by the ongoing work of bell hooks. In the field of literary studies, the work of scholars such as Hazel Carby and **Gloria T. Hull** is important to an understanding of the development of criticism on black women's writing and sexuality. Carby's *Reconstructing Womanhood: The Emergence of the Black Woman Novelist* (1987) is a good introductory text.

BLOOMSBURY GROUP. The early 20th-century group of artists and writers, which included **Virginia Woolf** and E. M. Forster, are known by this name. The name derives from the Bloomsbury area of London, where Woolf and her siblings set up a house in the 1910s. Here they intended to pursue a new aesthetic and political life. This neighborhood includes the British Museum, which then housed the British Library, setting of a well-known scene in Woolf's *A Room of One's Own*. The Bloomsbury group writers were popular and widely read in their own lifetimes, and also notorious for sexual experimentation. Many of the group's members were bisexual and lived in open marriages.

BLUESTOCKINGS. This name was given to a woman-centered group that congregated in London in the second half of the 18th century. It later became a somewhat pejorative term for any woman who expressed intellectual perception or feminist sentiment. The original bluestockings are an early example of liberal feminist endeavor, encouraging "good works" and limited public participation for women. The novelists Frances Burney and **Sarah Scott** both had connections to the bluestocking circle.

BOOKSTORES. Many women's bookstores and independent publishing houses have grown out of the second wave feminist movement around the globe. In a world where women are excluded from public space and public discourse, few women are able to access the space or the resources to influence literary culture. The idea behind women's bookstores was to create a subcultural space in which women could meet, exchange ideas and gain access to empowering literature. Such bookstores, with a consciously political agenda, were often communally run. Volunteer workers often staffed these businesses and they became centers for community organizing, activism and sometimes **independent women's presses**. Lesbian activists and writers were often driving forces behind such projects. **Judy Grahn** and others set up A Woman's Place in Oakland, California, in 1970, for both the publishing and distribution of women's, and specifically lesbian, literature. Old Wives Tales (San Francisco), Amazon (Minneapolis), Labrys and Woman-Books (New York City) and Sisterhood (Los Angeles) soon followed. London's Silver Moon bookshop was communally run and had, for a time, its own publishing facility.

BOOTH, EVA GORE (1870–1928). The writer and socialist activist Eva Gore-Booth was born into the colonial Anglo-Irish aristocracy. Her sister later became Constance Markievicz, the celebrated Irish revolutionary. In 1896 Gore-Booth moved to Manchester with her life partner **Esther Roper**. Both women made lifetime commitments to labor activism and the fight for women's suffrage.

Gore-Booth was a founding member of the Women's Trade Union Council, early member of the Independent Labour Party and editor of the journal *Women's Labour News*. Her first collection of poetry was published in 1898, and nine more followed throughout her lifetime. She also wrote more than 12 plays. Her drama and her poetry expressed her mysticism and sense of the feminine divine. Both Celtic pagan and Christian themes predominate. Her own commentary on her works shows that she consciously reinterpreted classical mythology to accommodate her political and spiritual intentions. Like Markievicz, Gore-Booth was a friend of W. B. Yeats, and the work of the two poets share many themes and concerns. In 1991 Frederick Lapisardi published *The Plays of Eva Gore-Booth*. Some of her political and cultural essays were printed by the League for Peace and Freedom under the subtitle *Peace and Freedom Pamphlets*. These remain in the British Library.

THE BOSTONIANS. The novelist Henry James published *The Bostonians* in 1886. Based in part on James' experience with his own sister, the novel details the struggle between a man and an older feminist for the affections, and control, of a young girl. The young woman is a powerful public speaker and committed feminist, whose family are of a lower class than her new friends. Her wealthy companion and patroness makes regular payments to her father in exchange for the girl's freedom from family obligations. The implications of this are somewhat sinister. In the group of politically active women to which the two partners eventually belong are other female couples who live in partnership. In the novel's eventual resolution, the young protagonist chooses marriage after a dramatic scene in which that choice is presented as in direct opposition to her public speaking. The implication that women's freedom and participation in the public sphere is equivalent to a sterile and exploitative romantic life is clear. The novel is highly significant here for its role in popularizing the mythic (and real) relationship between lesbians and feminism, and for its highly negative but very influential portrayal of that connection. *See also* BOSTON MARRIAGE.

BOSTON MARRIAGE. The term "Boston marriage" refers to life partnerships made between very wealthy women from the 18th to the early 20th century. Independent inheritances allowed a few women to forgo heterosexual marriage. Among women who were politically and intellectually active, and/or who loved other women, this option was particularly attractive. The phrase lends the title to Henry James' (1886) novel *The Bostonians*. The American writer **Sarah Orne Jewett** lived in a Boston marriage with partner Annie Adams Fields. **Eva Gore-Booth** and **Esther Roper** in Britain lived in a similar arrangement. Carol Smith-Rosenberg, Lillian Faderman and Josephine Donovan have all written on the practice of Boston marriage. *See also* ROMANTIC FRIENDSHIP.

BOWEN, ELISABETH (1899–1973). The Anglo-Irish fiction writer Elizabeth Bowen was born a wealthy member of the colonial aristocracy. After her marriage she spent much of her time in Oxford, where she befriended other modernist writers, including **Virginia Woolf** and **Rosamund Lehmann**. Her first published work was a collection of short stories, *Encounters* (1923). Throughout her working life Bowen depicted characters who inhabited a variety of sexually dissident positions. Sexuality is a subtle and complex issue in her work. She never depicted any easy or stable homosexual identities, but nor did she allow a facile heterosexuality to be assumed. Many of her female characters have complex relationships with each other that may be read as lesbian. **Jeannette Foster** gives a detailed reading of Bowen's first novel *The Hotel* (1927), which she sees as clearly "sexually variant." Bowen's brief love affair with **May Sarton** is depicted in Sarton's *A World of Light* (1976).

BOWLES, JANE (1917–1973). The American writer Jane Auer Bowles came of age in Manhattan's lesbian and gay subculture in the 1930s and 1940s. She entered a marriage of convenience with Paul Bowles and remained in it until her death, though both partners led separate sexual and romantic lives. Bowles was a highly intellectual existentialist writer, who had many literary admirers (including the playwright Tennessee Williams). One result of this, however, is that her works are not often examined with a lesbian reading practice, but are confined in a rarefied (male-dominated) critical world. She is best known for the novel *Two Serious Ladies* (1943), but also had one play performed in her lifetime, *In the Summer House* (1953) and published a number of short stories. Bowles' correspondence has been collected and edited by Millicent Dillon in *Out in the World: Selected Letters of Jane Bowles, 1935–1970* (1985).

BRADLEY, KATHERINE. *See* MICHAEL FIELD.

BRADLEY, MARION ZIMMER (1930–1999). The American novelist Marion Zimmer Bradley is best known as a writer of **science fiction** and fantasy. She published her first story in the science fiction magazine *Vortex* in 1952, beginning a tremendously successful science fiction/fantasy career. At the same period, however, she was writing lesbian **pulp** novels under the pseudonyms Morgan Ives, Miriam Gardner and Lee Chapman. As Lee Chapman, Bradley wrote *I Am a Lesbian* in 1962. She also made regular contributions to the homophile publications *The Ladder* and *Mattachine Review*. In 1960 Bradley edited the *Checklist of Lesbian Literature* with **Barbara Grier**.

Bradley's *Darkover Series* began with *Planet Savers* in 1962, the same year in which *I Am a Lesbian* appeared, and continued until her death. In science fiction and fantasy Bradley reimagines sexual possibilities for women. She is well loved throughout the American feminist community for her woman-centered reworkings of Arthurian legends in the *Avalon* series of fantasy novels, which began with *The Mists of Avalon* in 1982.

BRONTË, ANN (1820–1849). The English novelist Ann Brontë was born and raised in Yorkshire, where she attended a girl's boarding school in the 1830s. In the late 1830s and 1840s Ann worked as a governess at two different wealthy households in Yorkshire. She is included here both as a context to her sisters and for her novel *The Tenant of Wildfell Hall* (1848), which was a significant feminist achievement. The theme of *Tenant*, divorce, the abuse of married women and their rights, was so controversial that Brontë's own family distanced themselves from the work. Charlotte later described the book's theme as ill-advised and declined the opportunity to edit the novel for republication after Ann's death. It is clear that Ann was breaking new ground in the description of women's desire in this book and in many ways *Tenant* anticipated the concerns of novels that would become a popular arena for debating women's sexuality in the 1860s. She also wrote the novel *Agnes Grey* (1847), a protest against the working conditions of governesses.

BRONTË, CHARLOTTE (1816–1855). The English novelist Charlotte Brontë is perhaps the best known of a highly significant 19th-century Yorkshire literary family. The Brontë's grew up in a close-knit religious family with little outside society. Charlotte traveled to Belgium in the 1830s where she worked as a teacher in a girl's school. Her novel *Villette* (1853) is based on these experiences and contains a description of a passionate attachment between a young teacher and a senior pupil. This relationship ought certainly to be viewed in its historical context as a **romantic friendship** rather than a sexual relationship in the 20th-century sense, yet it remains an important landmark in literary relationships between women. Biographical scholarship contains hints that Charlotte herself may have experienced a romantic friendship with another young women in her early school life.

Charlotte is perhaps best known for her novel *Jane Eyre* (1847), which describes the life of a governess and her passionate attachment to her older, enigmatic male employer. The book presents a radicalized portrait of female sexual excess in the character of Bertha Mason, and numerous highly erotic descriptions of heterosexual passion in the narration focalized through the character of Jane. *Shirley* (1849) is a clearly gender dissident novel that places its eponymous female character in the transgendered position of a country squire and presents many feminist arguments through its dialogue and narration. The novel ends with two parallel heterosexual romantic resolutions.

BRONTË, EMILY (1818–1848). The English novelist Emily Brontë produced only one published work in her life time. *Wuthering Heights* (1847) is a Gothic portrait of a tragic romance, which reveals a fascination with sexual passion and death. Early in her life Emily produced a number of poems that seem to describe a **romantic friendship** with another woman. **Jeannette Foster** argues that Emily experienced a passionate and painful attachment to another young woman while at boarding school and that these emotions were translated into the doomed heterosexual passion depicted in her only novel.

BROPHY, BRIGID (1929–1995). The English essayist and novelist Brigid Brophy attended Oxford University in the 1940s, but was expelled for what may have been a lesbian scandal. She is most significant here for *The Finishing Touch* (1963), which depicts the sexually charged atmosphere of a girl's **school**. She published collected essays as *Baroque and Roll and Other Essays* in 1986.

BROSSARD, NICOLE (1943–). The Quebecois writer Nicole Brossard has foregrounded a **lesbian-feminist** politics throughout her work as an editor, poet and novelist, while at the same time working consciously within a (nationally) marginalized language and making critical experiments with form and representation. In 1965 Brossard founded the magazine *La Barre du Jour*, and since that time she has produced over 20 collections of poetry. Among Brossard's novels, which have been translated into English, are *Picture Theory* (1982, translation 1991) and *Mauve Desert* (1987, translation 1990).

BROUMAS, OLGA (1949–). The Greek-born poet Olga Broumas has spent most of her life in the United States, though both Greek and American cultural influences have been formative in her work. Following the tradition exemplified by **Renée Vivien**, Broumas uses classical Greek mythology and literature in forming her representation of the lesbian. At the same time, Broumas is a deeply political writer, who avoids any recourse to romantic, ahistorical ideas of lesbian life. Among Broumas' collections of poetry are *Beginning with O* (1976), *Caritas* (1976), *Perpetua* (1976) and *Sappho's Gymnasium* (1994).

BROWN, RITA MAE (1944–). The American lesbian activist and writer Rita Mae Brown was born in Pennsylvania but has lived much of her life in the southern United States, which is the setting for many of her novels. Brown was an early member of the National Organization for Women (NOW), where she was one of a group of outspoken lesbian activists. She resigned from NOW in protest against the homophobia that pervaded the organization in its early years. Brown's first novel *Rubyfruit Jungle* (1973) uses the form of the ***bildungsroman*** to detail one young working-class lesbian's search for an understanding of herself and her lesbian identity. A series of novelistic treatments of sex and gender dissidence followed, including *Southern Discomfort* (1982), which is perhaps the best example.

More recently, Brown has published three series' of crime novels, including the series begun with *Wish You Were Here* in 1990, and the "Sneaky-Pie" series, beginning with *Outfoxed* in 2000. Her one autobiographical work details her life as an antiracist, feminist lesbian activist.

BRYHER (1894–1983). The English writer and critic born Annie Winifred Ellerman chose the name Bryher in part to signify her transgender identity. Bryher was born in 1894 to a shipping magnate who was then the wealthiest man in England. In 1933 she inherited enough money to live comfortably for the rest of her life and to fund numerous artistic and literary projects. Like other lesbian, bisexual and transgendered women who have been considered historically significant figures in the development of the modernist lesbian identity, Bryher was privileged to have enough money both to live independently and to pursue literary projects.

In the 1920s, Bryher published two novels, *Development* (1920) and *Two Selves* (1923). Together, these detail the coming of age and reconciliation of the identity of a lesbian character. Thus they make significant contributions to the form of the lesbian novel, which is about the formation of identity. These move from what critics might call the ***bil-***

dungsroman in the modernist period, to the **coming-out** novel of the postmodern era. Bryher is equally significant, however, to the history of art cinema. She cofounded and edited the first English-language art film journal *Close Up* and collaborated on films with Kenneth Macpherson and her partner, the poet know as H.D. (**Hilda Doolittle**). In 1930 Bryher and H.D., along with the performer and activist Paul Robeson and his wife, made the experimental film *Borderline*, which attempts to challenge ideas of fixed categories of race and gender. It is possible that today Bryher would consider herself a transgendered rather than a lesbian figure. In any event, she made critical visual and literary interventions in modernist debates around gender identity.

In all, Bryher produced ten historical novels and one literary journal, *Life and Letters Today* (1934–1950). Her memoirs include *The Heart to Artemis: A Writer's Memoirs* (1963) and *The Days of Mars: A Memoir, 1940–1946* (1972), which details her experiences during World War II.

BUTCH. The phrase butch came into usage in English to denote a masculine lesbian in the early 20th century. By midcentury it was in common usage. **Sexological** theories of lesbian desire, beginning in the 1860s and 1870s, saw female same-sex desire as a "confusion" of gender identification. Thus, women who desired women must be more masculine than "normal" women. These theories were problematic for explaining cases in which feminine women desired other women. A culture of masculine and feminine lesbian coupling was in practice in France from at least 1880, when **Emile Zola** recorded it in his novel *Nana*. Throughout the early 20th century in Great Britain and the United States, working-class lesbian culture built itself around a bar culture that included a set of visual and behavioral butch and **femme** codes. At this same period middle-class and upper-class lesbians consciously distanced themselves from what they saw as the vulgar "obviousness" of femme and butch styles and behaviors.

In the mid-20th century, lesbian **pulp fiction** in the United States, as well as British novels such **Maureen Duffy**'s *Microcosm* (1966), depict the femme-butch traditions of lesbian bar culture. Leslie Feinberg's 1993 American novel *Stone Butch Blues* fictionalizes the life of a butch lesbian in the mid-20th century. From the late 20th century, lesbian writers such as **Joan Nestle** and **Pat Califia** began to publish work that sought to redefine femme-butch practices as radical and empowering. Nestle argues that femme-butch codes of dress and behavior made lesbian couples visible and challenged accepted heterosexual gender norms. Other lesbian activists continue to argue that femme-butch culture involved a sexism similar to that in the wider gender culture, through which femme lesbians suffered. Nestle herself acknowledges this, but believes it can be addressed without losing the radical potential of femme-butch practice. Lesbian theorists Sue-Ellen Case and **Judith Butler** have argued that all gender is performance and that butch lesbians and drag queens challenge heterosexual culture by making the instability of gender obvious.

BUTLER, JUDITH (1954–). The literary critic and philosopher Judith Butler holds an academic post at the University of California at Berkeley. She has been most famous and influential in questioning assumptions made by many **second-wave feminists** regarding sex and gender. One important theoretical step made by 20th-century feminists was to separate biological sex from socially constructed gender. For centuries the subjugation of women in the family, enforced sex and child-bearing and women's exclusion from the public sphere, as well as, of course, their enforced heterosexuality, had been explained through reference to what was called "nature." The common phrase "biology is destiny" was used by antifeminists to argue that, as women's bodies were made for child-bearing, nature intended them to remain in the home, embrace feminine passivity and accept male control. Twentieth-century feminist theorists demonstrated that gender was socially constructed and therefore was *part* of the social control of women rather than a justification for it. At the same time, however, feminism focused on the biological specificity of women's bodies in their formation of female power. In her book *Gender Trouble: Feminism and the Subversion of Identity* (1990), Butler points out that though feminism questioned the construction of gender it nevertheless rests on the idea of an essential category called "women." This, says Butler, is clearly a paradox. She also points out that notions of biological sex are equally constructed by culture. Discourses of biology, anthropology and anatomy have relegated all humans into two categories of sex, even when the physical reality is not that simple.

Judith Butler's work builds upon **psychoanalysis** (in particular on the **Lacanian** idea of the human subject as constructed through language) and on the work of the 20th-century French historian and philosopher Michel Foucault. She combines psychoanalytic ideas of the formation of the self—the human psyche—with Foucault's post-structuralist formation of the human *subject*—a product of historically specific discourses and power relations—as opposed to the Enlightenment idea of the *person* or *individual* who already exists prior to philosophy or the law.

Butler's *Bodies That Matter: On the Discursive Limits of Sex* (1993) seeks to explore the relationship between the gendered human subject and the physical body. She continues to see this body as a product of the psyche, rather than a home for it. Here she explores the way in which the limits of the body are imagined through **abjection** and the way in which sexed and gendered bodies are imagined through the performance and "reiteration" of sex and gender. Crucially, Butler argues that if gender positions must be constantly reiterated in order to retain their power and significance, then that reiteration leaves room for imperfection and thus subversion. The classic example here is the practice of drag. **Cross-dressing** individuals expose the constructed nature of gender by performing it in mixed, imperfect or overly perfect, exaggerated ways. This notion of the power of imperfect reiteration is further developed in Butler's The *Psychic Life of Power* (1997).

Butler's theory is widely taught and has influenced the direction of lesbian, gay, transgender and queer studies in the 20th and 21st centuries. She herself is a literary theorist. Her works often include controversial readings of novels and films. Fiction writers such as **Jeannette Winterson** and **Patricia Duncker** have been heavily influenced by her work. *See also* PERFORMATIVITY.

– C –

CALIFIA, PAT (1954–). Pat Califia has been a lesbian and transgender activist for virtually all of his adult life. Born into a working-class family in Texas, Califia first came out as a lesbian in the 1970s. She moved from Texas to San Francisco, where she wrote for the lesbian magazine *Sisters* from 1973. In the mid-1970s Califia began to speak and write publicly and positively about sado-masochistic (SM) sexual practice. Califia and other activists founded the SM pride organization Samois in 1978. Within a decade the debate around sex, power and role-play was a central flashpoint for feminism. Califia has always maintained that understanding sex as play with power can be liberating for all women. This flies in the face of an antipornography feminism that sees women as inherently attached to a position of feminine passivity and victimization through sexual power relationships.

Beginning in the late 1980s Califia began to articulate a transgender identity, but continued to write for lesbian publications after his sex reassignment surgery in 1990. Califia's work is never satisfied with the identity categories and understandings of power that organize the lives of the majority of individuals. As such, all of his work has been challenging, even within the communities from which he writes. In 1980, *Sapphistry: The Book of Lesbian Sexuality* announced Califia as an important sex activist. The 1998 collection of pornographic stories *Macho Sluts* quickly became a classic for a generation of sex-positive, gender transgressive lesbian feminists. Central to Califia's understanding of sexuality is his insistence that **pornography** (or **erotica**) can be an empowering and transformative category of literature for those whose gender and sexuality has been marginalized. Again, this has brought him into direct opposition to the views of a vocal majority of antipornography feminists.

Califia's book *Melting Point* (1994) was one of the publications named in the highly visible Canadian **censorship** case *Regina v. Butler*. This case regarded the confiscation at the United States border of a number of publications headed for a women's bookstore in Canada. The eventual legal decision supported the censorship of work defined as pornographic (such as *Melting Point*) but ruled that the law had been unevenly applied to lesbian and gay works in this case. A sense of Califia's versatility as a writer can be gotten from the 1994 vampire novel *Mortal Companion*. His 1997 *Sex Changes* uses both creative and critical writing forms to detail the history of the trans movement and outline an overview of **transgender** theory in the 20th century.

CAMERON, BARBARA MAY (1954–2002). The Native American lesbian activist Barbara May Cameron was raised on the Standing Rock reservation in South Dakota and moved to San Francisco as a young adult. Once there, she cofounded the organization Gay American Indians in 1975. Her poetry and essays have been anthologized in several collections of writings by women of color. The essay "Gee, You Don't Look Like an Indian from the Reservation," anthologized in Anzaldúa and Moraga's *This Bridge Called My Back* (1987), articulates the sense of marginalization Cameron felt within both Lesbian and Gay and Native American activist movements. The essay is widely taught and has been influential in the development of an understanding of lesbian activism in the United States. Cameron articulated power differences both in the movements within which she worked and in the larger structures that organized her world.

CARMILLA. See VAMPIRE FICTION.

CATHER, WILLA (1873–1947). The American novelist Willa Cather looked up to **Sarah Orne Jewett** as a kind of mentor early in her career. Cather's transgender identity was first expressed when she changed her name to William and began to cross-dress in her teenage years. She was raised among immigrant farmers in Nebraska, but herself came from a privileged family and received an excellent education, at least by late 19th-century standards for women. She had long-term relationships with both Isabele McClung and Edith Lewis.

Cather is acclaimed as an innovator and master of American prose fiction. In addition, her work subtly but significantly changed the possibility for the psychological and narrative representation of women in American fiction. *Oh, Pioneers!* (1913) presents a masculinized heroine and deliberately subverts the romance narrative, which had hitherto dominated the fiction created by women writers. *The Song of the Lark* (1915) plays upon colonialist ideas about ancient Native American civilization to create a woman-centered subconscious journey for its heroine. *Death Comes for the Archbishop* (1927) is Cather's acknowledged masterwork. *Sapphira and the Slave Girl* (1940) has been discussed by Toni Morrison in her *Playing in the Dark: Whiteness and the Literary Imagination* (1992). Morrison points out that this novel is underrepresented in the overall criticism of Cather's work and argues that this is because the novel raises highly uncomfortable questions about the interrelation of race and sexuality in American culture. Cather won the Pulitzer Prize for fiction in 1923. Her relationship with Edith Lewis lasted until her death in 1947.

CENSORSHIP. The lesbian identity, as it has evolved in modern Western culture, is more visibly about sexual behavior than economic social positionings. In reality, of course, the lesbian identity is a combination of sexual love between women and female economic independence. The focus on sex follows the overall control of women's economic lives through recourse to ideas of sexual being. In this context, we can see sexual censorship, the control of sexual representations in culture, as a further attempt to control material relationships through sexual ones. Therefore, lesbian sexuality, as it threatens to overturn the economic and sexual subordination of women, has been the subject of numerous efforts at control. Early efforts at sexological inquiry were subjected to prosecution for obscenity. Most notably Havelock Ellis' *Studies in the Psychology of Sex* was prosecuted in England in 1898 and the archives of Magnus Hirschfeld's Institute for Sexual Science in Berlin were destroyed by Nazi Youth in 1933.

The first American play to be successfully prosecuted for obscenity was Sholem Asch's **God of Vengeance**, which featured a lesbian character. The most notorious censorship trial of a lesbian (perhaps, more accurately, a transgendered) novel was the British trial around **Radclyffe Hall**'s ***The Well of Loneliness*** in 1928. The novel was also prosecuted, though unsuccessfully, in the United States in 1929. Censorship in U.S. case law was changed radically by the trial around James Joyce's novel *Ulysses* in *United States v. One Book Called* Ulysses (1933). **Jeannette Foster** discusses the prosecutions of two lesbian novels, *Love Like a Shadow*, by Lois Lodge in 1934 and *Mardigras Madness*, published under the pseudonym Davis Dresser 1935. Other landmark moments in the censorship of lesbian literature include The Committee for the Investigation of Current Pornographic Materials, chaired by one Senator Gathings in Washington, D.C., in December of 1952. This committee heard testimony from publishers, local police officers and members of the "concerned public" regarding literature defined as obscene. The transcripts of the so-called "Gathings Committee" hearings make interesting reading, as the committee needed to define ideas of obscenity and justifications for censorship. As is often the case, these are bound up with ideas of national security and racial power. Both pacifism and miscegenation, for example, are cited as dangerous. **Tereska Tores'** novel *Women's Barracks* (1952) was examined closely by the committee, along with other lesbian novels. More recently the Canadian Customs Service stopped the importation of a shipment of books destined for a lesbian bookstore, including works by **Judith Butler** and **Pat Califia**. This led to the case *Regina v. Butler* in 1994.

CHARKE, CHARLOTTE (1713–1760). The 18th-century English transgender actress Charlotte Charke is significant here for her autobiography, *A Narrative of the Life of Mrs. Charlotte Charke* (1755). Charke was raised in and around the Drury Lane Theatre by her father, the theater director Colly Cibber. After a break with her family and a time working for Henry Fielding at the New Haymarket Theater, Charke resorted to numerous odd jobs in order to support herself. She then carried her facility for cross-dressing stage roles into life, living for at least a short time as a man. After two heterosexual marriages, she lived as Mr. Brown with one Mrs. Brown from 1747 until her death. These and many other adventures are detailed in her autobiography. *See also* EARLY MODERN PERIOD.

CHATTERJI, BANKIM CHANDRA (1838–1894). The anticolonial Bengali novelist Bankim Chandra Chatterji is significant here for the nationalist novel *Anandamath* (1882), which features a **cross-dressing** heroine at least partly based on gender transgressive characters in classical **South Asian literature**. He also articulates a contemporary lesbian encounter in *Indira* (1873), a novella in which the eponymous heroine is an estranged wife who falls in love with the wife of her partner.

THE CHILDREN'S HOUR. This play, written by Lillian Hellman, was first produced in 1934. Some critics have argued that it was based on the real life Scottish Libel case of 1811, in which two teachers at a girl's school were accused of engaging in "unnatural acts" and sued their accuser for libel. The play details a similar story, in which the lives of two women are destroyed by accusations of lesbianism, which hold some truth for at least one of the characters. The

1961 film adaptation is perhaps better known than the play, which remarkably escaped prosecution for **censorship** when it was first performed on Broadway in New York City.

CHOISEUL-MEUSE, FELICITÉ DE (?–18?). The French novelist Felicité de Choiseul-Meuse published a number of erotic novels in the first decades of the 19th century. Most significant here is *Julie, ou j'ai sauvé ma rose*, which includes a young woman's encounter with lesbian romance. Interestingly, Choiseul-Meuse also published *Recreations morales et amusantes, à l'usage des jeunes demoiselles* (*Moral and Amusing Pastimes for Young Ladies*) in 1810.

CHRISTIAN, PAULA (19?–). Many lesbian **pulp** paperback originals were published under the name Paula Christian from 1959 until the late 1960s. Life history material reveals that many lesbians who read lesbian paperbacks in the postwar period remember Paula Christian's name. She was one of a cohort of women, including **Valerie Taylor** and **Ann Bannon**, who were not held to plot formulas by the paperback publishing houses. Here characters often achieve love and fulfillment in the conclusions of her novels. Some notable works include *Edge of Twilight* (1959), *Another Kind of Love* (1963), *Amanda* (1965), *The Other Side of Desire* (1967) and *Love Is Where You Find It* (1969). In the United States her works were published by Avon and Belmont, in the United Kingdom by Mayflower and Castle. In 1982 Christian published the novel *Cruise*.

CHRYSTOS (19?–). Native American activist and poet Chrystos has used her work to articulate the Native American identity as both urban and lesbian. She lives in Washington state where she is active in the land treaty rights movement. The theme of what she calls "love and lust" is a constant throughout the body of her work and creates an active and positive sexuality. Her collections of poetry include *Not Vanishing* (1988) and *Fire Power* (1995). She has been anthologized in *This Bridge Called My Back: Writings by Radical Women of Color* (1987) and *Living the Spirit: A Gay American Indian Anthology* (1988).

CLASS. An understanding of lesbian identity as socially constructed must also lead to the understanding that construction operated differently according to varying social positions of class, race, gender, ethnicity and nation. Likewise an understanding of sexual control as primarily economic must lead to an understanding that class is a primary building block of the lesbian identity. Virtually all of the novels that we think of as forming the lesbian identity during the **modernist** period were written by women in tremendous positions of economic privilege. Only during and after World War II did a recognizable working-class lesbian identity begin to appear in literature. An upper-class worldview pervades the work of writers like **Radclyffe Hall** and **Virginia Woolf**.

The tremendous boom in lesbian **pulp** fiction at mid-20th century marked out a lesbian literature that featured working-class characters, and was consumed by women and men of all social classes. The association with pulp fiction with "low" culture, and with the **femme** and **butch** identities that marked the working-class lesbian bar world, earned it an unfriendly relationship with an early **lesbian-feminism** dominated by middle- and upper-class women. At the same time, writings by early (1970s) feminist and lesbian and gay groups, such as the London branch of Gay Liberation Front and Boston's **Combahee River Collective**, display a radical understanding of the relations between class, race and sexuality. In 1962 **Maureen Duffy** broke ground with her English articulation of a working-class lesbian identity in *That's How It Was*. The American poet **Judy Grahn** expressed these same relations throughout her work in this era.

As lesbian-feminism began to come to terms with its class bias in the 1980s, writers such as **Gloria Anzaldúa**, **Joan Nestle**, and **Pat Califia** made literary innovations in working-class lesbian representation. These same writers also began to theorize the relationship between class and sexual identity. The American poet and novelist **Dorothy Allison** produced a radical articulation of working-class identity in her 1992 novel *Bastard Out of Carolina*.

An atmosphere of "tolerance" for lesbian, gay and transgender sexualities has grown since the 1980s, and this has led to an understanding of lesbians as a specific target for marketers. The economic independence of women is no longer a real threat to the material structures that underpin our society. Therefore sexually dissident women (at least those with any sort of economic privilege) are now more implicated in, than threatening to, capitalist structures of power. The huge marketing success of writers such as **Sarah Waters** (and the male-authored film adaptations of her work) are a testament to this new relationship. *See also* MANIFESTOS.

CLASSICAL GREECE AND ROME. The term "classical period" often refers to the extent of the culturally continuous Greek and Roman empires from roughly 600 B.C.E. to 400 C.E. In classical Greece women had very little power under the law. Upper-class married women in particular led highly privatized and restricted lives. Courtesans spent more time in public but also often had slave status. Some scholars argue that the evidence contained in Greek drama shows a much more powerful role for women than the law would suggest. Same-sex love in this period was associated primarily with men and seen as a more pure experience than heterosexual love. The latter is associated with spiritual being and the former with material distraction.

The most concrete examples of Greek lesbian literature in this period are those of **Sappho** and her possible disciples Gyrinno and Damophyla in the 7th century B.C.E. The later Latin writer Ovid portrays Sappho as a frustrated heterosexual lover who throws herself from a cliff and dies. The burnings of Sappho's writings by Christians and the popularity of Ovid throughout the early modern period ensured that this was the picture of Sappho that survived. The American-French poet **Renée Vivien** did much to dispel this myth, also translating the work of Sappho and her disciples into modern French.

During the period of the Roman empire, lesbianism, often derogatorily referred to as **tribadism**, was well known but most often associated with courtesans. This makes clear the association between female same-sex love and licentiousness and excess. There is some evidence that lesbianism was seen as unthreatening in a society that was primarily concerned with the legitimacy of children. Sex between women didn't produce children and may therefore have been tolerated, though rendered invisible through lack of literary and historical representation. Many examples of **cross-dressing** and **transgendered** women occur in classical literature. These may express anxieties about strict and oppressive gender roles as much as they express any real dissent in society, though this also certainly did occur. Virgil's *Aeneid* (19 B.C.E.) features amid its divine and earthly heterosexual marriages, an army of **amazon** warriors led by the **butch** and fearless Camilla, beloved of the goddess Diana. Diana herself, of course, along with the goddess Minerva, represent deviations from the passive heterosexual picture of womankind.

A significant lesbian literature from the Roman empire has not survived, which is not to say that it didn't exist. It is only by fortunate accident that the work of a poet like Sappho has been preserved.

COLETTE, SIDONIE GABRIELLE (1873–1954). The bisexual writer and cabaret performer known most often simply as Colette was born and raised in rural Burgundy in the late 19th century. Her first novels were published at the instigation of her first husband, Henry Gauthier-Villars. The so-called Claudine novels were published under this husband's pen name, Willy, and though Colette tried in later life to assert her right to have her name associated with them she was never successful in this. Some biographers claim that Gauthier-Villars coerced her into writing these sexually suggestive novels by locking her away until she had produced enough material each day. Like most of Colette's work the Claudine novels exist somewhere between fiction and **autobiography**. *Claudine a l'ecole* (*Claudine at School*, 1900) features a predatory lesbian headmistress and *Claudine a ménage* (*Claudine Married*, 1902) features a lesbian liaison, which the wife engages in to gratify her husband. These novels were an immediate and huge marketing success, even giving rise to a number of tie-in products bearing the name Claudine.

Colette divorced Gauthier-Villars in 1906 and set-up house in Paris on her own, making a sensation as a cabaret performer. Her shows included sexually explicit scenes including a lesbian kiss between Colette and her lover the Marquise de Belbouf (called Missy). Colette's relationship with Missy lasted for six years. She has also been romantically linked to **Natalie Clifford Barney** and Gabriele D'Anunzzio.

Colette produced over 60 books in her lifetime. Notable among these are *La Vagabonde* (1910), *Le Blé en herbe* (1923), *La Seconde* (1929) *Cheri* (1920) and *The Last of Cheri* (1926). These works focus on a variety of sexually dissident relationships, including an affair with the son of her third husband detailed in the Cheri novels. Each focuses on sexual dissidence and social isolation. Colette's work is known for presenting the tension between the independence and the sexual passion of her central female characters.

Most significant here is the 1932 volume *The Pure and the Impure*, which fictionalizes the group of Paris-based women writers that Natalie Clifford Barney called the **Academy of Women**. A thinly veiled and unfriendly portrait of the poet **Renée Vivien** is presented in this work. In distinguishing between the "pure" and the "impure" Colette focuses not on any Christian definition of sin, but on those who love well and in moderation and those whose characters tend to unhealthy excess. This model follows one common in Edwardian gay and lesbian writing and thought, which sees same-sex love through classical Greek writing as capable of the most pure and heavenly expression.

In later life Colette produced two memoirs, *L'étoile vesper* (1946) and *Le Fanal bleu* (1949). She was a members of the Belgian Royal Academy from the 1930s, and was the first woman ever admitted to the Parisian Goncourt Academy. On her death in 1954, she was granted a full state funeral by the French government.

COLONIALISM. The term colonialism refers most often to the violent takeover of many lands and cultures by the military and economic powers of Western Europe from the **early modern** period to the present day. Colonialism is significant here for a number of reasons. European sciences such as anthropology and sexology were based on a set of comparisons made between Europeans and colonized people. For example, **Sigmund Freud**'s *Totem and Taboo*, drawing upon both of these scientific disciplines, examines the sexual development of European children as parallel to the sexual life of "primitive" (i.e., colonized) people. Thus the comparison, often based on false or mythical information, between Europeans and racial **others** provided the basis for developing European ideas about sexuality, which in turn came to dominate the world. Works like H. Rider Haggard's *She* (1887) and Richard Marsh's *The Beetle* (1897) exemplify this development in interesting ways.

At the same time privileged individuals and subcultural groups from the metropolitan "centers" of the colonial world saw the colonies as places where sexuality was more fluid and its expressions more licentious. The concept of the "primitive," which was often used to justify the colonial endeavor, rested partially on the idea that colonized people were less sexually inhibited than Europeans, and thus in need of "civilizing." At the same time however, this idea led to numerous fantasies, often expressed in literary and other art forms, about the sexuality of colonized peoples and the sexual freedom that could be enjoyed in colonized sexual spaces. Lesbianism, from at least the 17th century, was a component of such fantasies. More recently in many former colonies debates around sexuality have both borrowed from and struggled against European ideas of heterosexual, gay, **lesbian**, bisexual and transgender identities. From the 1970s, a school of lesbian and gay scholarship used examples from colonized cultures (such as Native American practices of *bardache* and *winkte* identities, and South Asian concepts of *yaari* and *saheli* and *hijra* identities) to argue that lesbian and gay identities are universal and timeless. While a cross-cultural scholarship of sexuality has been and continues to be highly valuable, some theoretical moves tend to erase the cultural specificity of sexual identity and romantic and sexual practices, placing all within a "universal" set of definitions, which are in reality European.

Lesbian activism and scholarship is vibrantly expressed in a range of global languages and cultural contexts in the 21st century, though this remains largely unrecognized in the English speaking world. Among myriad expressions of lesbian sexuality in postcolonial contexts, a few examples of writers working in English are **Ashwini Sukhthanker**, **Ama Ata Aidoo** and **Gloria Anzaldúa**. Writing in numerous indigenous languages from Shona to Malayalam still awaits global recognition.

One difficulty that arises in former colonies is the association of lesbian identities with Western culture. Right wing groups in nations such as India and Zimbabwe have depicted lesbian and gay sexualities as a colonial menace brought in by decadent Europeans, thus attempting to disarm activists by associating them with a violent and damaging history. In reality, both heterosexual *and* lesbian identities, as we know them, are products of the 19th century and were first widely articulated by Europeans. Same-sex love, however, has taken and continues to take an endless variety of forms in all world cultures. In a reverse move, contemporary North American and European neocolonialists tend to present colonized countries as sexually backward and resolutely antifeminist. The repression of women's sexuality then becomes a justification for the violent takeover of a nation. The history of this practice stretches from the outcry in England over the South Asian practice of *sati* (widow burning) in the 19th century to the American and British outcry over the oppression of women in Afghanistan, which gained widespread attention only after the beginning of the imperialist war there in 2002. Thus views of women's sexuality are bound up with notions of race and nation and each informs the other. *See also* **MONTAGUE, MARY WORTLEY.**

COMBAHEE RIVER COLLECTIVE. This group of African-American feminist activists began organizing in Boston in 1974. With a strong lesbian focus, the collective organized around issues of gender, sexuality, race and **class**, fighting for community based battered women's shelters and engaging in antipoverty work. Their early articulation of a radical socialist, lesbian-centered **black feminism**, the "Comabhee River Collective Statement," has become a classic of the **second wave**. *See also* **MANIFESTOS.**

COMING-OUT STORY. The coming-out story, in both fictional and autobiographical form, is a product of lesbian and gay liberation movements of the mid to later 20th century. It is, in essence, a more specific form of the ***bildungsroman*** in which the eventual understanding of the central protagonist's identity is lesbian, gay, bisexual or transgendered. In this sense, lesbian coming-out stories follow lesbian uses of the *bildungsroman* by early 20th-century writers such as **Bryher** and **Radclyffe Hall**. The difference is that the coming-out story often locates itself within the specific context of liberation politics, with both its form of narration and its content. A distinct feature of this subgenre is the somewhat **essentialist** notion that the protagonist is inherently different from the outset. The process detailed by the narrative, then, is not one of becoming lesbian, but of articulating the always present, but hidden, lesbian self.

Rita Mae Brown's *Rubyfruit Jungle* (1973) is a classic of the lesbian coming-out genre. Pat Califia's most recent writings challenge stable notions of the lesbian identity and lesbian community by describing processes of coming out as a sado-masochist and transsexual person within his lesbian community. The hostility he experienced in his "second" coming out, belies the idea of the lesbian community as the liberated and accepting place that hosts the happy ending of so many coming-out novels.

COOPER, EDITH. *See* **MICHAEL FIELD.**

CORDOVA, JEANNE (?–). The activist and journalist Jeanne Cordova is notable for publishing the first American magazine to use the word lesbian in its title. *The Lesbian Tide* was produced by Cordova in San Francisco from 1971 to 1980. She also published *Square Peg Magazine* in Los Angeles from 1992 to 1994. Cordova has been active in virtually all political battles engaged in by lesbian and gay people in California since 1970 and has produced two novels, in addition to numerous journalistic contributions.

CORELLI, MARIE (1855–1924). The English novelist Marie Corelli achieved tremendous popularity in her own lifetime. She not only earned a very good living through fiction writing, but lived fairly openly, by the standards of the day, with her lifetime partner Bertha Vyver. Though friends with **Algernon Charles Swinburne** and host to a number of decadent events, she spoke out against decadent writing in her novels (cynically or otherwise), having one character denounce Swinburne as an English perpetrator of French immorality. **Emile Zola** is another novelist she mentions in this context. Clearly she did not see her own identity in the same terms in which decadent novelists were formulating representations of the lesbian. Corelli's first novel was *A Romance of Two Worlds* (1886), published in the same year as Henry James' *The Bostonians*. Here she weaves one of her own incidental love poems into the narrative, a poem in which both the speaker and the beloved are gendered female. Others of her love poems speak of love in clandestine terms. Corelli published dozens of novels in her own lifetime to tremendous popular, if not critical, acclaim. None of these dealt directly or openly with lesbian themes, though in both fiction and life she remained an outspoken critic of traditional, religious heterosexual marriage.

CORNWELL, ANITA (19?–). The black American journalist Anita Cornwell has written for the lesbian press since the 1960s. She has published articles in *The Ladder*, *The Gay Alternative* and *Dyke: A Quarterly*. Throughout her career she has articulated a specifically black lesbian sexual identity within the context of American structures of racial power. In 1983, she published the book *Black Lesbian in White America* with Naiad Press.

CORNWELL, PATRICIA. The American **crime** writer Patricia Cornwell has achieved global success with her series of novels featuring the medical examiner and sleuth Kay Scarpetta. Cornwell worked as both a crime journalist and an assistant to a medical examiner before beginning her publishing career. Scarpetta has been seen as a new kind of detective heroine, both markedly female and actively sexual, powerful and intellectual. In reality her position as "emancipated" female allows her to function flexibly as both detective hero and feminized victim. This is immediately evident in Cornwell's first novel *Postmortem* (1990). Dozens of novels have followed the success of this first work. The character Kay Scarpetta has a close maternal relationship with her niece, who turns out to be lesbian in later novels, and often plays an active role in Scarpetta's case work. Cornwell has been less than candid about her own sexuality, though a highly publicized affair with the wife of a politician seems to point to a lesbian aim. She also publishes popular fiction under the name Barbara Vine.

CORRESPONDENCE. Correspondence provides some of the oldest and also the most illuminating evidence of lesbian desire and female same-sex relationships that survived. A 12th-century Latin manuscript from Germany preserves two love letters written from one woman to another in verse form. Diane Watt has edited a collection of letters from one family called Paston, which illuminates the concerns and relationships between an extended family of women in the 15th century. Apart from the writings of **medieval women mystics** this provides some of the only evidence we have of passionate feelings between women in this period and place.

Correspondence from the 19th and 20th centuries has been extremely valuable to scholars of lesbian literature seeking to clarify women writers' understandings of their own desires and identities. The critical concept of **romantic friendship** was developed largely through the examination of **life-writing** and letters from women who could not or did not express feelings for each other in published works.

Some notable lesbian literary correspondences are Geraldine Jewsberry to Jane Welsh Carlyle, Edith Simcox to George Eliot, **Emily Dickinson** to Susan Gilbert, **Vita Sackville-West** to both **Virginia Woolf** and **Violet Trefusis**, the correspondence of **Gabriela Mistral**, **May Sarton** and that between Eleanor Roosevelt and the journalist **Lorena Hickock**.

CRIME FICTION. As a genre, crime fiction in the West developed from the mid-19th century. With the advent of modern urban culture came concerns about individual identity, the anonymity made available by cities and the transgression of social hierarchies of all kinds. Out of these concerns both the real-life detective and detective fiction were born at roughly the same time.

Female sexual excess had been associated with criminality from a much earlier period. Stories from the Newgate Calendar record the punishment of **cross-dressing** and bigamous women, as well as sex-workers, from the late 18th century. Daniel Defoe's 1722 novel *Moll Flanders* is an even earlier reflection of these same kinds of judicial events and the public fascination with them. Sensation novels of the 1860s, such as Wilkie Collins *Armadale* and Mary Elizabeth Braddon's *Lady Audley's Secret* focused on similar fascination and anxieties.

In the first half of the 20th century, developing ideas of human identity as sexual were expressed widely in detective fiction. Female masculinity was associated with criminality in both fictional and journalistic accounts. Excessive femininity was embodied in the criminal character of the femme fatale, best exemplified by the character of Bridget O'Shaughnessey in Dashiel Hammett's *The Maltese Falcon* (1930). Meanwhile Josephine Tey and Patricia Highsmith began to experiment with overtly lesbian and gay sexualities in crime narratives.

Once the **coming-out** novel had established a narrative identity for the modern lesbian, writers were free to employ lesbian characters who could do things apart from coming to terms with their lesbian identity. Lesbian detective heroes began to appear in the 1980s. The 1984 novel *Murder in the Collective* by Barbara Wilson is set in an **independent women's press** and its lesbian detective comes into contact with an array of **lesbian-feminist** characters as she solves a case of sabotage and murder. Manda Scott's *Hen's Teeth* (1996) and the novels of **Stella Duffy** are in a similar tradition and have received attention from mainstream audiences. **Patricia Cornwell** has developed a lesbian assistant for her detective, Kay Scarpetta, over a series of novels. **Rita Mae Brown** is an American lesbian writer who began by writing a coming-out novel and has moved through several romances into the crime genre. She now has three series of crime novels in print. *See also* POPULAR LITERATURE.

CROSS-DRESSING. Cross-dressing refers to the practice of dressing in the clothes of a gender that is not usually associated with one's biological sex. That is to say that women sometimes dress as men and men as women. Cross-dressing highlights the fact that one's gender has little to do with one's bodily morphology. From the 15th/16th-century poet **Ariosto**, through the **early modern** period and into the **nineteenth century**, many poems and novels in which women engage in romantic or sexual activity with each other explain this activity through cross-dressing. One partner is often "fooled" as to the other partner's gender. The titillating possibilities of gender confusion through cross-dressing have engendered a centuries long tradition of literature.

In early modern gender debates, those opposed to female emancipation focused around the confusion of gender roles. These are expressed specifically in terms of dress in the anonymous pamphlet entitled *Hic Mulier* (1620), which decries the practice of cross-dressing apparently popular in London at this period. By the 19th century, French writers like **Rachilde** were knowingly employing narratives of confusion and cross-dressing in order to achieve lesbian plot situations. Another tradition as exemplified by the French hero-heroine Joan of Arc, involves women cross-dressing in order to perform heroic acts normally reserved for men. The Bengali writer **Bankim Chandra Chatterji**, draws on this and similar South Asian traditions in his revolutionary novel *Anandamath* (1882).

Many of the most important writers in the lesbian tradition have been cross-dressing women, and we must recognize a strong transgender tradition in what was once seen in the simple category "lesbian writing." **George Sand**, **Colette**, **Radclyffe Hall** and **Leslie Feinberg** name just a few bisexual and lesbian writers who were/are also transgender people.

CROWLEY, ALEISTER (1875–1947). The English satanist and decadent writer Aleister Crowley is perhaps best known for a number of collections of poetry inspired by pagan spirituality and several books on magic published between 1900 and 1940. His *Diary of a Drug Fiend* (1922) details the decadent life and eventual salvation of a cocaine addict. In 1898 he published a poem entitled "The Lesbian Hell," which is very clearly influenced by the earlier French language publications of **Charles Baudelaire**. Like these, "The Lesbian Hell" presents sexual love between women as a kind of valorized ultimate sin, employing a common moral structure on the surface, but inviting a transgressive and decadent voyeuristic pleasure at the same time.

CULTURAL FEMINISM. Cultural feminism refers to the belief that women's oppression and potential liberation lies in the linguistic and material culture in which we live. From the turn of the 20th century, writers like **Renée Vivien** sought to revive an ancient cultural tradition that they saw as more empowering to lesbians and other women. The examination of mythology, language and visual art for female-centered traditions, which have been erased by patriarchal sciences of history, archaeology and linguistics, has been an integral component of 20th-century feminism. The practice of separatism— creating safe, women-only space within which to promote healing and empowerment—is also associated with cultural feminist projects such as women's music festivals, writing and publishing collectives and education centers. The Swedish-British author and visual artist **Monica Sjöo** and the American writer **Judy Grahn** have made important interventions in cultural feminism. **Mary Daly**'s 1973 *Beyond God the Father: Toward a Philosophy of Women's Liberation* and Merlin Stone's 1978 *When God Was a Woman* are examples of cultural feminist efforts to break down the patriarchal image of the masculine divine.

– D –

DALY, MARY (1928–). The American feminist theologian and philosopher Mary Daly was barred, like all other women in the mid-20th century, from attending graduate courses in theology in the United States. She therefore went to Switzerland where she gained multiple postgraduate degrees. On her return to the U.S., Daly published her first feminist critique of Christian theology *The Church and the Second Sex* (1968). Her groundbreaking work, however, was *Beyond God the Father: Towards a Philosophy of Women's Liberation* (1973). This was one of a handful of books that formed the ethics of the feminist second wave in the U.S. Daly's *Gyn/Ecology: The Metaethics of Radical Feminism* (1978) was such a profound intervention into the discipline of philosophy that she could no longer be ignored, even on mainstream curricula. This was followed by *Pure Lust: Elemental Feminist Philosophy* (1984). Daly taught for many years at Boston College, until her illegal dismissal in 1999 for holding women-only classes.

DANE, CLEMENCE (1887–1965). Clemence Dane is the pseudonym of the novelist Winifred Ashton. Ashton published *Regiment of Women*, a phobic portrait of a predatory lesbian schoolmistress in 1917.

DAUGHTERS OF BILITIS. The Daughters of Bilitis (D.O.B.) was a lesbian organization founded in San Francisco in 1955. It grew out of other **homophile** groups such as the Mattachine Society, but differed in its woman-only configuration and specifically lesbian aims. The name Daughters of Bilitis was derived from the long poem *Chansons de Bilitis* by **Pierre Louÿs**, and this choice is a clue to the level of education and class position of the majority of its members. Louÿs was an obscure writer in a foreign language and the eight founding members of D.O.B. assumed that those who recognized its significance would be welcome while the name would maintain a certain disguise in the face of the general public.

D.O.B. is significant here in that its stated aims involved implicitly the promotion of lesbian literature. Included in these aims was the intent to participate actively with social scientists in striving to understand the "problem" of lesbianism, and to promote understanding through medical and literary texts. Branches of D.O.B. kept extensive libraries that included both **sexological** and fictional volumes. In this way groups of lesbians developed and shared ideas about lesbian identity through reading practice. The lending library of the New York chapter of D.O.B., preserved as it was in the 1970s, is housed in the Lesbian Herstory Archives in Brooklyn, New York, under the title "red dot collection."

DAVENPORT, MARCIA (1903–1996). The novelist and music critic Marcia Davenport was the daughter of a wealthy cosmopolitan family. She produced biographies of Guiseppe Garibaldi (this was completed when Davenport was still a young girl) and Wolfgang Amadeus Mozart. She also wrote several novels, including a tale of working class immigrants to the United States, *The Valley of Decision* (1942), which was adapted to film. She is most significant here, however, for *Of Lena Geyer* (1936), a novel that fictionalizes her mother's lesbian affair. The novel was mentioned as formative by many lesbian readers later in the 20th century.

DE, SHOBHA (1948–). The popular Indian novelist Shobha De is significant here for the 1992 novel *Strange Obsession*, which details the unhealthy desire of the lesbian character Minx for a naïve young fashion model. Though decried as an unfriendly and damaging portrait, the tremendous popularity of this novel in India revealed a prurient public fascination with the topic.

DE BEAUVOIR, SIMONE (1908–1986). The French philosopher Simone de Beauvoir graduated from the Sorbonne with a degree in philosophy in 1929. She worked as a school teacher for nearly two decades before publishing her groundbreaking work *The Ethics of Ambiguity* (1948). De Beauvoir published several novels and philosophical treatises, using her formal philosophical training to argue existential and feminist principals. She had both a lifelong relationship with the philosopher Jean Paul Sartre and a number of love affairs with women. She is most widely known for *Le Deuxieme Sexe* (*The Second Sex*, 1949) in which she made the famous pronouncement that "one is not born a woman" but rather is made into one. Thus, de Beauvoir introduced the world to the concept of the **social construction** of gender, and almost single-handedly enabled the advent of the **second wave** of **feminist** thought. *The Second Sex* contains a chapter on lesbianism, which draws heavily on sexology and appears, in retrospect, less than empowering. It seems clear, in light of this treatment, that de Beauvoir struggled with her own sexual identity and self-image. Her picture of the lesbian contains nothing of the freedom or subversion of the modernist lesbian writers who came before her. The revelations contained in *The Second Sex* have enabled the development of a significant strand of lesbian thought that reaches to the work of **Monique Wittig** and **Judith Butler**.

DECADENT LITERATURE. The decadent tradition in literature was focused in France during the 19th century, though some English poets and novelists imitated decadent French writers. The decadent tradition was in some ways a reaction to romantic sentimentalism and 19th-century realism. Decadent writers presented characters who traveled widely throughout social strata and placed them in ornate and excessive settings. Violent criminality, drug use and excessive sexuality were common themes for these writers. Lesbian and transgender figures were important for decadent writers, who used them as signs of moral dejection and abject excess. The novelists **Théophile Gautier** and **Rachilde**, and the poets **Charles Baudelaire**, **Pierre Louÿs** and **Algernon Charles Swinburne** all worked in the decadent tradition.

DELARU-MARDRUS, LUCIE (1874–?). The French writer Lucie Delarue-Mardrus was one of a number of women who attended a lesbian salon held first by the poet **Renée Vivien** and, after Vivien's death, by **Natalie Clifford Barney**. Among her 47 novels is *L'Ange et les pervers* (*The Angel and the Perverts*, 1930), which features a transgender heroine and character portraits of Natalie Barney and Renée Vivien, each of whom was her lover for a time. She was also romantically linked with **Colette** and **Rachilde**. The great love of Delarue-Mardrus' life was the Jewish opera singer Germaine de Castro. During the Nazi occupation of Paris the two stayed together in hiding.

DIANA: A STRANGE AUTOBIOGRAPHY **(1939).** This American novel first appeared in 1939 and is remembered by many lesbians who lived and came out in the mid-20th century. Oral history accounts report the way in which women passed the book from one to another and relished the one lesbian kiss it described. It is unclear who wrote *Diana: A Strange Autobiography*, but it is highly significant as the novel that established the form for a whole genre of **pulp** fiction. The confessional, autobiographical prose is common to lesbian pulp paperbacks, as is the book's close association with medical and psychological ideas of sexual deviance. The first edition contained a preface by a sexologist and the narrator often describes her feelings and identification using sexological language. Over the next two and a half decades, a whole host of paperback original novels reproduced the formula established by *Diana*. Significantly, the protagonist ends the novel in a reasonably happy and well-adjusted state, though clearly seeing herself as an aberrant person. The novel was widely successful, printed in India and England and translated into French.

DIANIC WICCA. Wicca refers to the practice of European paganism popular throughout Europe and North America. The worship of both a male and female deity and of the material world (nature) provide a sympathy between Wiccans and some feminists and lesbians. Dianic Wicca refers to a more radical women-only practice, named for the Goddess Diana. The novels of **Marion Zimmer Bradley** have been influential for Dianic Wiccans, as has the work of Riane Eisler and **Monica Sjöo**.

DICKINSON, EMILY (1830–1886). The American poet Emily Dickinson is as well known for her eccentric life as for her work. Only two of her poems were published in her lifetime. As a young woman, she attended Mount Holyoke College and led a fairly happy life. After some trauma, the source of which is unclear, she became a recluse whose life was increasingly dominated by anxiety. At her death her family found over 1,700 poems carefully stitched into separate booklets in her room. A significant number of these, written between 1851 and 1886, are addressed to a female beloved. The fact that early editors altered the pronouns in these pieces indicates that they understood the work as expressing a transgressive lesbian desire. Mabel Loomis Todd was the first to edit Dickinson's work in the 1890s. Rebecca Patterson, in the 1950s, was the first to suggest a female lover, whom she identified as Kate Scott Anthon. **Jeannette Foster** discusses this theory. More recently, biographical scholars have proposed Dickinson's sister-in-law, Sue Gilbert, as the object of her love. Over 250 poems were included in letters to Gilbert throughout the two women's correspondence. Whoever Dickinson's lover may have been and whatever traumas and anxieties may have dominated her life, the stylistic innovations she made have had a tremendous influence on the development of American poetry. These were recognized as soon as the work was published, but took decades to fully comprehend. An example, quoted by Terry Castle, will serve to illustrate both Dickinson's formal excellence and her articulation of a lesbian poetic voice:

What could— it hinder so—to say?
Tell her—just how she sealed you—cautious!
But—if she ask "where you are hid"—until the evening—
Ah! Be bashful!
Gesture Coquette—
And shake your head!

DIDEROT, DENIS (1713–1784). The philosopher and novelist Denis Diderot is best known for his work on the celebrated Enlightenment project the *Encyclopédie*, which was intended as a complete compendium of the scientific/philosophical knowledge possessed by the "modern world." Diderot had a Jesuit education but later questioned the church and even the most basic tenets of religious devotion. He spent time in prison for his atheistic beliefs.

Diderot is significant here, and perhaps now well known, for his 1760 novel *La religieuse* (*The Nun*). The novel began as a practical joke played on a friend. Diderot and another acquaintance told a fabricated story about a girl who had been forced into a convent against her will. The listener was so intrigued by this story that Diderot began inventing a number of letters from this girl, which spun the story out. Thus the novel evolved in the first person and as an intimate psychological portrait. In this sense it is unique for its era. The story tells of the young Suzanne who is first sexually abused by her abbess, but then grows to enjoy lesbian sex after repeated episodes.

The existence of this novel shows that a clear understanding of lesbian sexual preference (if not identity) already existed in 1760, as did a tradition of producing lesbian characters for the titillation of men (and perhaps of women also). It was not published until 1796, after Diderot's death, though it may already have circulated in manuscript form before then. The idea of predatory lesbian vice in Catholic convents seems to be already widely held in 1791, when it is hinted at in Ann Radcliffe's *The Romance of the Forest*.

DOOLITTLE, HILDA (H.D.) (1886–1961). The poet, novelist and essayist Hilda Doolittle, known as H.D., was a major force in the establishment of the modernist lesbian identity. Herself a bisexual woman, she was married for many years to Richard Aldrington, but her primary life relationship was with the writer Winifred Ellerman, known as **Bryher**. Together with her early lover and friend Ezra Pound, H.D. defined the imagist movement in poetry. Her verse is syntactically stark but metaphorically elaborate, and it was these qualities that Pound called imagist. Throughout her work she draws on classical myth and imagery, in particular to create images of a feminine divine. Her first published collection of poems was *Sea Garden* (1916). This was followed by *Hymen* (1921), but perhaps her greatest poetic work was the later *Helen in Egypt* (1961).

Throughout her life, H.D. also experimented with prose form. The autobiographical novel *HERmione* was written in 1928, but not published until 1981. This work fictionalizes a crucial point in H.D.'s early life where she felt the need to choose between a female and a male lover. Choosing a woman companion, the protagonist, Hermione, leaves America for Europe at the end of the novel. These events are thinly veiled versions of H.D.'s own life events. Once in Europe she met Bryher and after the birth of her first child, went with her to Greece. The trauma of World War I affected her deeply and she experienced an emotional breakdown. Bryher took her to Greece to recover. It was here that H.D. experienced a mystical vision of writing (or images) on a hotel wall, which inspired her poetic writings thereafter. In her description of this vision, H.D. tells of the intensely close way in which she and Bryher communicated without words, and says that her experience of the vision depended on Bryher's participation.

H.D. produced three other autobiographical works. *Paint It Today* was published in 1921, *Asphodel* in 1922 and *Palimpsest* in 1926. In 1956 she published a memoir describing the analysis that she underwent with **Sigmund Freud** at his Vienna office in the early 1930s. *Tribute to Freud* is an honest, and not uncritical, but loving portrait of the founder of **psychoanalysis**. It is in this work that H.D. describes the vision of the "writing on the wall" that inspired her life's work.

DRAG. *See* CROSS-DRESSING.

DRAMA. The early history of sexually dissident women on the English-language stage is dominated by farces involving **cross-dressing** female characters. These might be exemplified by Thomas Middleton and Thomas Dekker's *The Roaring Girl* (1611). From the 18th century, the practice of having women play "breaches parts" created a space for cross-dressing women in the theatrical world and inspired women like **Charlotte Charke** to broaden the possibilities for their lives offstage.

As anxieties about women's (supposedly) increasing sexual activity and freedom increased in the 19th century, phobic portraits of lesbian characters appeared in some numbers. **August Strindberg** is a good example here. Toward the end of the 19th century, the movement for women's suffrage instigated a tradition of using the stage as a publicly accessible space in which to air debates around women's sexual oppression.

In the 20th century, plays like Edouard Bourdet's *The Captive* (1926) and Lillian Hellman's ***The Children's Hour*** (1934) began to articulate a modern lesbian identity for the stage, albeit in an ambiguous light. The scandal around the New York production of *The Captive* led to increased **censorship** efforts that persisted for some decades. *The Children's Hour* is remarkable in escaping these restrictions.

Significant figures in 20th-century lesbian drama are **Carolyn Gage**, **Sabina Berman** and **Judy Grahn**.

DU MAURIER, DAPHNE (1907–1989). The novelist Daphne Du Maurier was born into London's cultural elite during the Edwardian period. After her marriage she moved to Cornwall where many of her best-known novels are set. Her first published novel was *The Loving Spirit* (1931). She solidified her Gothic style with the popular *Jamaica Inn* in 1936, but she is most significant here for *Rebecca* (1938). *Rebecca* tells the story of a young wife's first year of marriage. The narrator's husband has been previously married to a woman named Rebecca. The wife, who narrates the novel but is never named, thinks at first that her husband is still in love with Rebecca. The dramatic climax of the narrative, reveals, however, that Rebecca was an immoral and decadent woman and that her husband shot and killed her. The housekeeper of the stately home where the story takes place, Mrs. Danvers, maintains a slavish loyalty to the dead wife and treats the narrator with murderous hostility. Underneath this story of heterosexual marriage lies a complex set of fascinations and desires that are all transgressive: the narrator's for Rebecca, Mrs. Danvers' for Rebecca and Rebecca's for an implied number of lovers both male and female. The tension and drive of the narrative is a deep and horrified desire for the absent presence of the dead Rebecca. This novel achieved a tremendous popular success and generated such a number of imitators that a whole sector of the publishing industry developed around the Gothic romance. Du Maurier herself had a number of female lovers, including the actress Gertrude Lawrence. She wrote several memoirs in later life, beginning with *Growing Pains* in 1977. These make her lesbian affairs almost, though not quite, invisible. Aside from her novels Du Maurier produced biographical studies of historical and literary figures, including Francis Bacon and Branwell Brontë.

DUFFY, MAUREEN (1933–). The English poet, playwright and novelist Maureen Duffy was raised in London's working-class East End but was able, with her mother's support, to attend girl's schools on scholarship. She took a degree from King's College London and published her first novel, *That's How It Was*, in 1962. This novel articulated a specifically working-class lesbian identity. Its action was set in the battle of Britain during World War II. *The Microcosm* (1966) is Duffy's best-known novel. It fictionalizes the subcultural setting of the real life London lesbian bar Gateways (also depicted in the lesbian-phobic film *The Killing of Sister George* in 1968). *The Microcosm* employs a modernist mix of narrative techniques and tells the intertwined stories of several characters. Duffy's novel *The Love Child* (1971), like *That's How It Was*, depicts the mother-daughter bond as central to lesbian development. She has written several radio plays, including *One Goodnight* (1981), based on the life of the 19th-century Irish writers and lovers **Edith Somerville** and **Violet Martin**.

DUFFY, STELLA (1963–). The actor and popular novelist Stella Duffy was born in London and raised in New Zealand. She has written four "literary" novels to date. These are *Singling Out the Couples* (1988), *Eating Cake* (1999), *Immaculate Conceit* (2000) and *State of Happiness* (2004). She is also well known in the lesbian reading community for a series of detective novels featuring the lesbian sleuth Saz Martin. These began with *Calendar Girl* in 1994. Duffy now lives in London where she writes, acts and teaches acting.

DUNCKER, PATRICIA (1951–). The English academic and writer Patricia Duncker was born and lived her early life in Jamaica. She achieved publishing success with her first novel *Hallucinating Foucault* (1996). Like all of her fiction, this novel blends Duncker's theoretical concerns and interests into both content and narrative form. She is described as a **postmodern** writer, because her work as a whole tends to undermine rather than to reinforce any of the identity positions through which we might categorize either her writing or her characters. Duncker's second novel *James Miranda Barry* (1999) fictionalized the life of the early 19th-century medical doctor and career colonial officer, James Miranda Barry. Barry was discovered at his death to be biologically female, and Duncker's novel imagines a history for his life as a man and the moment of his transgender movement. Duncker followed James Miranda Barry with *The Deadly Space Between* (2002), which was less well received. This novel describes the erotic and sadistic tension between a mother, her lover and her son. *Seven Tales of Sex and Death* (2003) continues her exploration of postmodern narrative and characterization, as well as her refusal to simply reiterate the identity positions and relationships in which people may expect to find her characters.

– E –

EARLY MODERN PERIOD. The historical term early modern generally refers to the period from the late European Renaissance to some time before the technological, cultural and scientific developments that mark the 19th century and the "modern" world. It is a somewhat arbitrary designation, but useful in literary terms as it marks a distinctive period in European poetry and drama and the beginnings of the modern novel. The widest dates we might give for the period are perhaps 1500 to 1800, though most scholars would argue for something narrower. This period saw the questioning of the divine right of kings, the growth of Western European global empires, the creation of the modern idea of race through those empires, the institution of colonial slavery and the beginnings of the industrial revolution and with it modern capitalism and warfare. As always, gendered and sexual identities were crucial to the maintenance of capitalism and colonial power in this period.

At this time the word **tribade** was perhaps most often used in English for a woman who had sex with another women, though **sapphist** and lesbian came into use during these centuries. Emma Donoghue notes that the Oxford English Dictionary, based on which most scholars measure the advent of particular words, draws only from high-culture, "literary" sources. Therefore the word lesbian was most certainly used in ballads, drama and broadsheet literature before the earliest date formerly agreed upon. This would point to an early understanding of the life of the ancient Greek poet **Sappho** as a women who loved other women sexually, rather than as the suicidal heterosexual presented in Ovid's popular story. Donoghue also documents the existence of a variety of slang terms for lesbian, which seem to have been in use at the time, most notably "tommy" for a woman who loved other women and "the game of flats" for sex between two women. Donoghue documents the use of the word lesbian (as an adjective) to 1732 and as a noun to 1736, both in successive editions of a long satirical poem called *The Toast* by one William King.

There was an extensive literature of same-sex devotion and friendship at this period as well as a burgeoning **pornography** involving lesbian sex. On the continent, medical research began to show a concern for nonreproductive female sexual anatomy (e.g., the clitoris), apparently as a response to tales of tribadism. Popular language about lesbian sex in the 17th and 18th centuries point to trouble imagining sex without the phallus. They therefore concentrated mostly on tribadism. Thus the idea of "flats" denoted sexual activity without the phallus. Early modern ballads, some of which survive in printed form, speak frankly about women's active sexual desire. A number of women began to publish literature seriously at this time. In *A Room of One's Own* (1928) **Virginia Woolf** incites all women writers to lay flowers at the grave of **Aphra Behn** because she was the "first" woman to make a living by her pen. Behn, along with **Anne Finch**, **Katherine Fowler Phillips**, **Lady Wortley Montague** and **Mary Wollstonecraft**, are notable figures in the literature of this period who express what might broadly be called lesbian desires in published writings.

In 1589, a woman writing pseudonymously as Jane Anger published a pamphlet entitled *Her Protection for Women*. The piece is notable as it is addressed by a woman to women readers. In it, Anger speaks of women as active sexual subjects and decries the empty superiority of men. Some scholars credit this pamphlet with sparking a spirited exchange of pamphlets on the question of the social, moral, sexual and spiritual position of women (often referred to as the *querelle des femmes*). The pamphlet entitled ***Hic Mulier; or, The Man-Woman*** (1620) is a later intervention in this same debate. On the continent **Christine de Pizan**'s *The Book of the City of Ladies* (1405) might be seen as an earlier initiation of the same debate.

Many lesbian characters emerged in English fiction at this time, though on the whole literature was still deeply concerned with cross-dressing women and gender confusion. Some scholars argue that the character Emilia in William Shakespeare and John Fletcher's *Two Noble Kinsman* is a lesbian, distinguished from Shakespeare's other cross-dressing female characters as a desirer of women. Thomas Middleton and Thomas Dekker's play *The Roaring Girl* (1611) is based on the life of the cross-dressing pick-pocket Mary Frith. Daniel Defoe's *Moll Flanders* (1722) details the life of a **cross-dressing** woman who is criminalized and never overtly expresses lesbian desire. John Cleland's *Fanny Hill: Memoirs of a Woman of Pleasure* (1749) follows a pornographic formula, which was common by this point, in which a young sex worker is first trained to passion by a more experienced woman and then exposed to men. The book caused a minor outcry and legal action, though it stayed in print after payment of a fine. A close reading of *Fanny Hill* is instructive. It is clear that the sexual instructress enjoys young women as much as young men, but she remains a minor character. Fanny is unsatisfied by female sexual companionship and proceeds to a worship of the phallus. Indeed pornography at this period makes the male organ a particular and central object of desire in a way that would cause homosexual anxiety among straight male viewers of pornography at later periods.

Henry Fielding's *The Female Husband, or the surprising story of Mrs. Mart, alias Mr. George Hamilton* (1746), describes transgender lesbianism as the most excessive of vices. "But if once our carnal appetites are set loose, without those prudent and secure guides [virtue and religion], there is no excess and disorder which they are not liable to commit . . . ," says the narrator by way of introduction. He goes on to say that he is sure that the story of *The Female Husband* is the "strangest" of those excesses we will have ever heard of.

The early modern period saw the growth of a fascination with gender transgression that was the precursor of modern ideas of gender and sexual identities. Two good historical investigations of the development of lesbian identity at this period are Valerie Traub's *The Renaissance of Lesbianism in Early Modern England* (2002) and Emma Donaghue's *Passions between Women: British Lesbian Culture, 1668–1801* (1995). A comparative literary study of French and English lesbian literature at this period is given by Elizabeth Susan Wahl in *Invisible Relations: Representations of Female Intimacy in the Age of Enlightenment* (1999).

EIGHTEENTH CENTURY. *See* EARLY MODERN PERIOD.

ELLIS, HAVELOCK. *See* SEXOLOGY.

EROTICA. The term erotica has been used to distinguish a form of writing that was intended to elicit sexual arousal but that was not **pornographic**. Viewed objectively, erotica is a political category that contains writings which are viewed as less dangerous, and therefore less open to censorship than pornographic writing. The writings of the Marquis de Sade are/were seen as pornographic, while the equally misogynist and sadistic *The Story of O* (1975) was seen, at a different historical period, as erotica. Lesbian or bisexual writers whose work has been classed as erotica include **Anaïs Nin**, **Chrystos** and **Liane De Pougy**.

ESSENTIALISM. Essentialism refers to the idea that one's identity is predetermined and stable, the essence of one's being. Essentialist feminists, for example, would argue that there are specific and undeniable traits that belong to women and that these create a specifically female way of being and viewing the world. Essentialism will always rest on a notion of biologically determined identity. That is to say, if we are special and immutable as women, it must be because we were "born that way." Many lesbian thinkers point out the dangerous implications of an essentialist view. In the first instance it allows society to be divided into any number or configuration of alienated groups, and in the second it disallows any analysis of the politics of power and exploitation implicated in the **social construction** of identity. Some see the most radical position as that which destabilizes the most commonly accepted identity categories, throwing into question what it means to be lesbian, bisexual or heterosexual, black or white, male or female. Throughout the history of literature, essentialist notions of gender and sexuality have given us the most enduring portraits of love. In much romantic poetry men and women are seen to be drawn to each other by forces beyond their intervention or control. Poets such as **Renée Vivien**, **Natalie Clifford Barney** and **Hilda Doolittle** and later theorists such as Luce Irigaray and Hélène Cixous, began to reimagine the nature of women in a way that did not involve an essential passive femininity or need to submit to male sexual power. While they freed up crucial tools for the expression of women's desire, they also created a new kind of essentialism. Later writers of erotica, such **Pat Califia**, seek to express women's desires in a way that departed entirely from any passive femininity and disrupted the categories of masculinity and femininity themselves.

EULENBERG SCANDAL. This public scandal erupted around Prince Eulenberg in Germany in 1906 and 1907. The Prince was a close friend of the Kaiser's and a journalist revealed his homosexual activities in 1906. The ensuing inquiries implicated a number of ranking officials including the army chief of staff and the head of the Berlin police. Several trials ensued and the scandal inspired a public debate of Paragraph 175 of the Viennese penal code (then extended to all of Germany), which prohibited male homosexual activity. The Eulenberg scandal is significant here in that it caused a backlash and a wave of **censorship** that slowed the publishing of gay and lesbian literature in Germany until the Weimar era. As with most similar public events, it also gave a voice and a public forum to those who advocated for the rights of lesbians and gay men.

– F –

FANNY HILL. See EARLY MODERN PERIOD.

FEINBERG, LESLIE (1949–). The American labor and transgender activist Leslie Feinberg is primarily a nonfiction writer though, ironically, it is the one novel for which s/he is best known. *Stone Butch Blues* (1993) describes the life of a fictional butch lesbian worker in the steel belt of America's northern states in the post World War II era. The novel details working-class bar culture, transphobia within the lesbian community, and the life of a transgender woman passing as a man. Feinberg says that s/he chose the medium of fiction in order to achieve an emotional depth and power not possible in nonfiction writing. *Stone Butch Blues* became an instant classic and raised awareness of transgender issues in the gay community and the wider community of the left. Among Feinberg's nonfiction works is the Marxist analysis of the transgender movement given in *Trans Gender Liberation* and the book *Trans Liberation: Beyond Pink or Blue* (1998). Feinberg argues that, in a liberated world, transgender and transsexual people would not have to move from one fixed gender category to another, but could articulate and continue to embody each of their unique journeys through and between genders.

FEMINISM. In the most widely accepted sense, feminism refers to the belief that an inequality exists between men and women in a given society and to the political practice that seeks to abolish that inequality. There are, however, a large number of feminist theories and practices that exist throughout the world. The European Enlightenment is seen by many as the birthplace of what we think of as feminism today. The idea of the free and sovereign individual whose rights were extolled by Enlightenment thinkers like John Locke, Thomas Paine and **Mary Wollstonecraft** is a simply defined and unproblematic subject of the doctrine of human rights, which evolved from the work of such thinkers. As people began to question the limits of these rights, from the standpoint of race, religion, gender and sexuality, extensions of human rights were fought for. In each of these cases, difference was often seen as something to overcome in order to achieve basic rights. The individual human was, in a sense, something that existed in the same essential way in each human being, "underneath our differences." Others have argued, however, that our differences are what make us who we are, that they cannot be legislated away and that they are never truly ignored.

As a product of this Enlightenment worldview, feminism often suffered a certain blindness about difference and many of the most widely known Western feminists saw gender as an essential category and ignored, or even repudiated, the idea of differences among women. Working-class women, women of color, out lesbians and bisexual women were historically excluded or at best patronized by a mainstream (white, middle- and upper-class) feminism that did not address their concerns. The most important developments in feminism in the 20th century were made by women who challenged the very roots of its idea of itself. Black feminists, lesbian feminists, socialist feminists and transgender feminists have taken the movement in important directions through their writings and their activism.

Mary Wollstonecraft's writings are important documents of early European feminism. The connections between lesbian networks and the **first wave feminist** movement were depicted unkindly by Henry James in *The Bostonians* (1886). **Eva Gore-Booth**, **Esther Roper** and Susan B. Anthony were important lesbian feminists of the first wave in Great Britain and the United States. The bisexual **Virginia Woolf** wrote in the early 20th century on feminism and literature and feminism and militarism. In the 20th century **Kate Millet**, **Alice Walker**, **Gloria Anzaldúa** and **Judy Grahn** have been tremendously influential, along with other lesbian, bisexual and transgender feminists too numerous to count. *See also* BLACK FEMINISM; COLONIALISM; CULTURAL FEMINISM; LESBIAN FEMINISM; MANIFESTOS; SECOND-WAVE FEMINISM.

FEMME. In lesbian writing the term femme, which came into common usage in the 20th century, most often refers to a feminine dressing and acting lesbian or bisexual woman. Some argue that the femme identity is made visible as lesbian only through coupling with a woman who inhabits a **butch** identity. It might also be argued, however, that femme dress and behavior is subversive. Like other forms of lesbian, gay and transgender role-play, femme both uses and parodies heterosexual gender norms. It could be seen an exaggerated parody of heterosexual femininity.

During the mid-20th century, a working-class bar culture in Europe and America made femme roles visible to the world. A historical study of Buffalo, New York by Madeline Davis and Elizabeth Lapofsky Kennedy describes the often violent struggle engaged in by femme-butch women in making a public space for themselves in the

1930s, 1940s and 1950s. **Valerie Taylor**'s novel *A World without Men*, written in 1963, describes the femmes in overtly femme-butch couples as overblown parodies of femininity. Many middle- and upper-class lesbians of the period found femme-butch roles to be uncouth and damaging. With the widespread popularization of the **second-wave feminist** movement from the late 1960s, femme-butch roles fell even further out of favor. They were described by feminists as damaging re-enactments of patriarchal power structures. Androgyny was seen by many as the way toward liberation.

By the 1980s the femme identity was nearly forgotten and the dominant image of the lesbian was of a butch or androgynous woman. In some political writings of the 1990s, lesbians attempted to reinstate a radical role-playing practice, coining the phrase "genderfuck" to express the way in which these practices destabilize, rather than reinforcing gender norms. In the popular media, however, the invention of the term "lipstick lesbian," to denote a women who was denying her lesbian heritage and political commitments and conforming to feminine norms, shows the almost total erasure of the idea of lesbian femininity.

Una Troubridge, **Joan Nestle** and **Lesléa Newman** are some lesbian writers who have consciously articulated femme identities. The femme has often remained invisible and silent in the most popular and widely recognized of lesbian narratives. **Radclyffe Hall**'s character Mary, love object of Stephen Gordon in *The Well of Loneliness*, is a case in point.

FIELD, MICHAEL. The two English poets Katherine Bradley (1848–1914) and Edith Cooper (1862–1913) lived together in Bristol where they attended university and later published several plays and volumes of poetry under the pen name Michael Field. The journal that the two women kept is still extant and discusses their romantic relationship in detail. It is clear that they saw themselves as belonging to a specific group of people, distinct according to a romantic inclination that marked a distinct identity. In this sense, Bradley and Cooper are early examples of women who inhabited something like a modern lesbian identity, rather than seeing themselves within the **romantic friendship** model. They were known to intimate friends by the masculine names Michael and Henry, and they referred to each other by masculine pronouns in journal entries and letters. In 1889 they published a book of verse, *Long Ago*, based on fragments of Sappho. Four years earlier, the scholar Henry Wharton had made the first translation of Sappho that used the correct pronouns and acknowledged that some of the poems expressed lesbian desire. In later life, Cooper and Bradley converted to Catholicism. In all, they produced 26 plays and several volumes of poetry, early on under the pseudonyms Arran and Isla Leigh (Bradley published poems as Arran Leigh before their partnership), but mostly as Michael Field. Though their relationship did not change, their later writings have a spiritual rather than a pagan and sensual character.

FIELDING, HENRY. *See* EARLY MODERN PERIOD.

FINCH, ANNE (1661–1737). Anne Finch, Countess of Winchilsea was an aristocratic woman who served in the court of King James II. She enjoyed a long and happy marriage and wealth throughout most of her life. Once she and her husband had retired to an inherited country estate, Finch felt that she could devote herself to writing poetry without opening herself up to public ridicule. Her poems and letters contain a great deal of feminist sentiment, meditations on the condition and capabilities of the female sex and acknowledgment of sexual prejudice. During her lifetime she was lampooned for being a woman who fancied herself capable of the high art of poetry. Most significantly here, she produced several poems that discuss the love between women, in what we might later think of as **romantic friendship**. "Friendship between Ephelia and Ardelia" is significant. Some scholars find romantic reference to her friend Ann Tafton in "Nocturnal Reverie." Finch produced only one volume of verse in her lifetime (1713) and today her work is in print only in anthologies.

FIRST-WAVE FEMINISM. The term first-wave feminism generally refers to the 19th- and early 20th-century feminist movement, which focused primarily on female suffrage and political participation and (less vocally) on ending the sexual and violent abuse of women within the family. On both sides of the Atlantic the feminist movement in the early 19th century was closely allied with the movement for the abolition of slavery. It's most active members were drawn largely from the middle and upper classes and its stated concerns often expressed a strong **class** bias.

An important figure in the early English first wave was the abolitionist and feminist Helen Taylor, who published *The Claim of English Women to Suffrage Constitutionally Considered* in 1867. This pamphlet followed the introduction of a women's suffrage bill to parliament by Taylor's husband John Stuart Mill. The literature of the period makes it clear that many people saw the relationship between women's public participation, their gender roles and their choice of sexual object. Anthony Trollope's *He Knew He Was Right* (1868–1869) contains a portrait of an "overly" masculine American feminist. At the same time it explores the power relationship between husbands and wives in light of the 1857 divorce act and the "surplus" in women, which made marriage for all impossible and the availability of work for some middle-class women a pressing question. In the United States a historical landmark is the 1848 women's rights convention at Seneca Falls, New York, where both women and men signed a Declaration of Sentiments calling for enfranchisement and other legal rights for women. From about 1880 to 1920 the movement for suffrage fought militantly in both Britain and the United States and eventually gained its victory. Important to this era were, in the United States, Susan B. Anthony and Alice Paul and, in Great Britain, the Pankhurst mother and daughters, of whom daughter Sylvia was also an active socialist.

Significant cultural interventions were also made during this period. The Utopian Socialist movement, on both sides of the Atlantic, sought to challenge traditional patriarchal family structures and the sexual mores of the era. In 1895 Elizabeth Cady Stanton published the *Women's Bible*. This edition of the bible was produced, at Stanton's instigation, by a committee of women scholars who identified all of the passages in the Bible that told women's stories or spoke to women about their duties and behavior. These passages were then retranslated by classical scholars and presented with commentary. Cady Stanton says in her introduction to the final volume:

> The only points on which I differ from all ecclesiastical teaching is [sic] that I do not believe that any man ever saw or talked with God, I do not believe that God inspired the Mosaic code, or told the historians what they say he did about women . . .

This is a clear critique of heterosexuality and its religious justification. The 19th-century feminist movement provided support to, and was supported by, a number of female couples who enjoyed **romantic friendships** or lived within **Boston marriages**. The English feminist couple **Esther Roper** and **Eva Gore-Booth** were one such. Henry James' *The Bostonians* (1886) is set within an upper-class feminist community. Again it presents unfriendly portraits of "improperly feminine" suffragists. His novel portrays the struggle over an innocent girl between a man and a suffragist who both love her. The man wins and the girl must give up her activism along with her female lover. The connections between feminism and the freedom of lesbian love were as clear in the 19th century as they were in the 20th.

FLAGG, FANNIE (1944–). The American actor and screenwriter Fannie Flagg admired southern novelist Eudora Welty and was inspired to write after attending a workshop with her. She is significant here for her novel *Fried Green Tomatoes at the Whistle Stop Café* (1988). This novel sets a story of the love between two white women in the segregated Jim Crow south. Like other works of its kind, it was adapted in a highly popular screen version that made its lesbian element invisible.

FLANNER, JANET (1892–1978). The American journalist Janet Flanner was born in Indiana and moved to New York City after World War I. In New York she became part of artistic and literary circles and met her long-term lover, the drama critic Solita Solano. Flanner and Solano moved first to Greece and then to Paris in the 1920s. From Paris, Flanner began the column "Letters from Paris" for the New Yorker in 1925. Throughout the period between the wars, she commented for American readers on the state of Europe and the rise of Fascism in Germany and Italy. During World War II she worked as a radio journalist and in 1945 she covered the Nuremberg trials. Flanner was a flamboyant **cross-dresser** and well-known member of Paris lesbian circles between the wars. She and Solano attended **Natalie Clifford Barney**'s salon and they are depicted in **Djuna Barnes**' *Ladies Almanack* (1928). Though Flanner is known mostly for her journalistic writings, she did write one novel, *The Cubical City* (1926) and also translated two of **Colette**'s novels into English.

FORREST, KATHERINE V. (1939–). The tremendously popular lesbian writer Katherine Forrest is best known for her Kate Delafield series of crime novels, which feature a Los Angeles detective. Forrest worked with Barbara Grier at Naiad Press in the 1980s and 1990s. Together the two women edited several **anthologies** of poetry and erotic writings. Aside from her successful detective fiction Forrest has written the lesbian romance novel *Curious Wine* (1983) and the **science fiction**/fantasy novel *Daughters of a Coral Dawn* (1984).

FOSTER, JEANETTE (1895–1985). The American scholar, poet, translator and fiction writer Jeannette Howard Foster was born in Illinois and gained a master's degree in literature from the University of Chicago at a time (1922) when relatively few women pursued postgraduate education. Foster worked at a number of academic jobs throughout her life, most notably as a secretary for Alfred Kinsey's Institute for Sex Research at Indiana University from 1948 to 1952. Throughout the 1950s and 1960s Foster published writings in several homophile publications, including *The Ladder*. Pseudonyms that Foster is known to have used include Jane Addison, Hilary Farr and Abigail Sanford. Throughout the postwar era Foster was a member of the **Daughters of Bilitis** and was involved in collecting lesbian popular fiction and establishing lesbian archive and library collections.

Foster is of incalculable importance to lesbian literary studies for her *Sex Variant Women in Literature*. First published in 1956, this work was the product of 40 years of independent research. In spite of her many academic positions, Foster never received any support for this enormous endeavor. When denied academic publishing, Foster self-published the work. It has since been reprinted by two separate small lesbian presses. *Sex Variant Women in Literature* details all genres of literature that represent love between women in Europe and North America from the Middle Ages to the mid-20th century. In this work Foster defined both the scope of the field of lesbian literary studies and a methodology for reading the literature within it. She does not define the category according to author identity, but rather according to the evolution of the depiction of same-sex love and transgender movement among women. Nearly 50 years after its first publication this work, which was barely conceivable to anyone but Foster at the time of its writing, is still a valuable resource for scholars of lesbian literature.

FREUD, SIGMUND (1856–1939). Austrian founder of **psychoanalysis**. Freud was trained as a medical doctor and published his first groundbreaking group of studies on hysteria together with his colleague Josef Breuer in 1895. These studies focused largely on young, middle-class Viennese women. The first of his works were translated into English in 1910. Freud's first case studies developed ideas of the relation between the conscious and unconscious mind, the repression of trauma and sexual drives, which would change the way in which 20th-century westerners understood the self. Freud argued that all humans are by nature bisexual and only achieve heterosexual **object-choice** through a complex series of psychic processes undergone during childhood. He saw the psychic journey of female children as more complex and open to "malfunction" than that of male children. In several key essays, he argued that the female child's first erotic attraction is to her mother, that her early **sexual aim** is masculine, characterized by clitoral stimulation, and that she must learn to give up this masculine aim and transfer her sexual desire onto her father (in the form of other men). Retention of the masculine aim, for Freud, is often implicitly associated with suffragism, the desire for paid work in the public sphere and the love of other women.

Anglo-American feminists have criticized Freud and his followers on the basis of their assumption that heterosexuality is the desirable outcome of psychic development and that women are more prone to neurotic and hysterical disorders than men. Several key thinkers in French feminist theory, such as **Monique Wittig,** Julia Kristeva and Luce Irigaray, derive important aspects of their work from an engagement with Freudian thought. In spite of very valid criticisms of Freud, it remains true that his ideas were important in giving early 20th-century lesbians, gay men and bisexual people a language with which to define themselves, to argue for their integrity as beings and to organize together. Many lesbian and bisexual women writers were influenced by Freud's work, including **Djuna Barnes**, **Radclyffe Hall** and **Violette LeDuc**. Particular essays and lectures of Freud's that are important in understanding his theories of female sexuality are "Some Psychical Consequences of the Anatomical Distinction between the Sexes," "Psychogenesis of a Case of Homosexuality in a Woman," "Fragment of an Analysis of a Case of Hysteria" (often referred to as "the Dora case"), "Female Sexuality," and "Femininity."

FRITH, MARY (1589–1663). Mary Frith was a notorious London pickpocket and **cross-dressing** woman, also called Moll Cutpurse, who lived during the 17th century. She is significant here as the inspiration for a number of fictions about cross-dressing, gender dissident women. Thomas Middleton and Thomas Dekker's play *The Roaring Girl* (1611) fictionalizes her life. Daniel Defoe's 1722 novel, *Moll Flanders* is also based partially on Frith.

FULLER, MARGARET (1810–1850). The American writer and advocate of women's rights Margaret Fuller was born into a Massachusetts Unitarian family. She became a central and outspoken member of the transcendentalist group of writers and philosophers, holding important salons at her home in Boston. Fuller's most important work is *Woman in the Nineteenth Century* (1845), in which she argues, among other things, for an expansion of the boundaries of femininity. This book had an immediate influence and can be said to have inspired the watershed women's rights convention at Seneca Falls, New York, in 1848. Fuller had several **romantic friendships**, which she consciously sought to define and place within a high culture tradition.

– G –

GAGE, CAROLYN (?–). Lesbian feminist playwright Carolyn Gage concerns herself almost solely with creating an empowering history for women through theater. Her plays most often rework the stories of powerful female historical figures, both those who have fed cultural myths about women and those who are less historically visible. Gage makes free with historical fact in her work, which is more concerned with empowering contemporary actors and audiences than with presenting accurate biographical accounts. This free play is openly acknowledged and is an integral part of a specifically lesbian feminist method. Gage seeks to make myth out of history in useful ways. This method has drawn criticism from historical scholars attached to ideas of factual history, as, for example, in the case of her popular play *The Second Coming of Joan of Arc*. As well as creating her own pieces, Gage is concerned with creating a theater for lesbian actors and directors. Her book *Monologues and Scenes for Lesbian Actors* (1999) is part of this conscious effort at creating a cultural reservoir of lesbian theatrical material. Some of her plays are collected in *The Second Coming of Joan of Arc and Other Plays* (1994).

GALFORD, ELLEN (?–). The novelist Ellen Galford was born and raised in the United States but has lived in Great Britain (primarily Scotland) since 1971. Her novels place lesbian characters in a variety of generic forms, from **historical fiction** to Gothic fantasy. *The Dyke and the Dybbuk* (1993) won the Lambda Award in 1994 and was short-listed for the American Library Association's Stonewall Book Award for fiction. This novel focuses on a Jewish lesbian political activist named Rainbow Rosenblum who is haunted by a *dybbuk*. In the course of dealing with this haunting, both Rainbow and the *dybbuk* must come to terms with the relations between 20th-century political realities, Jewish identity and tradition and lesbian community. Galford's other novels include the historical *Moll Cutpurse: Her True Story* (1984), *The Fires of Bride* (1986), *Queendom Come* (1990) and *Genealogy* (2001).

GAUTIER, THÉOPHILE (1811–1872). The romantic and decadent French writer Théophile Gautier had a far-reaching influence on the development of the modernist lesbian identity. As a young man, he published a book of verse entitled *Poésies* (1830). In 1835–1836 he serially published his novel *Mademoiselle du Maupin, double amour*. It thus appeared contemporaneously with **Honoré de Balzac**'s equally influential *The Girl with the Golden Eyes*. *Mademoiselle de Maupin* features both the **coming-out** of a gay man and the amorous adventures of a **cross-dressing** bisexual heroine. Jeannette Foster says of the eponymous heroine:

> Physically, we have for the first time in modern fiction the explicit description of a type which has since become associated with homosexual tendencies in women—the tall, wide-shouldered, slim-hipped figure endowed with perfect grace . . .

Indeed these same descriptors are used in characterizations by **Radclyffe Hall**, **Djuna Barnes** and numerous **pulp** writers. Gautier's immediate influence can be seen in the fact that Charles Baudelaire dedicated his *Les fleurs du mal* to him in 1857. *See also* DECADENT LITERATURE.

GIDLOW, ELSA (1898–1986). The journalist and poet Elsa Gidlow was born in England and raised in Canada. Gidlow moved to New York in 1920, where she spent time as an editor of *Pearson's Magazine*. She was an outspoken anarchist, early member of the homophile movement and an influential figure in the California-based radical spirituality movements of the 1960s and 1970s. Gidlow's first volume of poetry, *On a Grey Thread*, which expressed clearly lesbian sentiment, was published in the United States in 1923. During the 1950s she lived fairly openly in an intercultural lesbian relationship with her lover Isabelle Quallo, and was active in the homophile organization **Daughters of Bilitis**. For these reasons she was questioned, though never prosecuted, by the infamous House Un-American Activities Committee.

In the late 1940s Gidlow purchased land in Marin County, California, which she transformed into an artist's retreat called Druid Heights. The name reflects her interest in European Pagan spirituality, which she celebrated throughout her life. Through Druid Heights and her own activist, artistic and philosophical endeavors, Gidlow was a major influence on the beat culture of the 1960s. Gidlow was cofounder of the California-based Society of Comparative Philosophy. She was among the first California thinkers to popularize Buddhist spirituality among non-Asian Americans. She was also among the first **lesbian feminists** to embrace **Goddess** spirituality, and was a major influence on the emergence of the wider Goddess movement in the 1970s and 1980s. Druid Heights was a temporary home to male and female, queer and straight visual artists, writers and philosophers. The feminist theorist and activist Catherine MacKinnon spent time there.

Through Druid Heights Press, Gidlow published *Sapphic Songs: Seventeen to Seventy* (1976), *Sapphic Songs: Eighteen to Eighty* (1986) and *Elsa, I Come with My Songs: The Autobiography of Elsa Gidlow* (1986). After her death in 1986, several women continued to finance artist retreats for lesbian women under the Druid Heights name. This ended due to lack of funds in 1992. Gidlow's papers are housed at the Gay, Lesbian, Bisexual and Transgendered Historical Society in San Francisco.

GITTINGS, BARBARA (1932–). Barbara Gittings was a major figure in the American East Coast homophile movements of the 1950s and 1960s. She was active in the Mattachine Society and founded the New York chapter of the homophile organization **Daughters of Bilitis** in 1958. Gittings grew up in a wealthy diplomatic family and first sought therapy for an understanding of her lesbian desires. She rejected the offer of a "cure" and began her own research. Gittings has said in interviews that she found the **pulp literature** being published during the early 1950s to have been more useful than the medical and legal literature on lesbians that was available to her in libraries. This experience prompted a lifelong commitment to making lesbian and gay literature available in public libraries, so that young people might have access to positive representations of sexual dissidence.

Gittings edited the Daughters of Bilitis magazine *The Ladder* from 1963. She and her lover, the photographer Kay Tobin Lahusen introduced the practice of printing photographs of lesbians on the cover of *The Ladder*, again in an effort to increase positive representation. Gittings was also responsible for adding the word lesbian to the cover of the magazine, subtitling it "a lesbian review." From 1971 to 1986 Gittings was the head of the National Library Associations Gay Task Force. She was responsible for the initiation of that organization's lesbian and gay book award. It was Gittings who presented the first of these awards to **Isabel Miller** in 1971. *See also* JOURNALISM.

GODDESS. The worship of a female godhead has been important for **cultural feminism**, and for women's empowerment more generally for centuries. As early as the 12th century in Europe, the work of the **medieval woman mystic** Hildegard of Bingen suggested a female divine. In cultures where the image of a single male-gendered god functions as the ultimate moral and spiritual authority, feminists note the obvious devaluing and disempowerment of the position of women. Therefore from the 19th century female poets and novelists have attempted to revive a feminine image of the divine. **Christina Rossetti**'s 19th-century poem "Goblin Market" uses familiar Christian imagery in order to suggest that her heroine is analogous to Christ. **Renée Vivien**, **Natalie Barney**, **H.D.** (**Hilda Doolittle**) and other early 20th-century poets sought to revive pagan images of the feminine divine. In the 20th century a whole genre of Goddess-focused historical fantasy novels has evolved. These are perhaps best represented here by the work of **Marion Zimmer Bradley**. At the same time many cultural feminists have sought to write new histories that revive suppressed language, artistic imagery and mythic stories of the feminine divine. In this regard, the work of **Judy Grahn**, **Monica Sjöo** and **Barbara Walker** has been influential for many cultural feminists.

***GOD OF VENGEANCE* (1920).** This play by Sholem Asch was originally written in Yiddish and was a success in Yiddish theaters throughout Europe and in New York City. It tells the story of a Jewish-Polish brothel keeper and his family. The brothel keeper jealously guards his daughter's virginity, until she falls in love with one of the female sex-workers he employs. *God of Vengeance* was translated into English and performed in Provincetown, Massachusetts, and New York City in 1922. The English translation brought arrests by New York's vice squad and an obscenity trial that gained media attention throughout 1923. Eventually, the work was convicted on charges of obscenity, making it the first time that an American play was successfully **censored** by the law.

GOLDMAN, EMMA (1869–1940). The anarchist activist Emma Goldman was born in Lithuania, then part of the Russian empire, and immigrated to the United States as a young woman. As a young, working-class Jewish woman she experienced both racism and **class** oppression at first hand. This experience, together with her exposure to the leftist thought of 19th-century Russia, radicalized her. According to Goldman's own account, it was the hanging of anarchist revolutionaries in Chicago that finally prompted her to leave her family and join the movement. She was a fearless revolutionary, jailed six times and eventually deported by the United States.

Within radical leftist circles Goldman remained outspoken and controversial, particularly with regard to women and sexuality. She was an advocate of the doctrine of free love, which argued for the removal of sexual relationships from the confines of marriage. She argued against the institution of marriage as it imprisoned both women and men in unequal and unnatural power relationships. Goldman worked hard to promote the legalization and availability of birth control. Early speeches on the question of sexual deviance show that

Goldman was influenced by German **sexology**, and it is often argued that she was prohomosexual.

As a young woman, Goldman experienced relationships that can be classed as **romantic friendships**. Existing correspondence (particularly with a woman named Almeda Sperry) even shows some evidence of the physical expression of same-sex love. For this reason activists often claim her as a bisexual woman. It is certain, however, that Goldman viewed her own sexuality in entirely different terms. Later in life, she described lesbians in vehemently homophobic terms, as unnatural and unbalanced women. There is no evidence that she viewed her own relationships with women as sexual, or that these relationships continued into her later life.

Goldman published the anarchist monthly *Mother Earth* from 1906 to 1917. She was involved in the production of drama throughout her life. In 1931 she published an autobiography entitled *Living My Life*. Many papers by and relating to Goldman are housed at the Emma Goldman Papers Project at the University of California at Berkeley.

GOMEZ, JEWELLE (1948–). The African-American writer and activist Jewelle Gomez started her career as a journalist in the 1970s and began publishing poetry in the 1980s. Her first collections of poetry were *The Lipstick Papers* (1980) and *Flamingoes and Bears* (1986). She won two Lamda awards for her first collection of fiction *The Gilda Stories* (1991), which brought lesbian fantasy and **science fiction** a new récognition. *The Gilda Stories* features positive portrayals of lesbian **vampires**. Up until this point lesbian vampires had featured as figures of double horror in Gothic narratives, marrying female sexual excess with fear and death.

Gomez has been an antiracist, feminist and prolesbian activist since her undergraduate years at Northeastern University. She has served on the boards of numerous foundations and community projects that promote the artistic work of lesbians and other women and people of color. She has served as executive director of the Poetry Center and American Poetry Archives.

Among Gomez's other works are *Oral Traditions: Selected Poems Old and New* (1995), a collection of short science fiction entitled *Don't Explain* (1997) and the essays collected as *Forty-Three Septembers* in

1993. Her poems, stories and essays have appeared since the 1980s in the mainstream press, and also in national black and lesbian publications.

GRAHN, JUDY (1940–). The poet, cultural critic and activist Judy Grahn is important to the history of American lesbian literature not only as a writer but as a force in independent women's publishing and organizing. Like other lesbian writers, Grahn has said that she began writing because what she wanted to read did not yet exist. She felt the need to create a literature that represented the realities of her life. In the early 1960s Grahn was discharged from the United States Air Force for her lesbianism. Her first connections in the **homophile movement** were lesbians and gay men living in Washington, D.C., who had suffered the same discrimination. Grahn took part in the White House pickets organized by the Mattachine Society in the mid-1960s. Her first poems were published pseudonymously in *The Ladder* in this period.

Grahn moved to California in the late 1960s and was a founding member of the Gay Women's Liberation Group in 1969. She was a driving force behind the establishment of the first women's **bookstore** in the United States, A Woman's Place, and also of the Oakland Women's Press Collective. This collective published Grahn's *Edward the Dyke and Other Poems* in 1971, virtually a self-publishing effort. The title piece in this collection, the prose-poem "The Psychoanalysis of Edward the Dyke," was widely influential to the literature of **second-wave lesbian feminism**. The piece uses a surrealist technique to imagine the interaction between a transgender lesbian and a male psychoanalyst. The eponymous Edward responds to the psychoanalyst's rational language and logical (but erroneous) explanations with metaphorical language and poetic syntax that refuses to be placed anywhere on his map:

> "Narcissism," Dr. Knox droned, "Masochism, Sadism. Admit you want to kill your mother."
> "Marshmallow Bluebird," Edward groaned, eyes softly rolling. "Looking at the stars. April in May."

The piece takes the definition of lesbian as deviant and unnatural and gives that positioning a certain strength and critical power. "Edward the Dyke" was an early and influential American feminist response to psychoanalysis.

By 1975 Grahn's independently published work was widely read in lesbian feminist circles. The 1969 poems published as *The Work of a Common Women* are perhaps the easiest of access and most widely reproduced of Grahn's poems. This series of works attempts to undo the myth of the exceptional and untouchable woman as the subject of poetry and to celebrate the everyday power and strength of American women's lives. Rather than making "remarkable" women the subject of a feminist history, these poems celebrate the often unnoticed power we see in women everyday. Among this stunning series are, "Detroit Annie, Hitchhiking" and "Ella, in a Square Apron, along Highway 80." Grahn's acknowledged masterpiece is the longer poem, "A Woman Is Talking to Death" (1973). This poem contains a rare poetic vision of the interconnectedness of American racism, sexism and homophobia. The poet **Adrienne Rich**, among many others, names it as a revelatory influence on her own understanding.

From the 1980s some of Grahn's most important interventions have been in the area of cultural lesbian feminism. She produced the widely read *Another Mother Tongue: Gay Words, Gay Worlds* in 1984. This book functions as a sort of historical dictionary or encyclopedia that uncovers the roots and the suppression of a continuous and global gay culture. Like other **cultural feminists**, Grahn sees both the oppression and the potential liberation of lesbians and other women in the material and linguistic culture that pervades our lives. Her life work represents a sustained attempt to reshape the language and the metaphors through which we experience the world, in order to make it a safer and more empowering place. With the same aim in mind Grahn published *Blood, Bread and Roses: How Menstruation Shaped the World* in 1993.

Grahn has also produced a series of poetic dramas based on the Tarot. *Queen of Swords*, *Queen of Wands* and *Queen of Cups*. Her book of literary criticism *Really Reading Gertrude Stein* won the Lambda nonfiction award in 1990.

GRAMONT, ELISABETH DE (1875–1954). The writer born Antonia Élisabeth Corisande de Gramont became the Duchess of Clermont-Tonerre by marriage in 1896. She was a member of the early

20th-century circle of wealthy lesbian and bisexual writers based in Paris and centering first around **Renée Vivien** and later around **Natalie Clifford Barney**. Barney's papers point to De Gramont as one of the most moving affairs of her early life.

De Gramont was a wealthy society debutante. Her portrait was painted by Philip Alexius de Laszlo in 1902. In this painting she appears much like other young wealthy and aristocratic wives painted by Laszlo. A 1924 portrait by her friend the lesbian painter Romaine Brooks shows her in masculine dress. De Gramont was also close to the gay writer Marcel Proust and published a book about him, *Marcel Proust*, in 1940.

De Gramont seems to have begun her writing career at the age of 39 with *Histoire de Samuel Bernard et de ses enfants* (1914). Her best known work is perhaps *Mémoires, au temps des équipages* (1928). This was translated and published by Jonathan Cape as *Pomp and Circumstance* in 1929. *La jeune fille anglaise* and *Souvenirs du monde de 1890 à 1940* are later untranslated works, a novel and a memoir respectively. Other works include: *Almanach des bonnes choses de France* (1920), *Le Chemin de l'U.R.S.S.* (1933) and a book on Paul Valéry entitled *Un grand poète* (1946). *Souvenirs du monde* was published in 1966, 12 years after De Gramont's death.

GRIER, BARBARA (1933–). The American writer and publisher Barbara Grier is unique in her generation in insisting that her lesbian identity has been unproblematic. She relates the process of **coming out** as empowering and straightforward. This may be due to the support she received from her mother. Grier was mentored by the lesbian scholar **Jeannette Foster** in the 1950s, and later republished her works. She wrote for a number of **homophile** publications in the 1950s and 1960s. Her articles and stories appeared in *One*, *Mattachine* and *The Ladder* under the pseudonyms Gene Damon, Vern Niven and Gladys Casey.

In 1973 Grier established the lesbian Naiad Press with her partner Donna MacBride. Naiad gradually became the largest and most successful lesbian press in the world, reprinting older works and helping to establish new lesbian writers. In the 1970s Grier published a number of bibliographical studies of lesbian literature, including *The Lesbian in Literature* (1975) and *Lesbiana* (1976). She published a memoir *The Original Coming-Out Stories*, in 1989. Her lifetime's collection of books, papers and memorabilia is now housed at the James C. Hormel Gay and Lesbian Center in San Francisco California.

GRIMKÉ, ANGELINA WELD (1880–1958). The American poet, playwright essayist and activist Angelina Weld Grimké was born from a white mother whose family included white plantation slave owners and abolitionists and a black father, who raised her after his separation from her mother. Grimké's father was a lawyer and member of the National Association for the Advancement of Colored People (NAACP). Scholars speculate that her love for him and his disapproval of her sexuality led to intense conflict in Grimké's life. Her correspondence hints at this. One letter, to Mamie Burrill, speaks longingly of a time when Grimké can invite her to be her wife. After 1900 Grimké lived and worked as a teacher in Washington, D.C., where her most famous work, the play *Rachel*, was first performed in 1916.

Rachel was part of the response to the release of D. W. Griffith's fascist film *Birth of a Nation* in 1915. The NAACP organized nationwide pickets of the film and supported productions of Grimké's play. The play centers on a black woman who refuses to bear children, because she will not produce new human beings who will be subjected to racist violence. After its Washington premiere it was produced in New York and Massachusetts in 1917. The play was aimed at a white audience and intended to raise awareness of lynching and other racist violence and oppression. Several of her other plays and stories center on the refusal or failure of marriage.

Throughout the 1920s Grimké published poems, stories and essays in the NAACP journal *Crisis* and in *The New Negro*. By this time, at the height of the New Negro Movement (later called the **Harlem Renaissance**), Grimké was already a mature writer. Like other members of the movement, she was committed to the promotion and celebration of a specifically black American culture. She might therefore be seen as a major influence on the black cultural renaissance of the 1920s. Only 31 of her poems were published in her lifetime. Many of those that remained unpublished speak of her love for other women.

The first widely read work to discuss Grimké's sexuality and its relation to her unpublished work was **Gloria T. Hull**'s *Color, Sex and*

Poetry: Three Women Writers of the Harlem Renaissance (1987). Some of Grimké's poetry, plays and criticism have been collected and edited by Carolivia Herron in *The Selected Works of Angelina Weld Grimké* (1991), part of the Schomberg Library of Nineteenth-Century Women Writers. Grimké's papers, including her unpublished poems and letters, are housed at Howard University, in the Moorland-Spingarn Research Center.

– H –

HALL, RADCLYFFE (1880–1943). The English writer Radclyffe Hall is remembered chiefly for the controversy surrounding her 1928 novel *The Well of Loneliness*. During her own lifetime however, Hall was a celebrated poet and novelist, achieving widespread acclaim long before 1928. During the first two decades of the 20th century Hall published primarily poetry, five volumes in all. At the age of 21 she came into an enormous fortune, and thereafter moved among a circle of independently wealthy women in Great Britain and on the continent. She was acquainted with **Natalie Clifford Barney**, who is thinly disguised as a fictional character in *The Well*. Barney's circle most certainly influenced Hall's life as a lesbian/transgendered woman, though she herself credits primarily the science of **sexology** and her devoted Catholicism (she was a convert) with defining her identity and the purpose of her life.

Hall's first love and mentor was the wealthy socialite Mabel Batten. She met her life partner **Una Troubridge** shortly before Batten's death. Her first published novel, *The Forge* (1924), fictionalizes Hall and Troubridge's life in the form of a married heterosexual couple. *The Unlit Lamp* (1924), written before *The Forge*, but published after, is markedly the best of Hall's novels. It describes the love of a governess and her pupil and the struggle between the governess and the pupil's mother. The book never openly describes or defines lesbianism, but the relationship and the identity are implied. Publishers would not touch it, and friends advised Hall to write something less threatening first (hence *The Forge*). When it was finally published, *The Unlit Lamp* won the *Prix Femina, étranger* and Hall's reputation as a novelist was established, though her talents were still debated.

The 1926 novel *A Saturday Life* focuses on an unmarried woman called Sidonie. The illusion to inspiration from **Colette** (whose Christian name was Sidonie) seems obvious. *Adam's Breed* won the James Tait Black prize in 1926. The 1926 story "Miss Ogilvy Finds Herself" is clearly a study for what will become *The Well of Loneliness*. The story introduces the idea of female masculinity and also the historical idea that World War I allowed women a freedom and latitude that would change their social position forever. Both of these themes are pursued further in *The Well*.

Jay Prosser has argued convincingly that *The Well of Loneliness* should be read as a transgender, rather than a lesbian, novel. Indeed the novel is about a woman's struggle to express her masculinity as much as it is about her struggle to live a lesbian life. In 1928 most women did not distinguish between the two positions, that is to say, between **aim** and **object choice**. In 21st-century terms, however, Radclyffe Hall should be remembered as a transgender woman who risked her happiness in order to express her own masculinity.

After *The Well of Loneliness* and its notorious trial, Hall published the religious novels *The Master of the House* (1932) and *The Sixth Beatitude* (1936). Lest she be viewed as an uncomplicated hero, it must be acknowledged that both Hall and Troubridge were committed fascists and actively racist. This, and an affair that nearly destroyed her life with Una, led to a great deal of disillusionment in the final years of Hall's life, which were also the first years of World War II. Two excellent biographies are Michael Baker's 1985 *Our Three Selves: A Life of Radclyffe Hall*, which focuses on the Batten and Troubridge relationships and Diana Souhami's 1999 *The Trials of Radclyffe Hall*, the first to discuss the later affair with Evguenia Souline and to focus in depth on the fascination with fascism.

HAMILTON, ELIZA MARY (1807–1851). The Irish poet Eliza Mary Hamilton was born into a colonial family in Dublin. She was a contemporary of Maria Edgeworth, with whom her family was acquainted. Her poems were published in *Dublin Literary Magazine* in the 1830s. In 1838 a volume entitled *Poems* was published in Dublin. There is no biographical information to suggest Hamilton's lesbianism or bisexuality, but Terry Castle reproduces one poem "A Young Girl Seen in Church," which describes a remarkably active same-sex desire.

And then, the thoughts with which my heart had striven
Spoke in my gaze, and would not brook control.

I bent upon her my astonished eye
That glowed, I felt, with an expression full
Of all that love which dares to deify,—

This poem is not entirely remarkable in a strong tradition of **romantic friendship**, but nevertheless involves a direct and special articulation of female same-sex desire.

HANSBERRY, LORAINE (1930–1965). The American playwright Lorraine Hansberry was born and raised in Chicago, Illinois, and attended the Art Institute of Chicago in the 1940s. Her childhood was marked by the struggle of her affluent black parents to move into a segregated white neighborhood in the 1930s. This battle was eventually won, though the family suffered from the racism expressed by many of their neighbors. A similar situation is depicted in the play for which Hansberry became famous, *A Raisin in the Sun* (1959). Hansberry became the first African American to win the Drama Critics Circle award for best play in 1959. The title of this, one of only two plays brought to performance by Hansberry in her lifetime, comes from a poem by the gay **Harlem Renaissance** poet Langston Hughes: "What happens to a dream deferred / . . . Does it dry up / like a raisin in the sun? / Or fester like a sore— / and then run?"

Hansberry first moved to New York City in the 1950s, where she worked as a journalist for Paul Robeson's radical black paper *Freedom*. She soon married the Jewish songwriter Robert Nemiroff, but the two separated in 1957 when Hansberry began to acknowledge her lesbian identity. She joined the **Daughters of Bilitis** in 1957 and two letters in the D.O.B. magazine *The Ladder* are attributed to her. They are signed with the initials L.H.N. and L.N. and display Hansberry's sophisticated analysis of the relationship between homophobia and antifeminism. Indeed, Hansberry was an outspoken feminist who celebrated the work of **Simone de Beauvoir** and wrote journalistically about feminist issues. Sandra Gilbert and Susan Gubar, in *The Norton Anthology of Literature by Women* (1985), published an article by Hansberry satirically titled "In Defense of the Equality of Men" (1961). Hansberry intended this for publication in her lifetime, but it first appeared in print only in Gilbert and Gubar's anthology.

The article displays Hansberry's deeply political and historically grounded understanding of feminist thought. It anticipated Betty Friedan's *The Feminine Mystique* by two years and forms part of a link between early 20th-century **feminism** and the **second wave**. Lorraine Hansberry's life was cut short by cancer in 1965. The plays *Les Blancs*, *The Drinking Gourd* and *What Use Are Flowers?* were edited and published posthumously by Robert Nemiroff, who remained a close friend.

HARFORD, LESBIA (1891–1927). The Australian socialist-feminist activist Lesbia Harford was born Lesbia Keoghin 1891. Though trained as a lawyer, she spent much of her life working in garment factories. This work was a conscious political choice that Harford pursued in spite of very poor health. Her first love was a fellow academic, Kate Lush, to whom she remained attached throughout her life. She made two unsuccessful marriages, the second of which, to another socialist activist, gave her the name Harford.

During her lifetime, Harford published poems in the journal *Birth*. No collection was published, however, until 1941, 14 years after her death. A novel, *The Invaluable Mystery*, was written in the 1920s but not published until 1987. This work tells the story of a young girl whose German parents are imprisoned during World War I, because of their ethnicity. Like her poems, the novel reflects Harford's political convictions. Some argue that its strong feminist stance kept it from publication even by the radical press. Harford's early poems show that she understood and dared to express her lesbian desires.

In her last illness, Harford was cared for by Kate Lush. Most biographical pieces on her recognize her important contribution to Australian socialism, while downplaying her relationship with Lush.

HARLEM RENAISSANCE. The period now called the Harlem Renaissance refers to two or three decades of the flowering of urban African-American arts culture in the early 20th century. For a variety of historical reasons segregated black neighborhoods of northern U.S. cities became centers of intellectual, political and artistic communication and excitement during this period. At the time most artists, political activists and intellectuals referred to this as the New Negro Movement. The NAACP magazine *Crisis*, begun by W. E. B. DuBois in

1910 and still in print, was one focus for the development of Harlem Renaissance literature. The National Urban League began publishing *Opportunity: A Journal of Negro Life* in 1922. Both of these journals also initiated prizes for black American literature. *The New Negro*, another journal, was less long-lived. During this period the first all-black dramatic productions reached New York's Broadway theater district and black music gained widespread popularity among white audiences. An increasing number of black-owned and managed sports teams provided another cultural focus. Thinkers and writers of the Harlem Renaissance stressed the importance of reviving and celebrating a black American culture that was suppressed by a system of violent economic and cultural racism. Prizes for black art and literature were a part of this effort to validate black cultural production.

The decades of the Harlem Renaissance are now much written about as a time of sexual openness and fluidity. Within the entertainment culture of the period, particularly among singers of the increasingly popular blues style, was a network of women with a relative amount of wealth and power. Josephine Baker (who later emigrated to Paris), Bessie Smith, Gladys Bentley, Ethel Waters, Lucille Bogan, Moms Mabley and Ma Rainey were among a group of bisexual and lesbian Blues singers whose sexuality was widely (if not officially) acknowledged. Ma Rainey recorded the famous "Prove It on Me Blues," which discussed her sexuality openly, while yet daring her listener to "prove it."

The homosexual writer Claude McKay published a book entitled *Harlem: The Negro Metropolis* in 1940. This book is especially worth noting here for the section that McKay devoted to Harlem's prominent women. Madame C. J. Walker, who developed a line of cosmetics for women of color and became the United States' first woman millionaire, made important early contributions to Harlem's cultural and social life. Later, her daughter A'Lelia acted as a sort of patroness for many of Harlem's lesbians, gay men and transgender people.

The cultural politics of the Harlem Renaissance were complicated by a system of white patronage of black cultural production. Writers like Zora Neale Hurston, Langston Hughes and Claude McKay were supported by white patrons and many writers published through white-owned publishing houses. Hurston and McKay were accused of exoticizing their portrayals of black people in order to entertain white audiences, even as they attempted to articulate a specifically black cultural expression. The complex relationship between Harlem Renaissance writing and literary modernism is in part informed by the white fascination with what was then called "primitivism" (i.e., black culture).

Within this climate several black bisexual and lesbian women writers began to explore a new territory in the making of narrative and the expression of female same-sex desire. The poet and playwright **Angelina Weld Grimké**, like W. E. B. DuBois, was a generation older than most figures associated with the Harlem Renaissance, but must still be counted as a very important influence. **Nella Larsen** and **Alice Dunbar Nelson** are also significant here. The groundbreaking work on Harlem Renaissance writing and women's sexuality was **Gloria T. Hull**'s 1987 study, *Color, Sex and Poetry: Three Women Writers of the Harlem Renaissance*.

HEATHER HAS TWO MOMMIES. This children's book, written by **Lesléa Newman**, was first published in the United States in 1989. It describes the life of a little girl who was born to a lesbian couple after having been conceived by artificial insemination. The book caused some controversy in the U.S. and was used by the extreme political right as an example of the imminent breakdown of the family and the need for more restrictive laws. The original version of the book described the medical process of insemination in much the same way in which other children's books describe the heterosexual conception of children. Significantly, this section of the book was the subject of the widest number of complaints and was excised by an agreement between author and publishers in 1999 for the book's 10th anniversary edition.

HETAIRISTRAI. This Greek term for "masculine acting" women may have first been used by Lucian (160 A.D.) in *Dialogue of the Courtesans*. It was in any case well known in the **classical Greek** period.

HIC MULIER. This anonymous pamphlet, fully titled *Hic Mulier; or, The Man-Woman: Being a Medicine to Cure the Coltish Disease of the Staggers in the Masculine-Feminines of Our Times, Expressed in a Brief Declamation: Non omnes possumus omnes*, is a late addition to the exchange of pamphlets often referred to as the *querelle des femmes.* This debate on the position and worth of women may have been sparked by a pamphlet called *Her Protection for Women,* published under the name Jane Anger in 1589. *Hic Mulier,* published in 1620, is an argument against the London fashion for **cross-dressing**, which the writer sees as a sign of the breakdown of gender roles. These gender roles should, he argues, be the basis of a God-given social order. The writer invokes a biblically sanctioned and natural system of gender, saying that cross-dressers "have made yourselves stranger things than ever Noah's Ark unloaded or Nile engendered."

The Latin phrase at the end of the pamphlet's title translates "we cannot be all to everybody" and seems to point to the author's assumption that a woman dressing in men's clothing must want to be a man. Cross-dressing in women is associated with sexual accessibility and active desire. These are of course deplorable for the author who promotes a worship of fertile, passive, feminine women that borders on religious devotion. There is a clear indication here that gender transgression will upset the reproductive order. The pamphlet does figure the opposition of virgin to whore (demure to sexually aggressive woman) but also opposes mother (reproductive woman) to Butch (cross-dressing, masculine and therefore somehow infertile) woman. Interestingly the phrase "these new hermaphrodites" is used. Hermaphrodite here seems to carry the meaning we would ascribe to **transgender**, rather than the biological notion of intersex.

HICKOK, LORENA (1893–1968). The American journalist Lorena Hickok is remembered chiefly for her relationship with the administration of President Franklin D. Roosevelt in the 1930s and 1940s, and especially for her intimate relationship with first lady Eleanor Roosevelt. She should also be remembered, however, for an outstanding career as a woman journalist. At the start of her career Hickok, like many women journalists, was relegated to the society pages. In her case this was at the *Milwaukee Sentinel.* In 1917 she moved to the *Minneapolis Tribune* and by 1928 she was working for the Associated Press Wire Service. Here she was assigned to coverage of the White House and specifically the first lady. In 1933 Hickok left the Associated Press because she felt that her relationship with Eleanor impaired her journalistic objectivity.

Hickok was a political leftist and a certain influence on Eleanor Roosevelt's work as first lady. The cause of southern mine workers was certainly brought to E.R.'s attention by Hickok. Both remained staunch opponents of the political right throughout their lives. During the Depression Hickok toured the U.S. as a government-sponsored journalist writing pieces on the poor and unemployed. These pieces have been collected and edited by Richard Lowitt and Maurine Beasley in the volume *One Third of a Nation: Lorena Hickok Reports on the Great Depression* (2000). Together Hickok and Roosevelt wrote a historical study entitled *Women of Courage* in 1954. In the later years of her life Hickok wrote biographies for children.

For many years biographers of both women ignored the obvious evidence of the nature of their relationship contained in letters and journals. Doris Faber's 1980 biography of Hickok, *Life of Lorena Hickok: E.R.'s Friend*, performs the interesting feat of defining Hickok through her relationship to Roosevelt and then denying the reality of that very relationship. The book is, however, otherwise useful. Selected correspondence between the two women has been edited by Rodger Streitmatter and published as *Empty without You: The Intimate Letters of Eleanor Roosevelt and Lorena Hickok* (1998).

HIDALGO, HILDA (1928–). The Puerto Rican–American, academic, social worker and activist Hilda Hidalgo has raised the profile of both lesbians and other Latinas in the field of social work theory. In 1985 she published *Lesbian and Gay Issues: A Resource Book for Social Workers*, and in 1995 *Lesbians of Color: Social and Human Services*. She has also been anthologized in *Compañeras: Latina Lesbians*, edited by Juanita Ramos in 1994. Hidalgo is now retired, but remains a professor emerita at Rutgers University.

HIGHSMITH, PATRICIA (1921–1995). The American writer Patricia Highsmith was born in Texas to parents of German descent. After the 1950s she spent much of her time living in France and Switzerland. Highsmith achieved immediate fame with her first novel, *Strangers on a Train*, in 1950. The book was adapted for a film by Alfred Hitchcock. The story of two strangers who agree to commit murders for each other, and thus remain motiveless and untraceable, highlights Highsmith's lifelong preoccupation with identity and its instability. Highsmith published the lesbian romance *The Price of Salt* in 1953 under the pseudonym Clare Morgan. Many lesbian writers used pseudonyms at this period, but this seems especially interesting for Highsmith, with her particular preoccupations with disguise, masquerade and surveillance. The novel follows the romance of a wealthy married lesbian with a child and a young woman whom she finds working in a store. The two women elope together and are followed by a detective. This adds the uncanny sense of surveillance and ghostly looking that pervades all of Highsmith's novels. *The Price of Salt* was reasonably well received, gaining a review in the *New York Times*.

Highsmith is best known for her "Ripley series" begun with *The Talented Mr. Ripley* in 1955. Overtly lesbian themes were not taken up by her again until her final novel *Small G: A Summer Idyll* in 1995. This details the life of a gay and lesbian bar in Zurich. Highsmith's papers are held at the Swiss Literary Archives in Berne. **Marijane Meaker** has recently published a memoir detailing her relationship with Highsmith in the 1950s.

HINOJOSA, CLAUDIA (?–). The Mexican writer and activist Claudia Hinojosa has spent decades in the fight for the recognition of sexual diversity within her own country and for the right to the sexual empowerment of all women globally. She cofounded the Mexican lesbian and gay rights organization *Grupo Lambda* and often attends global conferences on sexual health as an outspoken lesbian. Her essays, including "Cries and Whispers: The Lesbian Quest for Visibility in Mexico," are widely anthologized.

HISTORICAL FICTION. Literary criticism has not focused sharply on the conventions and uses of historical fiction until fairly recently. The association of historical fiction with mass-market paperbacks, Gothic romances and working-class women's reading in general has perhaps kept it from prominence. Of course, not all historical fiction fits into the categories listed above, but when it does not it is often seen as something other than historical fiction. W. M. Thackeray's *Vanity Fair*, although it fits all of the criteria and performs many of the functions of a typical historical novel, is more often talked about as a classic of 19th-century satire.

Historical fiction seems to have helped lesbian writers to make two distinctly different moves in relation to lesbian identity. Works like **Isabel Miller**'s *Patience and Sarah* (1969) seem to present a lesbian identity, which is continuous through time, though it has been rendered invisible by the male-dominated discipline of history. That is, there have always been lesbians who have felt, thought and desired like us, we just need to uncover or reimagine their histories. Other lesbian historical fiction focuses on the contingency of lesbian identity, imagining how women who loved women felt and thought of themselves and their desires differently at different historical periods. The work of **Sarah Waters** might fit into this category.

We could date lesbian historical fiction from **Virginia Woolf**'s *Orlando* (1928). The novel itself is a historical fantasy focused on a miraculously long-lived **transgendered** character. It was written by the bisexual Woolf for the woman she loved, **Vita Sackville-West**, on whose life and family history the eponymous character Orlando is based. In the same year in which *Orlando* was published **Djuna Barnes** published *Ladies Almanack*, a satire on a group of Paris-based lesbian writers. The book places its allegorical characters in a vaguely **early modern** setting.

At midcentury the British lesbian writer **Mary Renault**, after writing a contemporary novel featuring two women lovers, turned to historical fiction featuring relationships between men in ancient Greece. The 1970s and 1980s saw the emergence of lesbian historical fictions of American racism in the Jim Crow South in **Alice Walker**'s *The Color Purple* (1982) and **Fannie Flagg**'s *Fried Green Tomatoes at the Whistlestop Cafe* (1992). Also in the 1980s lesbian writers in English on both sides of the Atlantic made use of the early modern period. **Ellen Galford**'s *Moll Cutpurse, Her True History: A Novel* (1987), makes fun, as the title suggests, of notions of historical truth and the line between biography and fiction. It follows a tradition of literary fascination with the **cross-dressing** figure of **Mary Frith**. Katherine Sturtevant's *A Mistress Moderately Fair* (1988) is an adult novel by a writer who normally produces historical children's fiction. This work is set in 17th-century London and details the relationships among two female lovers and their African servant.

Sturtevant's novel illustrates a commonplace regarding historical fiction of any time: that historical novels are really more about the time in which they are written than they are about the time in which they are set. In the case of lesbian historical fiction treatments of fictional plots and characters in historical settings have often illustrated the aims of 20th-century lesbian-feminism. Thus Walker, Flagg and Sturtevant all seek to illustrate the relationships between heterosexuality, femininity and racism. **Jeannette Winterson**'s two historical novels (*The Passion*, 1987, and *Sexing the Cherry*, 1989) create lesbian and transgender characters in terms that are clearly influenced by late 20th-century **queer** theory.

At the turn of the 21st century the lesbian historical novelist Sarah Waters achieved a tremendous market success with a succession of three novels featuring relationships between women in 19th-century England. For over 40 years the U.S. lesbian writer **Marion Zimmer Bradley** has been publishing lesbian fiction alongside a series of highly popular **science fiction** and historical fantasy novels which re-examine women's roles while mostly avoiding overt lesbian content. Diana Wallace's volume *The Woman's Historical Novel: British Women Writers 1900–2000* (2004) gives an excellent overview of British women's historical fiction throughout the 20th century, including in-depth readings of Mary Renault, Jeannette Winterson and **Sylvia Townsend Warner**, as well as brief readings of several other significant lesbian figures.

HOMOPHILE MOVEMENT. The homophile movement refers to the lesbian and gay activism that took place in North America, Europe and Scandinavia in the mid-20th century. In this period, lesbian and gay activists began to see themselves as part of a network of global (in reality primarily Northern Hemisphere) groups that were engaged in a struggle for human rights. In the United States, groups began to emerge in the 1940s. Most had strong leftist connections at first. The Mattachine Society was founded in California in 1950. Connections with the American Communist Party caused a rupture in the early Mattachine Society, and more politically central leadership had taken over by 1956. The California-based Knights of the Clock were a specifically antiracist homophile group founded in 1950. They circulated regular reports to members until 1953. In 1955, the specifically lesbian organization Daughters of Bilitis (D.O.B.) was founded in San Francisco. Eventually D.O.B. had branches on both coasts of North America and in the Midwest.

Homophile groups often produced magazines, journals and newsletters. The Mattachine Society produced *One Magazine* throughout the 1950s, and at first women were important contributors. One, Incorporated was founded with the aim of promoting homophile education and publishing. The D.O.B. began publishing the specifically lesbian magazine **The Ladder** in 1956. This magazine is an example vehicle for the study of the process through which the homophile lesbian movement became the lesbian/lesbian feminist movement of the 1960s and early 1970s.

The One publication *Homosexuals Today, 1956* lists a number of homophile organizations that were then in existence throughout Scandinavia and continental Europe. Editor Marvin Cutler also briefly alludes to men's homophile groups in East Asia. Little evidence is given for these however.

HORROR. The designation horror generally refers to any fiction or nonfiction that focuses on the abject, the violent, the supernatural or all three. As Patricia White and other theorists point out, horror is a genre that inherently questions what is normal through its focus on the abnormal. White argues that lesbians abound in horror because they represent "an excess of female sexuality which cannot be contained without recourse to the super-natural." A classic example here is Henry James' novella *The Turn of the Screw,* which presents the suggestion of a pedophilic lesbian relationship between a ghostly former governess and her young charge. The narrator here is a new governess who may be unreliable. The reader is left wondering whether these desires are actually her own and the ghostly governess imagined. Lesbianism here appears as an instability and excess of narrative function. A whole category of horror fiction works on the association of haunting with lesbian desire. **Daphne Du Maurier**'s 1939 novel *Rebecca* and Shirley Jackson's 1959 *The Haunting of Hill House* are two good examples here.

Any news story involving violent and frightening lesbians has a doubly prurient appeal, in being both transgressively sexual and frighteningly horrific. In the United States the high profile murder trial of Alice Mitchell, who was accused of cutting her female lover's throat in Memphis in 1892, engendered an increase in tales of horrific and murderous lesbians. The idea of the murderous lesbian, already developed through characters like Sheridan Le Fanu's **vampire** story, *Carmilla*, quickly gained a prominent place in **pulp** magazine fiction. The character of Tascela, who features in Robert Howard's 1936 story "Red Nails," is a classic example. Marijane Meaker's pulp novel *The Evil Friendship* (1958) is another example. It tells the story of the excessive childhood relationship between real-life crime writer Ann Perry and another young girl. The two girls, who wrote fiction together, were obsessed with each other's company and ended by murdering one of their mothers. The parents had feared a lesbian relationship and sought to separate the girls, who believed that murdering the mother was a way to keep them from being separated. Peter Jackson's film *Heavenly Creatures* (1994), based on the same story, suggests that the fantasy life of the girls, fed by their exclusive obsession with each other and their creation of fictional worlds, was out of control to the degree that they were no longer capable of responsible action. The success of this film and its relation of lesbian desire, fantasy and horrific violence, are part of a long tradition of public fascination with these themes.

Alongside (or within) a tradition of evil lesbian characters there rests the potential to exploit horror's destabilization of the normal. Lesbian vampire fiction and lesbian **crime fiction** have presented increasingly positive and powerful characters throughout the 20th century. These characters, presented by writers like **Jewelle Gomez** and **Kathy Acker**, often question ideas of good and evil, normal and abnormal, and even the boundaries of the horror genre. The stories and novels in which they appear often avoid simple divisions of characters into the good and the bad and also avoid simple moral resolutions.

In addition to numerous genre-based anthologies, critical perspective is presented alongside a selection of lesbian and gay horror fiction in *Bending the Landscape: Horror* (2001), edited by Nicola Griffin and Stephen Pagel.

HULL, GLORIA T. (?–). The African-American feminist scholar Gloria T. Hull has been instrumental in recovering the works of black American women writers of the early 20th century and making them visible to critical attention. In 1979, she published groundbreaking work on **Angelina Weld Grimké** in the article "Under the Days: The Buried Life and Poetry of Angelina Weld Grimké. This brought the suppression of Grimké's lesbian identity and its expression in verse to scholarly attention. Until Hull's work in 1979 Grimké was known only as a critic and playwright. In 1981 Hull, together with Patricia Bell Scott and **Barbara Smith**, edited and published *All the Women Are White, All the Blacks Are Men, But Some of Us Are Brave: Black Women's Studies*. Again, the work broke academic and critical ground and remains, over 20 years later, widely taught. Hull is best known for decades of work on **Alice Dunbar Nelson**. Among other books on Nelson she has edited her diaries and published them as *Give Us Each Day: The Diary of Alice Dunbar Nelson* (1984). Hull's *Color, Sex and Poetry: Three Women Writers of the **Harlem Renaissance*** appeared in 1987. Her work has contributed enormously to the struggle for the recognition of black American women's literature and literary criticism.

HULL, HELEN ROSE (1888–1971). The American writer Helen R. Hull was born and raised in the Midwest but lived her adult life in New York City with her lifelong partner Mabel Louise Robinson. For many years Hull taught at Barnard, the women's college attached to Columbia University. She was a member of the early 20th-century New York feminist club heterodoxy, to which **Emma Goldman** also belonged. In 1918 Hull published a short story called "The Fire" in *Century* magazine. Like her first novel *Quest* (1922), this story tells of one young woman's lesbian schoolgirl crushes and her parents' censure of them. *Labyrinth* (1923) presents a feminist portrait of an alienated housewife. This novel contains some sexually dissident characters, though they are largely peripheral.

HYBRIDITY. The term hybridity is derived from biological science and refers to cross-breeding between species that are defined as distinct. The idea that black and white races were biologically distinct was a major argument in support of colonial slavery. Thus the need to police, or make invisible, reproductive sexual contact between black and white people became a major anxiety for colonists. Colonial power was, in a very real sense, maintained through various controls of sexual access, and the children that resulted from intercultural unions caused anxiety for those who sought to justify slavery through a biological notion of distinct racial categories.

Postcolonial theorists such as **Gloria Anzaldúa**, Homi Bhabha and John Young have borrowed the concept of hybridity as a means of questioning the identity categories that support racism, nationalism and racial heterosexual power. Anzaldúa uses the Spanish language term *mestiza*, arguing for a *mestiza* consciousness that refuses to remain inside any of the categories assigned to people in colonial or postcolonial situations. An important new field of **queer** postcolonial theory argues for a radical repositioning (or un-positioning) of racial categories that have always been inextricable from regimes of sexual control.

– I –

IDENTIFICATION. As understood in the discipline of **psychoanalysis**, identification refers to the process by which an individual subject incorporates what is outside into her/his definition of her/himself. Classically, a child's two parents and their opposing genders allow the child two positions through which to create a gender identity. For example, the theory says that a girl ought to incorporate her mother's femininity and her father's masculinity into her own definition of herself as things to identify with and against, respectively. This is the source of questions about "role models" for children raised in single-parented, same-sex parented, or transgender-parented households. In actual fact, of course, gender identification takes place, for better or worse, in a much wider field than the nuclear family. The idea of gender identification is deeply ingrained in most cultures, though many also have traditional practices through which a person might switch gender allegiance. In fictional and life-writing narratives that tell of a character's sexual development, critics often trace a series of identifications. Early lesbian/transgender writers such as **Radclyffe Hall** sought to create the lesbian identity in narrative through the story of a child's unique identification with father and mother.

IDENTITY. The concept of identity is derived from Enlightenment discussions of the individual self and arose once religious definitions of being began to be supplanted by ideas of nationality, race, gender, sexuality and class as primary definitions of the individual. Maria

Edgeworth uses the word identity in the modern sense to speak of the national identity of Irish people in her 1800 preface to *Castle Rackrent*. Feminists of the **early modern** period, from the *querelle des femmes* to the Enlightenment writings of Olympe De Gouges and Mary Wollstonecraft, used the idea of woman to create a specific identity for the gendered citizen. Nineteenth and early 20th-century **sexologists** first began to develop ideas of sexual identity through creating taxonomies of gender positions for transgender people and those who desired people of the same sex. In the mid-20th century, American sociologists began to employ the notion of ethnic identity to studies of various urban neighborhoods. This concept of identity, once it merged with the **homophile movement** of the same period, grew into what we think of as sexual identity. Identities are definitions more than they are the realities of people's lives. They are used by marketers to sell things (a growing effort aimed at the lesbian and gay market is a pertinent example) and as categories by bureaucracies. As the shortcomings of various identity definitions become apparent these categories change. Thus women who love and desire other women have moved from **tribade** to **invert** to **sapphist** to **lesbian** over the past two centuries.

INDEPENDENT WOMEN'S PRESSES. One of the tenets of **cultural** and material **feminism** is that women must gain control of the means of cultural production. With the **second wave** of feminism a number of women's presses, printers and binders were set up to promote the production and distribution of women's books in what was otherwise a male-dominated global publishing industry. When **Judy Grahn** established A Women's Place, the first women's **bookstore** in the United States, a printing press was quickly set up in the basement. Early women's presses in the United States included Daughters, which first published **Rita Mae Brown**'s *Rubyfruit Jungle* and the specifically lesbian Diana Press. Kitchen Table Women of Color Press, Spinster/Aunt Lute and Shameless Hussy followed, along with the specifically lesbian presses Long Haul (first publisher of **Dorothy Allison**), Firebrand and Alyson. Iowa City Women's Press included printers and binders in its women-only cooperative structure, so that women might control the entire length of the book production process.

In Great Britain, The Women's Press and the lesbian Onlywomen Press were early products of the second wave of feminism. The British Virago, like the American Feminist Press, was first set up to reprint classics of women's writing that were otherwise lost. The Feminist Press has since moved into publishing original work. Kali for Women was set up in India in 1984 by Urvashi Butalia and Rita Menon, who have since cowritten *Making a Difference: Feminist Publishing in the South* (1995).

INDIAN LITERATURE. *See* SOUTH ASIAN LITERATURE.

INVERSION. This term, used by the **sexologist** Havelock Ellis, described what would now be called a variety of transgender persons. Conflating the idea of **object-choice** with the gendered **aim** of those he studied, he argued that women who desired other women must be, to some degree, more masculine than women who desired men, thus their gender was "inverted." **Radclyffe Hall** used the idea of the invert to create her famous character Stephen Gordon in *The Well of Loneliness* in 1928. It was still in use when Ann Aldrich wrote *We Walk Alone* in 1955. **Jeanette Forster** distanced herself from the term "inversion" in her 1957 *Sex Variant Women in Literature*, borrowing the term "sex variance" from **sexologist** George Henry. By the late 1960s the term had mostly fallen out of usage, being replaced by the term "lesbian" for a woman who desired other women, and "**butch**" for a masculine woman.

– J –

JAY, KARLA (1947–). The lesbian activist and academic Karla Jay was born into a working-class Brooklyn neighborhood just after World War II. She attended university in New York and took part in the student uprisings of 1968. Jay's years as a leftist lesbian activist are detailed in her recent memoir *Tales of the Lavender Menace: A Memoir of Liberation* (1999). She was an early member of the radical feminist group the Redstockings and published an important early collection entitled *Out of the Closets: Voices of Gay Liberation* with Allen Young in 1972. She worked as an activist in both New York and California in the early 1970s. Jay has since made several important interventions in the field of lesbian studies. Her doctoral dissertation focused on **Renée Vivien** and **Natalie Clifford Barney**. It was published as *The Amazon and the Page* in 1988. With Joanne Glasgow she edited the critical collection *Lesbian Texts and Contexts: Radical Revisions* (1990), which has been an important teaching tool for lesbian studies.

JEWETT, SARAH ORNE (1849–1909). The American prose writer born Theodora Sarah Orne Jewett was raised and educated by wealthy parents in southern Maine. Jewett's father was a doctor and he often took her on his country rounds when she was a small child. The sense of traveling the land and celebrating the working people who lived on it, which she gained on these excursions, stayed with Jewett throughout her life and is expressed in her fiction. Jewett was educated both at home and in local girl's academies. Her first short stories were published under the pseudonyms Alice Eliot and A. C. Eliot in *Riverside Magazine for Young People* and *Atlantic Monthly*. These were collected in the 1877 volume *Deephaven*, which was her first published book.

Jewett is significant to American modernism in that she developed a new and freer narrative style that helped others see their way to breaking the conventions of 19th-century realism. Virtually all of her work is in the form of what she called "sketches," replacing sustained plot development with lyricism and an almost impressionistic sense of place. Other works include *The Country Doctor* (1884), *A White Heron and Other Stories* (1886), *The King of Folly Island* (1888) and *The Country of the Pointed Firs* (1896) for which she is perhaps best known. Jewett was well respected as a writer during her own lifetime. She received an honorary doctorate from Bowdoin College in Maine in 1901. **Willa Cather** viewed her as a role model and mentor.

Jewett's life partner was Annie Adams Fields whom she met during Field's marriage and lived with from the time of Mr. Field's death until her own. Scholars have described their relationship as a **Boston marriage**. The two women made annual tours of Europe throughout their life together. Fields was the first editor of Jewett's letters after her death.

JOURNALISM. We trace the history of lesbian journalism back to feminist political pamphlets of the **early modern** period. Certainly **Aphra Behn** and **Mary Wollstonecraft** ought to be counted. A strong and vibrant tradition only began to emerge, however, in the 19th and early 20th centuries when changing economic realities opened many middle-class professions to women. The 19th century saw a boom in the newspaper business, with a lack of clarity about whether journalism was a "genteel" profession. Nevertheless as the novels of Anthony Trollope and George Gissing reveal, women were already making their mark as journalists by the 1860s and were, relatively speaking, well accepted within the profession by the turn of the 20th century. Countless lesbians have of course contributed to the development of journalism while remaining unrecognized as such.

The sexually open and experimental period of the **Weimar Republic** in Germany in the 1920s saw the national distribution of several exclusively lesbian periodicals. The most notable of these *Die Freundin* (*The Girlfriend*, published from 1924 to 1933) and *Frau Liebe und Leben* (*Woman Love and Life*, published from 1928.) These contained poetry, fiction, editorials and articles. They also provided a forum for lively social and political debate in the form of letters and reader responses, and a place for lesbians to communicate with each other in classified advertisements. The Berlin-based Scientific Humanitarian Committee provided the support network for many of these periodicals and their journalistic contributors. This lively period of lesbian journalism was ended by the Nazis in 1933.

In Great Britain during this same period the privately circulated journal ***Urania*** provided a similar forum within the framework of a **transgendered** philosophy that included lesbianism as one of its foremost exempla. *Urania* illustrates the shifting and diverse ways in which sexuality and sexual identity were conceived in this period. The relation between transgendered and lesbian **identities** expressed in this journal differs significantly from the way in which these identities would be consolidated in the late 20th century. Early French efforts include *Akademos* (from 1909) and *Inversions* (1924–1925).

The paper entitled *Friendship and Freedom*, which appeared briefly in Chicago in 1925, appears to have been entirely for male homosexuals. The earliest known exclusively lesbian magazine in the United States was ***Vice Versa***, which produced nine issues in 1947 and 1948. Beginning in the 1950s lesbian journalism in the English-speaking world began to gain the kind of mass audience it had in Weimar Germany. **Homophile** organizations like the Mattachine Society began to publish privately distributed newsletters in the United States in the 1950s. Mattachine's newsletter, *One*, like the organization itself, at first included lesbian members, subscribers and contributors. Its initial publication was also supported by a California-based lesbian and gay organization called Knights of the Clock, which had a specifically antiracist mission. Lesbians quickly began to feel, however, that they were being underrepresented in a gay and lesbian forum. By 1956 the lesbian organization Daughters of Bilitis had formed and begun publishing its own newsletter, *The Ladder*, by private subscription. Later scholarship focuses on the middle-class, and implicitly white-dominated nature of *The Ladder*'s mission and concerns. This would represent a departure from efforts like *Vice Versa*. A good collection of postwar lesbian journals exists in the Lesbian Herstory Archives in Brooklyn, New York.

American journals and organizations of the 1950s enjoyed links with vibrant homophile publishing organizations in France (including the journal *Arcadie*), Germany, Holland (including the journals *Vriendschap—Friendship* and *De Schackel—The Link*), Denmark, Sweden and Norway. The Mattachine compilation *Homosexuals Today*, edited by Marvin Cutler in 1956, mentioned a speech given by one Dr. Robert Lindner on a number of homophile organizations then extant in Thailand and Indonesia. Like the European and Scandinavian examples, however, these appear largely dominated by men. There is no mention of British homophile publishing in this volume. American journals of the 1950s were closely allied with medical and sociological researchers, as one tenet of the homophile movement was that cooperation with researchers would bring greater understanding of the "problem" of the homosexual. A British organization called Minorities Research Group published *Arena 3* in the 1960s. In oral history accounts some British lesbians mark this magazine as an important point of identification. Though later in date than *One* and *The Ladder*, in style and content *Arena 3* can be placed with other homophile publications.

Beginning in the 1960s a more radical group of journals and newspapers appeared. Their distribution was both more open and more widespread. *The Advocate* began publishing openly in the United States in the 1960s and is now a mainstream lesbian and gay journal that endorses democratic presidential candidates. The Gay Liberation Front, which based its politics on a radical leftist, class-conscious and anti-imperialist understanding of sexuality, published newsletters in North America, Europe and Australasia from 1972. At the same time the women's movement gave rise to a number of national publications in these same countries in which lesbians participated from the outset. Quickly again, however, some lesbians felt marginalized both by a lesbian and gay movement dominated by gay men and a women's movement dominated by middle-class, white women. The radical feminist British journal *Spare Rib*, which published from 1972 to 1984, is a good example of publications fueled by this dissatisfaction. *Spare Rib* experienced a number of damaging ideological struggles in the final years of its publication. Chief among these was the homophobia experienced by lesbians involved in the magazine.

Again a group of specifically lesbian newspapers, magazines and journals arose out of this radically leftist political atmosphere in response to the sexism, homophobia and racism experienced in other arenas. In the United States *The Lesbian Tide* was published privately from 1971 to 1980, and is said to be the first American magazine to bear the word lesbian its title. Among publicly distributed papers, magazines and journals were/are: *Lesbian News* (from 1975), *Sinister Wisdom* (from 1976), *Tribad* (1977–1979) and *Azalea: A Magazine for Third World Lesbians* (from 1977). The committedly antihomophobic and antiracist political newspaper *Off Our Backs* (published in Washington, D.C., since 1970) has provided an important forum for lesbians, though the stance the paper took during the "**sex wars**" of the 1980s alienated a large portion of its lesbian audience.

The 1980s and 1990s saw a continued diversity of lesbian journalistic publishing as well as the mainstreaming of some lesbian journalists. *Lesbies net Nieuws* began publishing in Holland in 1981. *Trikone* addressed a diasporic South Asian lesbian audience beginning in 1986. *Lesbo* has published in Slovenia from 1995. Meanwhile, a number of slick national magazines, such as *Curve* in the United States and *Diva* in Britain, exploited a growing atmosphere of tolerance by providing opportunities for advertisers to access a lesbian market and toning down the political orientation of earlier productions. In the United States in the 1990s lesbian journalist Donna Minkowitz became nationally known for her column in the *Village Voice* (which earned her a Pulitzer Prize nomination) and Deb Price was syndicated nationally as an out lesbian.

Important figures in the history of English language lesbian journalism include **Djuna Barnes**, **Lorena Hickock**, **Janet Flanner**, Laura DeForce Gordon and Margaret Gordon. Clare Potter's *Lesbian Periodicals Index*, published in 1986, is an invaluable resource for material published up to that point. A list of scholarly journals addressing lesbians and lesbian sexuality is provided in the bibliography at the back of this volume. *See also* SEXOLOGY.

– K –

KAMA SUTRA. Dates for the *Sanskrit* text *Kama Sutra* are unclear, though it seems to have been compiled sometime before 600 C.E. (some of the material may be older) by a scholar whose family name was Vatsyayana in Uttar Pradesh. *Kama* refers to the material, sensory pleasures of life and *Sutra* to a book of guiding principles. The *Kama Sutra* contains sections on food, cleanliness and music, as well as acts of sex. It thus denoted a cultural period and place when sexuality was not necessarily protected, isolated or valorized above other sensual experiences and abilities.

The *Kama Sutra* is relevant here for two reasons. First, it classifies women as sexual objects and actors in a number of ways. Vatsyayana categorizes women as single, married or widowed, thus defining them patriarchally through their relation to men. It also describes women of various temperaments. As Vanita points out in *Same-Sex Love in India*, however, it also characterizes women as *swayamdutika*, one who represents herself, *samasyabandhu*, a woman who lives in relation to another woman and *svairini*, a strong woman who stands alone. In addition Vatsyayana also describes what he terms a "third" sexual nature, which might either manifest as masculine or feminine.

Secondly, the *Kama Sutra* has a long tradition of cross-over into other cultures. It first entered English in the **orientalist** Sir Richard Burton's translation in 1883, and has been a major focus for Western myths about "Eastern" sexualities. Mira Nair's 1996 film bearing the title *Kama Sutra* and playing on associations with the ancient text was accused of obscenity and censored in India. Many scholars both inside and outside of India labeled it an internalization of orientalist ideas about Indian sexuality.

KAMANI, GINU (?–). The Indian-American writer, critic and teacher Ginu Kamani was born in Bombay and now lives in Oakland, California, where she has been writer-in-residence and writing teacher at Mills College for several years. She is most significant here for her collection of stories *Junglee Girl* (1996), which explores women's sexuality in a shifting cultural context. Kamani's criticism and teaching focuses consistently on intersections of race, gender and sexuality in women's lives. In 2001 Kamani wrote the play *The Cure* with Asian-American playwright Joel Tan.

KLEPFISZ, IRENA (1941–). The Polish-American Jewish lesbian activist Irena Klepfisz was born in the Warsaw Ghetto during the Nazi occupation there. Her father died saving other Jews from Nazi gunmen. Klepfisz has distinguished herself as a writer of holocaust poetry and an outspoken lesbian feminist. She has written about anti-Semitism in the women's movement as well as the atrocities committed by Israel in Palestine. She was founder of the lesbian-focused feminist journal *Conditions*. Klepfisz writes in a bilingual mixture of Yiddish and English. Her poems have been published as *A Few Words in the Mother Tongue: Poems Selected and New, 1971–1990* (1990). She has also published a volume of memoirs, *Dreams of an Insomniac: Feminist Essays, Speeches, and Diatribes* (1991). Together with Melanie Kantrowitz she edited the anthology *The Tribe of Dina: A Jewish Women's Anthology* (1989).

– L –

LACAN, JACQUES (1901–1981). The French **psychoanalyst** Jacques Lacan is a significant figure in the psychoanalytic movement and in 20th-century French philosophy, primarily for his blending of **Sigmund Freud**'s theories with those of the linguist Ferdinand de Sausseure. In Lacan's version of Freud's primal scene it is the intervention of the symbolic father, possessor of the phallus, the primary signifier that heralds the child's entry into language and the symbolic order. This places the mother implicitly (and explicitly) in a position that is prior to language, without signification. In Lacan's theory, woman (or the feminine position) is defined by her lack of the phallus. She is **the other** (mother), through separation from which the male child defines himself and the world. Passive femininity is then, in a negative sense, crucial to Lacan's picture of the human subject. Thus the kind of active desire expressed by many lesbians is theoretically impossible. As a woman the lesbian lacks the phallus, the ability to function as the active subject of desire. Lacan would not have argued that any possession of a real phallus allows an individual to signify through language, but rather that its possession is invested with that power by the mythic structures which govern our culture. However the distinction between the real and imaginary phallus often blurs in practice. Lacan's theories are typical of the Freudian school in the sense that they present a universalizing theory that claims to hold true across the specificities of culture and historical periods. Many feminist and lesbian feminist psychoanalytic theorists continue to suffer from this cultural blindness.

Lacan is significant here in that his theories influenced, both positively and negatively, a number of French feminist and lesbian theorists in the 1980s. Significant among these are Hélène Cixous, **Monique Wittig**, Julia Kristeva and Luce Irigaray. Notions of phallic lack and phallic possession have been played with by a number of lesbian writers in English as well. Significant among these are the theorist and pornographer **Patrick Califia** and the philosopher **Judith Butler**.

THE LADDER. See JOURNALISM.

LADIES OF LLANGOLLEN. Two Anglo-Irish women, Eleanor Butler (1739–1829) and Sarah Ponsonby (1755–1831), eloped from the west of Ireland to Wales in the 1780 and, settling near the village Llangollen, came to be known by this name. The two kept extensive journals and corresponded with many of the leading literary figures of their day. Their idea of a contemplative and simple rural life appealed to notions of romance that were popular in British culture of the period.

Elizabeth Mavors 1971 biographical study of Ponsonby and Butler, *The Ladies of Llangollen*, established the scholarly concept of **romantic friendship**. Mavor argues that due to various shifts in cultural production and consumption at this period, women had developed a romantic and literary sensibility that most men did not share. Therefore she argues, they naturally turned to each other for the fulfillment of romantic desires and fantasies that weren't necessarily sexual. **Anne Lister**, however, who mentions the Ladies of Llangollen in her own diaries, clearly saw herself as the subject of a sexuality that was best kept private. Ponsonby and Butler are significant here for their own **life-writings**, but also for their many appearances in the literature of this period.

LARSEN, NELLA (1891–1964). The American novelist Nella Larsen spent her literary career exploring her culturally mixed ancestry. Educated in both the United States and Europe, she later became the first African-American woman to win a Guggenheim fellowship. During her lifetime she published two novels, *Quicksand* 1928 and *Passing* 1929. The second, *Passing*, begins from an encounter between two women who, though at the moment of encounter are passing for white, know each other to be of African-American descent. One of these figures is permanently passing in a marriage to an abusive and racist white man, who is unaware of her family history. A subtle and powerful form of desire develops between the two women. They evolve into a relationship in which racial aspirations and disappointments are conflated with romantic and sexual desires for each other. One cannot say of this novel that repressed lesbian desire stands in for relationships of racial crossing, nor vice versa. Larsen has adeptly intertwined the two so that the novel raises a number of disturbing questions, rather than producing any fixed identity categories for its characters. Both of Larsen's novels are highly interactive in this sense. In true modernist fashion they challenge readers to engage actively with the work before them. Though Larsen also wrote children's literature, her reputation as a writer did not match her technical excellence and cultural relevance. After many years working as a nurse she died unrecognized.

LAWRENCE, D. H. (1885–1930). The English writer D. H. Lawrence is remarkable here for his oppositional engagement with the lesbian identity that had begun to emerge in **modernist** fiction in the early 20th century. Like many modernist writers Lawrence was deeply influenced by the emerging discipline of **psychoanalysis**, as well as the **sexological** discourses of gender and desire that were also influential during this period. In general his depictions of sexual relations between women and men involve violent psychic struggles that can only be resolved by the woman submitting to the worship of the phallus, which she secretly desires. The story "St. Mawr" (1925) as well as the 1920 novel *Women in Love* are typical in this sense. Lawrence described sexual relationships with a frankness and intensity that, along with his unique and mystical prose style, gained him a devoted audience in his own lifetime. **Anaïs Nin** wrote in defense of his work.

In journalistic essays such as "Cocksure Women and Hensure Men" (1929) Lawrence articulated his reaction to the increasing popularity of **feminism** and the movement of women into the public sphere. "Cocksure Women and Hensure Men" describes the breakdown of culture through the breakdown of traditional gender roles. The extended metaphor of barnyard fowl connects domestic arrangements with nature (biological destiny). Following this same formula, Lawrence created several unkind portraits of lesbians and masculinized women characters. *The Rainbow* (1915) details the relationship between a schoolgirl, Ursula Brangwyn, and a teacher. The history of their affair is narrated in a chapter entitled "Shame" and Lawrence makes a clear and unfriendly connection between lesbianism and women's rights. The teacher, Winifred, is both the active (almost predatory) partner in the relationship and an adherent of the principles of the women's movement. *The Rainbow* was the first of Lawrence's novels to be withdrawn from publication for indecency.

The 1923 story "The Fox" again depicts a lesbian relationship involving one women who is more active, and this time clearly predatory. The influence of sexological pictures of female inversion is clear here. Like Havelock Ellis, Lawrence seems to place lesbians into categories according to how much or how little they deviate from femininity. This deviation from femininity correlates with a desire for other women. The more passive partner in "The Fox" is eventually "saved" by a man who kills her lover and marries her. Like Ursula Brangwyn, however, she remains cold toward men after her lesbian affair.

The influence of "The Fox" was sadly extended by a loose Canadian film adaptation, which was tremendously successful in 1967. Combined with the 1968 British film *The Killing of Sister George*, this created a cinematic picture of threatening predatory lesbians, which dominated English-language film culture in the late 1960s. Both **Kate Millet** in *Sexual Politics* (1968) and Anne Smith in *Lawrence and Women* (1978) give feminist readings of Lawrence that are now dated but remain historically significant.

LEDUC, VIOLETTE (1907–1972). The French novelist Violette LeDuc is best known for her autobiographical work *La Bâtarde* (*The Bastard*, 1964). This work details the lesbian affairs that LeDuc had as a young woman in a chapter that was excised in its first edition. It also exemplifies the author's fascination with her own **abjection**. *La Bâtarde* was preceded by several novels, including *L'Asphyxie* (1948) and *Ravages* (1955). Her private **life-writing** details an unrequited love for the philosopher **Simone de Beauvoir**, who helped to promote LeDuc's work.

LEE, VERNON (1856–1935). Vernon Lee is the pseudonym for the English travel writer, short story writer and cultural critic Violet Paget. Paget was raised by parents who traveled around Europe and she continued this habit in her adult life, living for long periods in Italy. She was a close friend of Henry James, and their friendship has been fictionalized by Colm Toibin in his novel *The Master* (2004), which also deals with James' sexuality. Paget had several affairs with women, but the longest was with Clementine Anstruther Thomson.

As Vernon Lee, Paget published *Studies of the Eighteenth Century in Italy* in 1880. Two volumes of Gothic short stories were published under the same pseudonym. First came *Hauntings: Fantastic Tales* (1892) and then *Pope Jacynth and Other Stories* (1904). Travel writings include the full-length *The Spirit of Rome* (1906). Later in her life she produced the literary study *The Handling of Words, and Other Studies in Literary Psychology* (1923).

LEGUIN, URSULA (1929–). The American science fiction and fantasy writer Ursula K. LeGuin is significant here for her **science fiction** novel *The Left Hand of Darkness* (1969), which describes a world on which people change gender in a cyclical, seasonal fashion. She is also the recent English translator of the poems of **Gabriela Mistral**.

LEHMANN, ROSAMUND (1901–1990). The English novelist Rosamund Lehmann used her life's work to stretch the possibilities for what women characters could do in novelistic narrative. Though Lehmann began publishing poetry in 1917, it is for her **novels** that she is justly remembered by literary critics. Rachel Blau DuPlessis, in her critical work *Writing Beyond the Ending* (1985), argues that the history of the 20th-century women's novel might be broadly viewed as the story of how women writers struggled to write beyond the culturally ingrained idea that novelistic plots featuring women must resolve themselves in either the marriage or the death of the heroine. Lehmann's work might be viewed as integral to this struggle. Her plots and the characters within them consciously resist placement within the traditional **romance** narrative. Throughout her work she mentions lesbianism alongside single womanhood, paid work, birth control and free sexuality generally as empowering possibilities for women. Her first novel, *Dusty Answer* (1927) establishes a narrative pattern where several thematic sections present a number of intertwined stories around one character's development. The central narrative section in *Dusty Answer* tells the story of a lesbian affair. **Jeannette Foster** claims that this first novel is autobiographical. *A Note in Music* (1930) and *Invitation to the Waltz* (1932) followed *Dusty Answer*. *The Weather in the Streets* (1936), which carries on the narrative of *Invitation to the Waltz*, raises, more briefly than *Dusty Answer*, the idea of lesbian sexuality. Overall, Lehmann is less significant for her individual lesbian portraits than for her reshaping of the narrative possibilities for women characters and the way in which she used formal experiments to stretch the possibilities of what could be represented in the novel.

LESBIAN. The term lesbian is derived from the name of the island of Lesbos (now part of the nation of Greece) where the poet Sappho lived and worked in the 7th century B.C.E. The surviving fragments of Sappho's poetry that tell of her love for other, younger women were well known to European **classical** scholars, though her works were twice destroyed by the church. The heavily Greco-Roman "classical" bias of European scholars during the **early modern** period and after eventually led to this being the primary description of women who loved each other. Emma Donoghue documents the first usage of lesbian, in the modern sense of woman who loves other women romantically and sexually, to 1732, in a long satirical poem by William King entitled *The Toast*. Both **tribade** and forms of the word lesbian were clearly associated with female same-sex desire in French at least a century before the publication of *The Toast*.

LESBIAN CONTINUUM. This term was coined by the poet and essayist **Adrienne Rich** to describe a variety of behaviors and feelings between women, and a variety of female identities that could be ascribed to women with these feelings. Rich's idea, expressed in the essay entitled "Compulsory Heterosexuality and Lesbian Existence," was to move away from the idea of an opposition of identity between straight and lesbian women (with bisexual women squarely in the middle), which had often divided the 20th-century **feminist movement**. Her argument emphasized the political, social and cultural aspects of lesbian identity, instead of focusing on the sexual. This had the advantage of uniting all women who felt an emotional and or political solidarity with other women. Critics of the notion saw it as denaturing the lesbian position by removing or de-emphasizing its most radical aspects. Nevertheless the term is still often used.

LESBIAN FEMINISM. We might name the first lesbian feminist as the German activist **Anna Rüling**, who gave a speech in Berlin in 1904 entitled "What Interest Does the Women's Movement Have in Solving the Homosexual Problem." This speech was sponsored by the Scientific Humanitarian Committee, and might thus be seen as part of the homosexual rights movement then gaining momentum in Germany. What is significant is that it is a directed attempt to create a framework that sees lesbian rights and feminism as interrelated concerns. This would be the broadest definition of lesbian feminism.

The term most often refers, however, to an activist and cultural movement that arose out of the **second-wave feminist** movement. From the start there were attempts within gay liberation and second wave feminism to address lesbian issues and lesbians were crucial to the early development of both movements. As popularity spread in North America and Great Britain, however, active homophobia in the women's movement and sexism within the gay liberation movement combined to spur lesbians on to independent organizing. An important moment in the United States was the formation of the group the Lavender Menace, later Radicalesbians. Their **manifesto** was produced in response to Betty Friedan's comment that the lesbian issue was a "lavender herring" within the women's movement. Lesbian feminism sees lesbianism and the oppression of lesbians within the context of patriarchal oppression. The imperative toward gender role conformativity, and the unequal legal power relationships involved in heterosexual coupling, which most feminists acknowledge as in some way oppressive, are quite clearly related to fears about female same-sex commitments and masculine women. Suzanne Pharr's *Homophobia: A Weapon of Sexism* (1988) is an important text that draws a basic map of these connections.

Lesbian feminism is often seen as related to radical feminism and **cultural feminism**, which seek to recreate culture in more woman-centered terms. Separatism (safe space for women), radical activism and any number of lesbian-centered cultural moves are often equated (both rightly and wrongly) with lesbian feminism. Arlene Stein has written extensively on lesbian feminism, first in the essay "Sisters and Queers: The Decentering of Lesbian Feminism" (1992), and then in her book *Sex and Sensibility: Stories of a Lesbian Generation* (1997). Important feminist journals that reflected a lesbian feminist community were *Spare Rib* in Britain and *Off Our Backs* in the United States. *See also* JOURNALISM; SEXOLOGY.

THE LESBIAN TIDE. *See* JOURNALISM; CORDOVA, JEANNE.

LIFE-WRITING. The designation life-writing has been developed by literary and historical critics to encompass the genres of diary and journal writing, autobiography, testimony, memoir and any other works that purport to tell the truth about the writer's life. The French critic Philip Lejeune defines what he calls "the autobiographical contract" as the agreement between writer and reader that the author, narrator and protagonist of a written piece are one and the same person. Traditionally, autobiography has rested on the idea of a privileged and communicable truth about a subject's life. Because of its association with unassailable truth, life-writing has been used as both a method of recovering from trauma and a method of communicating with others about the trauma experienced by individuals and communities. Thus, increasingly as the 20th century progressed, lesbians and feminists used life-writing as a means of making their oppression visible to the wider world.

Anne Lister's late 18th- and early 19th-century diaries, edited and published by Helena Whitbread in 1988, created a sensation due to their explicit descriptions of lesbian sex. Previously, numerous collections of letters and journals had helped lesbian historians to develop the idea of a tradition of idealized **romantic friendship** between 19th-century women. The idea of romantic friendship downplayed the role of genital sex, placing 19th-century female couples in a nonsexual place on the **lesbian continuum**. Lister's diaries are significant in the history of lesbian life-writing in their descriptions of an active knowledge of lesbian desire and sexual practice.

In late 18th- and 19th-century France a number of fictional/pornographic productions began to arise that purported to be autobiographical accounts of lesbian lives. This tradition remains active in the 21st century, though it no longer dominates lesbian literature. **Denis Diderot**'s *La Religieuse* (1760) and "Diana Frederics'" *Diana: A Strange Autobiography* (1939) represent two historical ends of this tradition. The early 20th-century American works of **Mary MacLane** are significant in that they bridge the gap between bisexual autobiography, where the lesbian encounters are coded, and prurient fiction that plays on its lesbian suggestions.

Beginning in the 1950s, lesbian autobiography began to move into the realm of politically determined testimony that detailed the oppression of lesbian women and argued for lesbian liberation. Kate Millet's 1974 *Flying* is a highly politically determined piece of bisexual life writing. Millet followed *Flying* with *Sita* in 1977 and *The Loony Bin Trip* in 1990. Michelle Cliff's *Claiming the Identity They Taught Me to Despise* (1980) explores the notion of racial and sexual identities through ideas of repression and **hybridity**. **Audre Lorde** takes the notion of hybridity into the realm of genre, inventing a new generic category for her *Zami*, which she subtitled a biomythography. Biomythography may have been anticipated by **Djuna Barnes** with *Ryder* (1928). Lorde's new category allows her to exploit the association of life-writing with testimony and factual truth while also claiming the kind of "true" psychological character portraits and conflation of personal and historical events available only in fiction. **Leslie**

Feinberg's transgendered lesbian life history *Stone Butch Blues* (1993) might also be placed in the category of biomythography, though Feinberg insists that it has no autobiographical content. **Dorothy Allison**'s first novel *Bastard Out of Carolina* also blurred the lines between autobiography and fiction to stunning effect. Her *Two or Three Things I Know for Sure* (1995) contains a number of autobiographical essays.

Some forms of life-writing present a special authorial difficulty in that they are mediated through a scribe or anthropologist who writes down the spoken words of another. How much input has the mediator had and what is her/his agenda in recording the story? The life stories of many **medieval women mystics** who describe female companionships were recorded in this way. *Singing Away the Hunger: Stories of a Life in Lesotho* (Mpho M'atsepo Nthunua dictated to K. Limakatso Kendall, 1996), which details a complex social system of erotic relationships between women that exists in Lesotho alongside and together with heterosexual marriage, also presents this problem of mediation. Kendall is careful not to impose her own cultural definitions of heterosexuality and lesbianism in this case, but she still performs an obtrusively authorial function.

Many lesbian memoirs provide highly valuable insights into the reality of lesbian lives in particular times, places and literary circles. **Sylvia Beach** is significant for her participation in the Paris **modernist** movement. **Karla Jay**'s *Tales of the Lavender Menace: A Memoir of Lesbian Liberation* (1999) tells of her participation in the emergence of lesbian-feminism in the 1970s. **Daphne Du Maurier** and **May Sarton** are also significant memoir writers in English. For a beginning resource on lesbian autobiography see Nicky Hallet, *Lesbian Lives: Identity and Autobiography in the Twentieth Century* (1999).

LISTER, ANNE (1791–1840). Anne Lister came independently into a large property in West Yorkshire, including the estate named Shibden Hall, in 1817. She was a committed intellectual, doing much reading and writing and also keeping extensive private diaries from 1806. It is these diaries that have recently interested lesbian scholars. First edited and published by Helena Whitbread in 1988 as *I Know My Own Heart: The Diaries of Anne Lister 1791–1840*, these diaries describe a conscious lesbian life. Lister is quite clear that she can only love women, and she describes her physical intimacy with female partners in detail. Some sections of the diaries (and Lister's letters to lovers) are written in code. It is clear that at times, some would use her lesbian life to slander her. It is equally clear, however, that Lister was in no danger from the law or the violence of her neighbors. No doubt, this safety can be attributed as much to her wealth and position as anything.

Like other 19th-century women with romantic attachments to other women, Lister sometimes uses the word wife to describe the relationship she would like to have with her lovers. Ann Walker, a wealthy neighbor, moved in with Lister in 1834 and became a long-term partner, living, indeed, much as Lister's wife. Lister's diaries record a visit to the so-called **Ladies of Llangollen** (Eleanor Butler and Sarah Ponsonby). Jill Liddington's monograph *Presenting the Past: Anne Lister of Halifax* (1994) identifies from Lister's papers a network of lesbians and bisexual women with whom she was in contact. These women seem to have been conscious of the need for a degree of secrecy about their attachments and their sexual adventures. Lister often admits to infidelities in her diaries and to her commitment to her long-term partners. Anne Lister, and the information her papers provide about lesbian life in the early 19th century, should be placed in the context of her social class. Most of the information we have from this period comes from upper-class women, and their wealth was clearly their ticket to sexual freedom.

LORDE, AUDRE (1934–1992). The African-American poet, essayist, activist and teacher Audre Lorde was born in New York City to West Indian parents. Her childhood in upper Manhattan is semifictionalized in the "biomythography" *Zami: A New Spelling of My Name* (1982). The novel also details her experiences of coming out as a young black lesbian in New York City's 1950s gay subculture, and struggling to make a living and write in the postwar period. Lorde's critical ability to present radical and complex concepts in accessible language has made her essays tremendously influential for feminism and feminist literary studies. The essays "Poetry Is Not a Luxury" and "Age, Sex, Race and Class" are good examples of Lorde's critical work and are widely anthologized. Lorde taught in Jackson, Mississippi, at the height of the violent white reaction to the civil rights movement in the late 1960s. The experience solidified her commitment as a political artist and activist. Lorde first suffered from breast cancer in the 1980s. Her experiences of her illness inspired *The Cancer Journals* (1985), which earned her a wide audience of women who might not otherwise have read her work. She was appointed poet laureate of New York State in 1991, and served in this post until her death. *The Collected Poems of Audre Lorde* were published in 1997.

LOUŸS, PIERRE (1870–1925). The Belgian writer Pierre Louÿs had a tremendous influence on modernist lesbian identity. His work, and its decadent fascination with the classical lesbian figure, influenced both **Renée Vivien** and **Natalie Clifford Barney** profoundly. Louÿs' *Chansons de Bilitis* (*Songs of Bilitis*, 1894) was a long fanciful poem that pretended to be a translation of a lost classical document. It describes, in part, the love and "marriage" between two women. Louÿs also published the long poem *Astarté* (1891) and the novel *Aphrodite* (1896), both of which drew on classical ideals of excessive and powerful feminine sexuality. Though he is less well thought of today, his contemporaries respected him. He founded the journal *La Conque* to which both Algernon Charles Swinburne and Paul Valéry contributed. Graham Robb refers to his work as "soft porn" and "cliché-ridden sleaze." Yet Louÿs was supportive of Renée Vivien's work and thus clearly had some respect for a developing lesbian empowerment in both life and verse. Natalie Barney dedicated her *Five Short Greek Dialogues* to him in 1902. Finally, it is clear that some lesbians still enjoyed and identified with his work in the mid-20th century. The homophile organization **Daughters of Bilitis** took its name from his well-known poem, knowing that this title would proclaim their lesbian focus to those who had the knowledge to read the sign.

LOWELL, AMY (1874–1925). The American poet and critic Amy Lowell was born into a wealthy and well-connected Boston family. She is significant as a patron and critical promoter of the modernist movement, as well as a poet in her own right. Lowell's first collection of verse, *A Dome of Many-Colored Glass*, was published in 1912. *Swords, Blades and Poppy Seed* followed in 1914, *Men, Women and Ghosts* in 1916 and *Pictures of the Floating World* in 1919. *What's O'clock* was published in the year of Lowell's death, 1925. She was awarded the Pulitzer Prize for poetry posthumously for this final work. Early in her life Lowell, like other contemporary lesbian and bisexual poets, wrote love poems to the actress and singer Eleanora Duse. Her lifelong partner was Ada Dwyer Russell.

– M –

McCULLERS, CARSON (1917–1967). American novelist and playwright Carson McCullers was born Lula Carson Smith. She dropped the feminine Lula from her name at the age of 13. She is famous for young heroines who, like herself, resisted the transition from tomboy youth to adult femininity. At a young age McCullers moved from Georgia to New York City. She is best known for her development of the fictional genre that came to be known as the **Southern Gothic**. Her novels combine a strong regional sense of the southern United States, a sense of social dislocation in terms of gender and class and a concern with the effects of American racial violence.

McCullers published *The Heart Is a Lonely Hunter* in 1940 and *The Member of the Wedding* in 1946. Both of these **novels** feature adolescent girls who maintain a forthright and adventurous masculinity along with their changing bodies and desires. *The Heart Is a Lonely Hunter* weaves the story of its young female protagonist, Mick, together with a group of isolated characters embroiled in the politics of 1930s ethnicity, race and **class**. In *The Member of the Wedding*, which is McCullers most popular work, young Frankie (note the masculinized names of her protagonists) expresses her difficult adjustment to adult gender through an obsession with her brother's wedding. She would like to be part of a "we" and does not fantasize about herself as part of a couple. She does attempt a liaison with a soldier (like her brother), but her longings here are vague and when confronted with the reality of heterosexual encounter she flees. In the final scene of the novel a kind of resolution is depicted through Frankie's invitation of another girl into her kitchen. *The Ballad of the Sad Cafe* (1943) centers around a **butch** female character, Miss Amelia Evans who, like Frankie, had a motherless childhood. *A Clock without Hands* (1961) concentrates on the experience of racial integration in a small southern town.

McCullers was married twice to the same man, though both had numerous relationships with other people of both sexes. She was romantically linked to Gypsy Rose Lee and Greta Garbo, as well as Annemarie Schwarzenbach, to whom she dedicated her *Reflections in a Golden Eye* (1941). In later life McCullers grew close to the gay southern playwright Tennessee Williams, who encouraged her in writing stage adaptations of her novels and the play *The Square Root of Wonderful* (1958). She suffered from very poor health from an early age and died after a long and debilitating illness.

MACKENZIE, COMPTON (1883–1972). The British writer Edward Montague Compton Mackenzie was educated at Oxford University and spent several years as a young man living with the English bohemian elite on the Italian island of Capri. Here he met and befriended Romaine Brooks, Natalie Clifford Barney and other lesbian artists and writers. Mackenzie published two comical novels based on his experiences at this period. The first was *Vestal Fire*, which appeared in 1927 to little comment. The second, *Extraordinary Women* (1928), is a farce about a promiscuously flirtatious young woman named Rosalba. This novel satirizes a number of well-known lesbian literary characters of the day. It appeared in the same year as **Radclyffe Hall**'s *The Well of Loneliness*. While *The Well* was prosecuted for obscenity, *Extraordinary Women* drew no comment from the British Home Office. The general critical consensus on this has been that Mackenzie's novel was less than friendly, presenting lesbians as flawed and broken creatures and was therefore not a threat. Terry Castle disagrees, calling extraordinary women "a light-hearted farce," but then has difficulty explaining the different legal reactions to the two novels.

MACLANE, MARY (1881–1929). The journalist and writer Mary MacLane was born in Canada and raised in Minnesota and Montana. She had a good classical education and chose to use it in writing for a mass audience. In 1902 she published the sensational *The Story of Mary MacLane*, which was quickly translated into at least 30 languages. This autobiographical work stretched the boundaries of what it meant to be a woman in the modern world and was reasonably frank (for the period) about MacLane's romantic desires, which were bisexual. Her description of her desire for a teacher whom she calls "the anemone lady" highlights the way in which many people still conflated same-sex desire with transgender movement at this period. She says that "I feel in the anemone lady a strange attraction for sex. There is in me a masculine element that, when I am thinking of her, arises and overshadows all others." We can see here the idea that anyone who desires a woman must be masculine, and/or the idea that active desire for another is a masculine sentiment.

In 1903 MacLane published *My Friend Annabel Lee* and *The Devil's Letters to Mary MacLane*, cementing her reputation as a daring and unconventional woman. She also wrote **journalism** for papers in Chicago (where *The Story of Mary MacLane* was first published) and later New York. In 1917 came *I, Mary MacLane*, another autobiographical piece in which the author discusses her lesbianism (using the word lesbian) and mentions reading and translating **Sappho**. Here lesbianism is seen as psychic, and not necessarily physical, though she does admit to "lesbian kisses." There is a kind of Edwardian ideal of same-sex desire as pure Greek love in MacLane's construction of her own sexuality in *I, Mary MacLane*. After a long career as a journalist and a brief attempt at screen writing, MacLane died in Chicago in 1929.

MADCHEN IN UNIFORM. See WINSLOE, CHRISTA.

MADELAINE, MARIE (BARONESS VON PUTTKAMER) (1881–1944). The German poet Marie Madeleine became a baroness by marriage to a wealthy general and thereafter divided her time between Germany and France. Of over eight volumes of her verse, only one is translated into English. This first volume *Auf Kypros* (*On Cyprus*) contains much of Marie Madeleine's juvenilia. A strong thread of lesbian desire and a number of narratives and characters built on the lesbian theme runs through this collection, which was first translated into English as *Hydromel and Rue* by Ferdinand E. Kapper in 1907. Terry Castle cites **Paul Verlaine** and **Charles Baudelaire** as influences on the young poet, who is clearly working in a **decadent** tradition. One of the poems in *Auf Kypros* describes a passing woman and her female lover. Another, "Vagabonds," voices an older women's regret for having seduced a younger woman and thus initiated her into lesbian desire. The collection also includes a poem entitled Sappho, which is an imitation of the classical poet's verse. Thus she makes a similar move to the one made by **Renée Vivien** at roughly the same period.

MAGAZINES AND PAMPHLETS. *See* JOURNALISM.

MALLET-JORIS, FRANÇOISE (1930–). The writer Françoise Mallet-Joris was born in Belgium and spent most of her life in France. She has published poems, novels and numerous song lyrics. She won the *Prix Fémina* in 1958 for *L'empire Céleste* and served on its committee in 1969 and 1971. She has been a member of the *Académie Goncourt* since 1971. There she holds the chair that once belonged to **Colette**.

Mallet-Joris is significant here for her first novel *Les remparts des béguines* (1949), which was first translated into English as *The Illusionist* in New York in 1952. This novel depicted the love affair between a teenage girl and her father's mistress, and it caused a "scandal" when it was first published. The novel cemented Mallet-Joris' popularity and was clearly read by American lesbians in the 1950s. Excerpts are included in the anthology *Carol in a Thousand Cities* (1960), edited by Ann Aldrich. The novel appeared in later paperback versions as *The Loving and Daring*. Mallet-Joris has also written a number of historical biographies that focus on women overlooked in traditional histories.

MANIFESTOS. The term manifesto is derived from the Italian and its common usage, for a statement of the political beliefs and goals around which a group is organized, reveals its roots in 19th-century socialist and anarchist activism. There are, however, pieces of writing produced prior to this period, which declare a revolutionary political stance and which might be called manifestos in retrospect. The roots of lesbian feminist manifestos can be traced back to early expressions of feminism that arose during the European and American revolutions of the late 18th century.

Both the French Olympe de Gouges and the English **Mary Wollstonecraft** produced what could be called the first feminist manifestos in 1791. The bourgeois playwright Olympe de Gouges published "A Declaration of the Rights of Women and Female Citizens" as a clear response to the Revolution of 1789. In the declaration de Gouges calls for "mothers, daughters, sisters, representatives of the nation" to be granted representation as a national assembly. She declares that the corruption of governments is a direct result of the denial of representation for women. The declaration also articulates the relationship between women's economic and political powerlessness and the control of women's sexuality and reproduction, saying, for example, that when a single woman has children "ancient and inhuman laws refuse to her for her children the right to the name and wealth of their father." Most radically De Gouges presents a new and gender equal "Form for a social contract between man and woman," which would replace the legal practice of marriage. Her political activism led to her arrest by the revolutionary government. She was executed as a royalist sympathizer in 1793.

There is no clear evidence that Mary Wollstonecraft had read de Gouges declaration, though she had spent time in Paris in the years prior to the publication of her own *Vindication of the Rights of Women* in 1791. Wollstonecraft, too, focuses on the detrimental effects that the prevailing sexual morality of the period had on women. She focuses largely on the upper classes and on ideas of virtue and innocence. The eighth chapter of *Vindication* is entitled "Morality, undermined by sexual notions of the importance of a good reputation." ("Sexual" here carries a meaning we would understand as gender, rather than as sex or sexuality.) Like de Gouges, Wollstonecraft, herself a single mother, decries the vulnerable position of single women: "If an innocent girl become a prey to love, she is degraded for ever . . . nor has she violated any duty—but the duty of respecting herself."

In Seneca Falls, New York, in 1848 a group of **first-wave feminists** held the first United States women's rights convention in a small church. Historical accounts tell of the excitement of the participants as they traveled to the events. Once there they signed the "Declaration of Sentiments," a feminist manifesto written by Elizabeth Cady Stanton. The signatories were both women and men who were active in the abolitionist and feminist movements. Black abolitionist Frederick Douglas was a signatory. In listing the wrongs done by "man" to "woman," the declaration includes these points:

After depriving her of all rights as a married woman, if single and the owner of property, he has taxed her to support a government which recognizes her only when her property can be made profitable to it. . . .

He has created a false public sentiment by giving to the world a different code of morals for men and for women, by which moral delinquencies which exclude women from society, are not only tolerated but deemed of little account in man.

The latter is the only hint at the politics of sexuality. "The Declaration of Sentiments" is much more concerned with the legal and economic aspects of women's oppression. However, all three of these early documents make connections between legal, economic social and sexual aspects of the oppression of women. In discussing the legal and social situation of single women and their children, they pave the way for feminists to think themselves out of the idea that heterosexual marriage is women's sole destiny.

The manifestos of lesbian feminism came out of antiracist, feminist and gay movements in the mid-20th century. The earliest of these is lesbian Valerie Solanas' 1967 (first published in 1968) *S.C.U.M. Manifesto*. S.C.U.M. (Society for Cutting Up Men) plays on the political history of the manifesto to articulate a radical and violent feminist rage that was read by some as satirical and by others literally. In it, Solanas masterfully inverts traditional assumptions about gender and psychology. "Screwing is, for a man, a defense against his desire to be female." When Solanas later shot the artist Andy Warhol and was institutionalized, the feminist movement distanced itself from her. Her manifesto, however, has remained in print and is often studied academically.

In New York in 1970 a group calling themselves first the Lavender Menace (in response to Betty Freidan's labeling discussions of lesbian rights "the lavender herring") and then Radicalesbians, produced "The Woman-Identified-Woman Manifesto," which was first distributed at a meeting of the National Organization for Women (NOW). In response to the invisibility of lesbians in the women's movement and to the open homophobia of some of its members, "The Woman-Identified-Woman Manifesto" sought to explain the connections between sexism and homophobia and to argue for the need for antihomophobic activism in the women's movement. In powerfully symbolic language the manifesto begins "What is a lesbian? A lesbian is the rage of all women condensed to the point of explosion." The writers went on to argue that heterosexuality and homosexuality are culturally contingent (constructed) categories that would not exist in a world without sexism where people were free to love as they desired to. There is a strong leftist vocabulary here. Words like "caste" and "exchange" signal that this manifesto is part of a strong American tradition of socialist-feminist politics.

At the same period (1970) the Gay Liberation Front (GLF) began organizing, with branches around the globe. The Front had close ties to the anti-Vietnam War movement and was marked by a strong leftist politics. Early GLF branches began producing manifestos in their first year of existence. The London branch created a document that reveals a strong lesbian feminist politics. It describes wives as slaves and expresses the hope that "it will lead to the furtherance of a scientific analysis of sexism and of our oppression as gay people." Like many gay organizations of the postwar era, the London GLF expresses here a dislike of gender role-play among lesbians and gay men, though it also acknowledges that gender is fluid and that gay men and women will naturally be masculine and feminine to different degrees.

In 1974 the Boston-based **Combahee River Collective**, which included **Barbara Smith**, Beverly Smith and Demita Frazier, published "The Combahee River Collective Statement." The name of the organization and the title of the statement refer to battle led and won by the abolitionist Harriet Tubman during the American Civil War. The statement outlines a strong tradition of black American women's revolutionary activism and declares its members to be "feminists and lesbians" who belong to that tradition. Smith, Smith and Frazier, who wrote the statement, outline the racism of the "mainstream" women's movement and the sexism experienced by many women in the movement for black liberation. They express a solidarity with black men and black communities and a strong commitment to socialist politics. The Combahee River Collective continued its antiracist, antisexist, antipoverty activism in Boston until 1980.

In 1992 New York AIDS activist and lesbian **Sarah Schulman** formed the activist organization the Lesbian Avengers, which was part of a newly militant late 1980s early 1990s **queer** activist movement, galvanized around the world by the struggle for the lives and the rights of HIV-positive people and in Great Britain by both the AIDS emergency and the Conservative Party's "Section 28" legislation, which prevented any government-funded body from promoting "homosexuality or pretend family relationships." The Lesbian Avengers produced "The Dyke Manifesto" in 1993, calling for "creative activism." This manifesto implicitly decries the culture of mass lesbian consumption and calls for a reawakening of a radical leftist lesbian politics. Some branches, however, significantly declared themselves open to members from any political affiliation, a move that would have been alien to many lesbian feminist organizations in the 1970s.

Running alongside this tradition of focused political activism is a lesbian and feminist tradition of satirical manifestos that are often equally politically affective. Jo Freeman's "The Bitch Manifesto," declares itself to speak for "an organization which does not yet exist. The name is not an acronym. It stands for exactly what it sounds like." The early 21st century web production "Dyxploitation" contains the similarly satirical "The Dyxploitation Manifesto" and "Blueprint for the Revolution." *See also* BUTCH; FEMME; JAY, KARLA.

MANLEY, MARY DELARIVIER (1663–1724). The English novelist, playwright and political commentator Mary Delarivier Manley is most relevant here for a piece she wrote in 1709 satirizing the court of the bisexual Queen Anne. *Secret Memoirs and Manners of Several Persons from the New Atlantis, an Island in the Mediterranean*, pokes vicious fun at all aspects of English political culture and court society, including a section on "The Ladies of the New Cabal." This section caricatures a number of lesbian and bisexual women who surrounded Queen Anne, including the playwright and philosopher Catherine Trotter. The piece gives, albeit satirically, a number of justifications for female same-sex relationships. The primary one is that while liaisons with men compromise your virtue, liaisons with women do not. Women in the piece also complain that men's caresses are not "poetical" enough. This reflects Elizabeth Mavor's argument that later, in 18th-century Britain, a gender specific intellectual culture of sensibility drew women to each other. The piece is light hearted, if somewhat unfriendly. It does link lesbianism with the general decadence of court life. However, it also inadvertently provides later generations with evidence that a clear subculture built around female same-sex relationships existed in the English court at this period.

MANSFIELD, KATHERINE (1888–1923). The New Zealand–born bisexual short story writer, musician and poet Katherine Mansfield spent the latter half of her life in England and France. She had a first very brief marriage and then lived with and later married the literary critic John Middleton Murray (1899–1927). She was also the lifelong companion of a woman named Ida Baker. When Mansfield was a young woman studying music in London her parents grew so worried about her "unnatural" relationship with Baker that Mansfield's mother traveled from New Zealand to force her into treatment. This did not deter Mansfield from her relationship with Baker, nor from any number of unconventional sexual relationships with both men and women. In Mansfield's diaries and letters Baker is often referred to by the pseudonym Leslie Moore (or the initials L.M.).

Mansfield was conversant with other writers associated with the **modernist** movement, especially **D. H. Lawrence**, with whom she and Murray had a long and sometimes difficult friendship. She is sometimes spoken of as a rival of **Virginia Woolf**'s and much is made of one patronizing comment made by Woolf about Mansfield's writing. Overall though, the evidence shows that the two women respected each other's work. Mansfield's early stories appeared in the modernist magazine *The New Age* and later work appeared in *Rhythm* and *The Blue Review*.

Mansfield's first collection of stories was *In a German Pension* (1911), followed by *Bliss, and Other Stories* (1920) and *Garden Party, and Other Stories* (1922). The title story "Bliss" tells of a vaguely dissatisfied middle-class housewife, who is first attracted to a lovely young female dinner guest and then realizes that the woman is having an affair with her husband. "Bliss" contains powerful descriptions of a lesbian desire that the disillusioned housewife Bertha Young does not understand: "What was there in the touch of that cool arm that could fan—fan—start blazing—blazing—the fire of bliss that Bertha did not know what to do with." Mansfield did once attempt a novel-length work, which was to be entitled *Aloe*. This was never fully developed though, and it survives as the short story "Prelude." In this story she experiments with a decentralized narrative without a focalizing character. In experiments like these and in her dialogue with writers like Lawrence and Woolf we can see her important contributions to the development of what would come to be known as the modernist aesthetic. Mansfield is highly regarded as a master of the short story form and her work is still widely studied by students of fiction in English. She died in France of tuberculosis after a long illness. A good literary biography of Mansifeld is Sydney Janet Kaplan's *Katherine Mansfield and the Origins of Modernist Fiction* (1991).

MARCHESSAULT, JOVETTE (1938–). Quebecois playwright and novelist Jovette Marchessault was possibly the first openly lesbian French Canadian writer to achieve widespread recognition. Her several prize-winning novels include *Comme une enfant de la terre* (*Like a Child of the Earth*, 1976), and *Le Voyage Magnifique d'Emily Carr* (*The Magnificent Journey of Emily Carr*, 1990). In 1983 she and **Nicole Brossard** mounted an exhibition, celebrations, dedicated to women's writing.

MARTIN, VIOLET (1862–1915). The Anglo-Irish novelist Violet Martin was born into a wealthy colonial family in 19th-century Ireland. She is well known for several novels and collections of stories that she wrote together with her cousin and life partner **Edith Somerville**. These novels satirized Irish class relations from a distinctly upper-class perspective.

THE MASCULINE PROTEST. The masculine protest refers to the identification of feminist sentiment as a revolt against femininity and heterosexual positioning. In other words, women might take on the dress and manners of men as a way of (consciously or unconsciously) refusing their oppression as women. The idea was popular in the 19th and early 20th centuries. **Jeannette Foster** names Oliver Wendell Holmes, Henry James and Olive Schreiner as authors who used the idea of the masculine protest in characterization and plot.

MATTACHINE SOCIETY. *See* HOMOPHILE MOVEMENT.

MAUPASSANT, GUY DE (1850–1893). The French short story writer and novelist Guy De Maupassant had a career in the military before working as a civil servant. The novelist Gustave Flaubert mentored him for a time. He published his first short story "Boule de suif," in a collection edited by **Émile Zola**. Like Zola, he employed a realist literary style in the hundreds of stories and six novels he published during his lifetime. Maupassant is most significant here for the story "Paul's Mistress" (1881). Like decadent depictions of the lesbian, Madeline, the object of the story, enables fantasies of degradation and sexual excess. The resolution of the story introduces the **crossdressing** Pauline, for whom Paul is abandoned. At the same time, Maupassant provides a carefully detailed depiction of Parisian gay and lesbian subculture in the 1880s. "Paul's Mistress" has remained almost continually in print since its first publication. In 1960 it was included in the **pulp** anthology *Carol in a Thousand Cities*, edited by **Marijane Meaker** (as Ann Aldrich.) Clearly then, Maupassant's images of lesbian characters have been influential for lesbian readers.

MEAKER, MARIJANE (1927–). The tremendously prolific novelist Marijane Meaker has published under several pseudonyms throughout her life. As Vin Packer she published the lesbian **pulp** classic *Spring Fire* in 1952. The Vin Packer name appeared on several other pulp novels throughout the 1950s. As Ann Aldrich, working for Fawcett Publications, she published a number of exposés of the lesbian subcultural world. These include *We Walk Alone through Lesbos' Lonely Groves* (1957), *Take a Lesbian to Lunch* (published in 1970, but written earlier), and the anthology *Carol in a Thousand Cities* (1960). *The Evil Friendship* (1958) is a sensational treatment of New Zealand's Parker-Hulme case, in which two young girls in a romantic relationship were tried for the murder of one of their mothers. These books tend to objectify the lesbian, speaking to an implied heterosexual audience and "explaining" lesbian deviance. For many years Meaker has also published young adult fiction as M. E. Kerr. In 2000 Meaker published a memoir detailing her relationship with the novelist **Patricia Highsmith**, *Highsmith: A Romance of the 1950s*. Meaker herself is presented as a thinly veiled and very unsympathetic lesbian character in **Ann Bannon**'s *I Am a Woman* (1959).

MEDIEVAL PERIOD. In medieval Europe, the vast majority of recognized writers were men. The occasional poet or correspondent stands out. A number of romances and ballads that involve same-sex liaisons survive, and these tend to be about gender crossover, disguise and confusion. **Jeannette Foster** notes the romance *Huon of Bordeaux* in this regard. This particular long verse poem is interesting in that it does involve explicit descriptions of same-sex sexual activity. Foster also asserts that a group of Middle-Eastern tales, written down in the 16th century as *La Fleur Lascive Orientale*, probably entered Europe around this time. By far the most significant figure before the early modern period in Europe is the Italian-French renaissance writer **Christine de Pizan**. See also MEDIEVAL WOMEN'S MYSTICISM.

MEDIEVAL WOMEN'S MYSTICISM. The group of historical figures known collectively as medieval women mystics span several centuries and the breadth of Europe. They are significant in asserting a specifically female voice in a world dominated by the patriarchal structure of the church. Insisting on a personal relationship to God through mystical vision, many of these women were able to escape heterosexual marriage and claim the (divine) right to define their own lives and thoughts. This process was not unproblematic. As women, many women mystics had no access to literacy. Most of their words come to us as written down by confessors, often translated from their own vernacular languages into church Latin. The spiritual path of a female mystic often began with resistance to imposed marriage. This so-called "**militant virginity**" marks this group of women as making an organized resistance to heterosexuality.

The German Hildegard of Bingen (1098-1179) gained a tremendous amount of power within the European church and lived much of her life in the company of a special female companion. She wrote works of theology and medicine, as well as morality plays and complex musical compositions. The English Julian of Norwich (1342–c.1416) asserted a special, and often very sensual, relation to Christ. Like other women mystics she dwelled in a fascinated and erotic fashion on the violence of the passion. The Italian Angela of Foligno (1248–1309) took these erotic and highly sexualized visions of Christ to extremes. Like Hildegard and others, she describes what we would call sexual orgasm. The medieval women mystics are the first European women to express this kind of desire and release in literature, though of course they did not have the over-arching framework that defined this experience as sexual. Angela of Foligno lived in an all-female lay community, which she herself created. The English Margery of Kempe (c. 1373–1458) eventually negotiated a nonsexual marriage with her husband, after a long struggle during which she was sometimes defined as mad. Eventually she was acknowledged as being blessed with divine vision. Her *Book of Margery Kempe* could be the first autobiography in the English language. Medieval women mystics are highly significant in the history of women's sexuality in literature because they asserted a sexual independence, organized their lives around relationships with other women and forged a unique language for the expression of female desires out of seemingly hostile cultural material. *See also* MEDIEVAL PERIOD.

MENDÈS, CATULLE (1841–1909). The novelist Catulle Mendès was married, for a time, to Judith Gautier (1846–1917), daughter of the writer **Théophile Gautier**. Mendès is considered less talented than either Gautier, or Honoré de Balzac, but is in some ways more fascinating. Writing in the **decadent** tradition, at least two novels focusing strongly on lesbianism, his ideological bluntness lays bare the more subtly expressed fantasies and anxieties of his contemporaries. The earlier of Mendès' two lesbian novels, *Lila and Colette* (1885), is the sort of romanticized classical fantasy of lesbianism that **Pierre Louÿs** published in verse a decade later. *Méphistophélia* (1890) follows a lesbian drug addict in a downward spiral through debauchery, drug abuse and sexual disease. We see the final, abject state of the eponymous character in the novel's first scene. A lengthy flashback then shows us her path through decadence into degradation.

MEW, CHARLOTTE (1869–1928). The English poet Charlotte Mew lived in both the Victorian and Edwardian ages and she is often seen as a transitional figure, having written both Victorian sentimental verse and disillusioned war poetry after 1918. She published the collection *The Farmer's Bride* in 1916. She is perhaps best known for her poem "The Cenotaph" (1919) in which the deaths of young soldiers haunt the French fields on which they are no longer visible.

Though her poetry had little or no lesbian content, Mew was a cross-dresser who had a number of passionate attachments to women, including the writer May Sinclair. She lived with her sister throughout her life, which ended in suicide.

MICHAELS, REA. A number of **lesbian pulp** paperbacks were published under this name by Lancer-Domino in the United States in the early 1960s. Among these were: *Cloak of Evil*, *Duet in Darkness*, *How Dark My Love*, *The Needs We Share* and *The Twisted Year*. What distinguishes these pulps and makes them rich objects of study is their use of race in the characterization of forbidden lesbian desire. Paperbacks authored by Rea Michaels are preserved in a number of archives and special collections in the U.S.

MILITANT VIRGINITY. This expression is applied to a refusal on the part of young women to submit to marriage, usually pleading the excuse of religious devotion and purity. The expression was first used with reference to the European **medieval period**. Many young women claimed a special relationship with God, which prohibited their "defiling" themselves with earthly marriage. Often these women claimed mystical visions and revelations (many of which survive in written form) and went on to live with other like-minded women in all female communities, even developing so-called special friendships or companionships in couples. *See also* MEDIEVAL WOMEN'S MYSTICISM

MILLAY, EDNA ST. VINCENT (1892–1950). The bisexual American poet and playwright Edna St. Vincent Millay was born and raised in New England. She attended Vassar College for women on scholarship. Insistently calling herself Vincent as a child, Millay seems to have been untroubled by her sexuality. She was notoriously scornful of psychoanalytic theories of deviance. Her poetry expresses love and desire for both women and men. Millay's first collection of poems was *Renaissance and Other Poems* (1917). Her second, *A Few Figs from Thistles* (1922), expressed a strongly feminist worldview and was widely commented on. Millay often worked in a formal poetic style and is still taught as a consummate poetic stylist.

MILLER, ISABEL (1924–1996). Isabel Miller is the pen name under which the Michigan-born writer Alma Routsong wrote lesbian fiction. Like other postwar lesbian writers in the North America, Routsong published fiction throughout the 1950s under her birth name but used an invented name to write about love between women. In this case, the writer chose a specifically lesbian and feminist form for her pseudonym. Isabel is an anagram for lesbia and Miller was the maiden name of Routsong's mother.

In 1969 Routsong, as Isabel Miller, published her first lesbian novel, *A Place For Us*, in New York City. She used her own money to finance a limited first edition of 1,000 copies. These were sold independently and through the New York chapter of the **Daughters of Bilitis**. In 1971 the novel won the first ever American Library Association Gay and Lesbian Book Award, having been picked up by a major publisher and released under the title by which it is best known, *Patience and Sarah*. *Patience and Sarah* is a factually based historical **romance** about two women who homesteaded together in New York State in the early 19th century. One of these women was the folk painter Mary Ann Wilson, whose work is still highly prized. Routsong researched all of the limited information on Wilson and her partner, Miss Brundage, before creating two fictional characters based on them.

Much later in life Routsong published a collection of short stories entitled *A Dooryard Full of Flowers and Other Short Pieces* (1993). The title piece in this collection continues the story of Patience and Sarah. A novel called *Laurel* was published after her death in 1996.

MILLET, KATE (1934–). The bisexual writer and literary critic Kate Millet is deeply important to the history of feminist literary criticism in English. She published her doctoral dissertation, *Sexual Politics*, in 1968. The work gives a feminist analysis of Western culture in general, and of the work of **D. H. Lawrence**, Henry Miller and Norman Mailer in particular. Prior to *Sexual Politics*, no developed language for a gendered reading practice existed in literary criticism. All of Millet's other writings are autobiographical to some degree. *Flying* (1974) describes Millet's coming out as a bisexual woman during the second wave of feminism. When she did come out publicly as bisexual, many used her admission to discredit feminism by associating it with "sexual deviance." The women's movement was divided over the issue of whether or not to support her. The novel *Sita* (1977) is a thinly veiled description of a lesbian affair. Since 1971 Millet has made a significant contribution to **cultural feminism** by maintaining and expanding the Women's Art Colony Farm in upstate New York.

MIN, ANCHEE (1957–). The Chinese actress and writer Anchee Min grew up during the Cultural Revolution, and worked as an actress in Madame Mao's movie studio during the 1970s. Min immigrated to the United States in 1984, where she quickly began publishing English-language memoirs and novels. Most significant here is *Red Azalea: Life and Love in China* (1994). This autobiographical novel is a kind of ***bildungsroman*** about the life and romantic attachments experienced by a bisexual woman during the Cultural Revolution. Min published her first fictional novel, *Katherine*, in 1995 and the study *Becoming Madame Mao* in 2000.

MISTRAL, GABRIELA (1889–1957). Gabriela Mistral is the pen name of the Chilean educator, diplomat, poet, feminist and Nobel laureate born Lucila Godoy y Alcayaga. Her published collections of poetry include *Sonetos de la muerte* (1914), *Desolación* (1922) and *Ternura* (1924). Themes that are most remarked upon in Mistral's work are motherhood (what most critics describe as an unfulfilled desire for children), death and a feeling for oppressed people, especially children. Alongside these themes the poet expresses a great deal of romantically sensual feeling that is clearly homoerotic.

Mistral is acknowledged to have been an important influence on Pablo Neruda, Chile's most famous poet. She was a consultant on education to the Mexican revolutionary government and was appointed as Chilean consul to several nations during her lifetime.

For decades during her life and after her death, most accepted criticism ignored the lesbian nature of Mistral's life and work. Much was (and still is) made of an affair with a male railroad worker called Romelio Ureta, which is said (based on scant evidence) to have taken place when Mistral was in her late teens. After this there is no evidence of relationships with men. Mistral's will left all of her foreign property to an American woman, also the executor, whom the will describes as "one particularly loved close friend." This woman was named Rose and one wonders whether lines like the following, from the poem "Give Me Your Hand," refer to her: "I'm called Hope and you're called Rose / but losing our names we'll both go free / a dance on the hills and nothing more / a dance on the hills is all we'll be." Certainly no one who could write

> In this sweetness I feel
> my heart melt like wax
> In my veins runs
> not wine, but slow oil
> and I feel my life slipping away
> still and soft as a gazelle

was entirely ignorant of sexual pleasure. In the absence of male relationships and in the presence of strong female attachments, critics claim Mistral for the lesbian canon.

A facing page Spanish-English translation of Mistral's poems was published by the fantasy writer **Ursula LeGuin** in 2003. The relationship between Mistral's work, her identity and the way in which she functions as a national figure in Chile is discussed in Lucia Fiol-Matta's (2002) book, *A Queer Mother for the Nation: The State and Gabriela Mistral*.

MODERNISM. This term, as distinct from the term modernity, is used to describe a movement in literature and the visual arts that took place in Europe and the Americas in the late 19th and early 20th centuries. The widest set of dates for the modernist period might be from 1870 to 1940 and the shortest 1910 to 1930. Traditional definitions of literary modernism focus on a heightened sense of the self and exploration of human consciousness (influenced by the popularization of psychology and **psychoanalysis**), radical experiments with narrative form and narration and a questioning of the most cherished techniques and assumptions of 19th-century realism. This last quality relates particularly to the modernists' questioning of objective truth and their heightened explorations of human subjectivity. Less remarked are other sets of questions, for example, around empire and race. Many modernists were fascinated by racial otherness. Some white modernists like **Radclyffe Hall**, **Una Troubridge** and Olive Schreiner courted fascism and eugenicism, while others romanticized "primitive" peoples. At the same time the New Negro Movement, now usually referred to as the **Harlem Renaissance**, was an important arena for black American modernism, though it is not always recognized as part of the modernist movement.

Before the advent of women's literature and women's studies programs the "great" modernists were generally agreed to be James Joyce, **D. H. Lawrence**, T. S. Eliot and perhaps Virginia Woolf. Feminist scholars have noted that the period was marked by deep conflicts around gender, sexuality and the new social roles open to women. Bonnie Kime Scott argues that we might see modernism as characterized more by experiments with gendered and sexual roles than by experiments with narrative and subjectivity. Thus we could consider both **Djuna Barnes'** *Nightwood* and Radclyffe Hall's ***The Well of Loneliness*** as important modernist texts because they both radically resituate femininity, even though *The Well of Loneliness* makes no new or interesting innovations with form and narrative.

The fact is that a great many sexually dissident women were involved in the variety of modernism's new interventions in form, from Blues singers like Bessie Smith and Ma Rainey, to visual artists like Frida Kahlo and writers like **Virginia Woolf** and **Nella Larsen**. What these women shared was an ability and a desire to place women at the center of stories and images. They made women's desire (often for each other) visible and active and in so doing changed what the idea "woman" meant. Modernism is marked by a questioning and destabilizing of the category woman (for example in Woolf's *Orlando* and Hall's *The Well*) and by a proliferation of narratives structured around the active desires of women characters (for example Barnes' *Nightwood* and Larsen's *Passing*).

MONNIER, ADRIENNE (1897–1999). The writer and editor Adrienne Monnier is most famous for her bookshop La Maison des Amis des Livres, which she opened in Paris in 1915. This bookshop was located across the Rue de L'Odéon from her life partner Sylvia Beach's English-language shop, Shakespeare and Company. Both shops were frequented by the most influential writers of the modernist movement, including **Colette** and James Joyce. During the 1920s and 1930s, Monnier edited and published a number of literary journals, though most of her own writings remained unpublished until years later. In 1962 she published a book of poems, *Poésies*. In 1976 her essays and memoirs were collected as *The Very Rich Hours of Adrienne Monnier*. Sylvia Beach's memoirs describe their literary life together, but do not discuss their relationship. Beach also makes it clear that there was a certain rivalry between she and Monnier and **Gertrude Stein** and **Alice B. Toklas**, who also held a literary salon during this period.

MONTAGUE, MARY WORTLEY (1689–1762). The aristocratic journalist and poet Mary Wortley Montague lived the early part of her life in London, where she studied Latin and wrote poetry during her teens. She played an important part in the literary life of 18th-century London, publishing an essay in the *Spectator* in 1713 and a collection of essays, *The Nonsense of Common Sense* in 1737–1738. She wrote one play, *Simplicity, a Comedy*, which was never performed. *Six Town Ecologues: With Some Poems* was published in 1747. When her husband was posted to Turkey as a diplomat in the early years of the 18th century, she included a number of travel accounts in letters to friends in England. These were first collected a year after her death and are still available as *The Embassy Letters*. It is these letters from Turkey that have earned Wortley Montague a place in lesbian criticism. As a woman, she had access to the women only environments of public baths, and as a European she viewed these women as exotic others through a somewhat masculinized gaze. Passages such as the following have been read as overtly homoerotic:

> I perceived that the ladies with the finest skins and most delicate shapes had the greatest share of my admiration, though their faces were sometimes less beautiful than those of their companions . . .

The overall tone of such passages is more aesthetic than sexual and, one suspects, has as much to do with the sexualized nature of **orientalist** fantasy as with Wortley Montague's own desires. Montague was a popular and well respected writer in her own lifetime and immediately after. Her *Collected Works* were first published in 1803.

MOORE, MARIANNE (1887–1972). The cross-dressing American poet and editor Marianne Moore was born in Missouri, but lived her adult life mostly in the northeastern United States. She attended Bryn Mawr College in Pennsylvania, where she began to write. Some of her early poems were printed in the London-based modernist journal *The Egoist*, which the writer H.D. (**Hilda Doolittle**) was editing at the time. Her first collection, *Poems,* was published in London in 1921. An expanded edition of this work was published in New York as *Ob-*

servations in 1924. Moore edited the New York-based modernist magazine *Dial* from 1925 to 1929. Later collections of her poems include *What Are Years?* (1941) and *Like a Bulwark* (1956). Moore's papers are held at the Rosenbach Foundation in Pennsylvania.

MOOTOO, SHANI (1958–). Shani Mootoo is a writer and visual artist whose work reflects the development of her migrant identity. Mootoo is a member of the South Asian diaspora who was born in Ireland, raised in Trinidad and has spent her adult life between Canada and the United States. She began her creative career in Canada as a visual artist and videographer. In 1993 she published a collection of stories called *Out on Main Street*. The title story of this collection is narrated by a South Asian–West Indian **butch** and here Mootoo begins her fictional exploration of the **hybrid** nature of identity. Her work explores the spaces between the identities that we normally think of as fixed and binary: straight/gay, male/female, black/white, member of this nation/member of that nation. Her explorations of hybridity make Mootoo an important figure in the ongoing **postcolonial** lesbian exploration of identity, which is perhaps best exemplified by the writer and critic **Gloria Anzaldúa**.

Mootoo is best known for her highly successful novel *Cereus Blooms at Night* (1996). This work explores a complex set of relations among racial, national, gendered and sexual positions in a West Indian community. It is also deeply concerned, like many postcolonial novels of this period, with ideas of childhood and memory. One of Mootoo's abiding themes is childhood sexual abuse.

MORAGA, CHERRIE (1952–). The poet, playwright and community activist Cherrie Moraga was born in California of Chicana and Anglo descent. After her Anglo father left the family, her mother tried to give her children all possible advantages by encouraging them to use English and take advantage of their fair skins. Passing for white in racist America thus became a formative experience for Moraga. Coming out as a lesbian in the 1970s was, for her, also a process of coming out as Chicana and reconnecting with her mother. All of Moraga's work is strongly community based and focuses on interactions between ethnicity and sexuality. Her most widely read book of poems is *Loving in the War Years* (1983). Among her plays is the award winning *Watsonville: Some*

Place Not Here (1996). Moraga has made a lasting contribution to feminism through her editing and publishing work. Together with **Gloria Anzaldúa**, she edited *This Bridge Called My Back: Writings by Radical Women of Color* in 1981. The struggle to find a publisher for this work led to Moraga founding Kitchen Table Women of Color Press with **Barbara Smith**. Now over 20 years old, this press has made an incalculable contribution to feminism through its publishing. Moraga edited *The Sexuality of Latinas* (1993) with Norma Alcaron and Ana Castillo.

– N –

NAMJOSHI, SUNITI (1941–). Indian lesbian feminist writer and academic Suniti Namjoshi focuses her work on creating empowerment through the reworking of cultural myth. Her poems, short stories and longer fiction all utilize mythic formal structures and often directly rework both South Asian and European popular myths. Namjoshi has held academic posts in India, Canada and England. Collections of her poetry include *The Authentic Lie* (1982). Her best-known work is the collection of short stories *Feminist Fables* (1981). These short stories rework traditional myths by placing women at the center of the narrative. They also mythologize certain common contemporary events experienced by women. *The Conversations of a Cow* (1985) employs a similar structure. *The Mothers of Maya Diip* (1989) is a book-length utopian satire about matriarchy.

NELSON, ALICE DUNBAR (1875–1935). The American poet, journalist, fiction writer and activist Alice Dunbar Nelson was born in New Orleans into a social class locals refer to as *gens du couleur libre* (free people of color). Her background was thus both European and African and she enjoyed an upper-middle-class education. She was a graduate of Straight University, which still exists in New Orleans as the African-American Dillard University. After university, Dunbar Nelson worked as a school teacher, first in New Orleans and then in New York. The first of her three marriages was to the well-known poet Paul Lawrence Dunbar. **Gloria T. Hull**, who has published extensively on Dunbar Nelson, also documents a number of relationships with women.

An active suffragist and antiracist journalist, Dunbar Nelson published poems and articles in the NAACP journal *Crisis* and in several other journals and newspapers. Her short stories were published as *Violets and Other Tales* (1895) and *The Goodness of St. Rocque and Other Stories* (1899). During her lifetime, however, she was best known for her poetry. She found it difficult to find acceptance for her fiction, which did not produce stereotypes of black people that were intelligible to whites. Her work also often boldly challenged racism and segregation. She treated explosive and racially loaded themes such as rape and lynching in ways that made American readers uncomfortable. Hull identifies "You! Inez!" as a rare moment in which Dunbar Nelson's lesbian desires were expressed in her poetry. She also argues that the unpublished novel *This Lofty Oak* is based on one of Dunbar Nelson's female lovers.

NESTLE, JOAN (1940–). The American activist and **femme** lesbian writer Joan Nestle was born into a working-class Jewish community in New York. She participated in the femme-**butch** lesbian bar culture of the postwar era, which is documented in her autobiographical writings. She has joined in struggles against homophobia, **censorship**, sexism, racism and American imperialism since the 1950s. Nestle's work is crucial to an understanding of the development of **lesbian-feminism** in America on several counts. As the **second wave of feminism** began to devalue lesbian gender roles, Nestle retained and articulated her lesbian femme identity, which she saw as a source of erotic power. In both erotic and political writings she has asserted the validity of femme-butch role-play. In the early 1980s this earned her vicious condemnation from some feminists. Nestle resisted and thus her work became a major flashpoint for the "**sex wars**" of the 1980s. She has since edited *The Persistent Desire: A Femme-Butch Reader* (1992), a collection that has been important to lesbian studies. Nestle's *A Restricted Country: Documents of Desire and Resistance* (1987) mixes autobiography with academic and political writings in a way that allows Nestle to draw the connections between lived experience and critical and political consciousness. The various pieces in this collection talk about growing up Jewish in America, Nestle's experience of her own mother's sexuality, her femme identity and empowerment and the history of lesbian-feminism. Nestle's work is often both sexually explicit and overtly political at the same time, thus stretching definitions of **pornography** and erotica in unexpected ways. Her work displays an understanding of sex as play with power and the possibilities of enjoyment and empowerment that this realization holds. Other publications include, *A Fragile Union* (1998) and, with Tristan Taormino, the edited collection *Best Lesbian Erotica* (2000).

Nestle's other important contribution to **cultural feminism** has been the Lesbian Herstory Archives. She and Deborah Edel founded the archives in their New York apartment in 1973. They remained there for 20 years, and are now housed in a building of their own in Brooklyn. The working processes of the archives are deliberately antipatriarchal. All material is housed by the first name (rather than the patronym) of its author. Any and all lesbians are invited to house documents and life history material in the archive, which does not seek to value any individuals, histories or stories above any others. Among other important materials and documents, the archives house the lending library of the New York Chapter of **Daughters of Bilitis**, as it was in the 1970s, and extensive material on **Valerie Taylor** and other writers of lesbian **pulp** fiction.

NEWMAN, LESLÉA (1955–). The American lesbian **femme** writer Lesléa Newman has published several volumes of short stories and numerous children's books. She is best known for the children's book ***Heather Has Two Mommies*** (1989). This short book, which describes for children the experience of same-sex parenting, caused a minor controversy when it first appeared. Newman's other publications include the short story collection *A Letter to Harvey Milk* (1988), *Out of the Closet and Nothing to Wear* (1997) and *The Little Butch Book* (1998). Her stories have been collected as *Best Short Stories of Lesléa Newman* (2003).

NEWSPAPERS. *See* JOURNALISM.

NIN, ANAÏS (1903–1977). The Spanish-American writer Anaïs Nin is best known for her life writing, published in several volumes as *The Diaries of Anaïs Nin* between 1966 and 1985. These diaries were a success due to Nin's close relationships with several key modernist figures (especially Henry Miller) and her avid **erotic** fantasies. Best known of these is a series of erotic writings that were published after her death as the two volumes *Delta of Venus* and *Little Birds*. The work collected in these books was commissioned by an anonymous private client. Nin is, however, a significant literary figure on several other counts. In 1932 she published *D. H. Lawrence: An Unprofessional Study*, which defended the writer against the harsh criticism then prevalent. Nin respected Lawrence's attempts to represent complex relations of gender, sex and power. She herself famously said that she wrote "as a woman only." Thus Nin's writings have made controversial study for feminists, as they tend to reproduce a sexualized idea of femininity that some find problematic. It is largely for this reason that she is not taught in women's studies courses. It can be said, however, that Nin creates an active and desiring feminine subject in a way that is subtly unintelligible within the prevailing regimes of gender and desire. The lesbian elements of her narratives are significant in this regard.

Nin's novels are highly interesting both as formal experiments and as explorations of desire and memory. Her style is often called surreal, and might be compared with **Djuna Barnes'** style in the novel *Nightwood*. Her novels *House of Incest* (1936) and *Ladders to Fire* (first published in the United States in 1959, but written much earlier) describe Nin's erotic fascination with June Miller, wife of the writer Henry. Like Barnes, Nin describes the abject and fascinated longing and pursuit of one woman for another. Nin is often portrayed, especially in the film *Henry and June*, as a bourgeois wife writing erotica out of boredom. In reality, she was a driven and prolific writer. When she could not find a publisher for the 1939 novel *Winter of Artifice*, she acquired a press and printed it herself. Her journals were continuously maintained from the age of 11 until her death. She stored back volumes in a vault in Brooklyn. Late in life Nin undertook many lecture tours of U.S. universities. After her death, a scholarly journal, *Anaïs: An International Journal*, was dedicated to her work. It began in 1983 and ceased publication in 2001.

NINETEENTH CENTURY. The 19th century saw the development of ideas of sexual identity that have carried through to **postmodern** literature. Both the sweeping project of fictional realism and the tradition of **decadent literature** play important roles in the development of psychological and cultural models of female sexuality. In the early years of the century a literature of ideal friendship, pure same-sex love and **romance** combine with an erotic tradition of gallant romances in Europe. Early modern writers such as **Denis Diderot** inspired a host of male writers with a fascination for lesbian erotica and **pornography** in France. Much of this literature focused on transgender women and the suggestion that they *might* be led into sexual situations with other women by accident, as it were. **Theophile Gautier**'s *Mademoiselle de Maupin* (1835) fits into this category. **Honoré de Balzac**'s novel *Seraphitus-Seraphita* (1834) presents an androgynous female character who is loved (not physically) both by a man and a woman. Balzac's *The Girl with the Golden Eyes* (1835) gives a more overtly lesbian, but less positive, portrait. During these same years **Charles Baudelaire**, **Paul Verlaine** and **Pierre Louÿs** all published poems involving the overt depiction of lesbianism. The 20th century regarded Verlaine and Baudelaire as great poets and Louÿs as a pornographer, but it was Louÿs' work that was remembered by American lesbians in naming the 1950s organization Daughter of Bilitis.

The one French woman writer who stands out during this early 19th-century period is the cross-dressing bisexual **George Sand**. Sand's novels, though never overtly lesbian, extended the range and power of women's active desire. Many later 19th-century female writers in both the French and English speaking world mentioned an admiration for her in letters and diaries. Citing Herbert Lewandowski, **Jeanette Foster** documents the existence of an 1858 novel called *La Sapho* by the French Writer Céleste Venard de Chabrillan which Lewandowski describes as overtly lesbian. I have been unable to verify this, but if true it represents an early use of **Sappho** in this way. Together with the earlier diaries of **Anne Lister**, this would point to the development of the lesbian identity throughout the duration of the 19th century.

Later in the 19th century, Paris became known for an active lesbian subculture and a number of well-known lesbian writers. Two women writers stand in out in late 19th-century France. The American-French poet **Renée Vivien** revived the reputation of Sappho as a lesbian icon, translating her work into modern French and modeling her own lesbian life after her. Vivien's contribution to the development of the modern lesbian identity is thus immeasurable. Her own work was openly lesbian and her lifestyle flamboyant and publicly known. The more popular fiction writer **Rachilde** published *Monsieur Vénus* in 1884. The novel featured a cross-dressing heroine. Rachilde also wrote many widely read reviews of gay, lesbian and transgender literature. Rachilde and Vivien participated in the growing lesbian literary subculture of Paris after the turn of the 20th century. **Emile Zola** depicts lesbian characters in both *La Curée* (1874) and *Nana* (1880). *Nana* contains what is perhaps the first description in literature of a modern lesbian bar (restaurant) scene. Interestingly the women in this establishment play clearly defined masculine and feminine roles. **Catulle Mendès**, in *Mephistophèlia* (1890), also depicts lesbian subculture in detail.

Well-educated members of the English-speaking world, both male and female, often read French in the 19th century. Nevertheless, the reading of French novels is used in countless 19th-century English stories to signal the moral laxity, or even depravity, of characters. This makes it clear that the messages about lesbian sexuality and female transgender movement (among other forms of **sexual dissidence**) that were being written in France had an influence in England and America.

Women's writing that survives from the first half of the 19th century in England and America, both published and private **life-writing**, most often depicts love between women as an idealized form of friendship. This has led scholars such as Carol Smith-Rosenberg and Lillian Faderman to argue for **romantic friendship** as a precursor to the lesbian identity, which arose later. The one very notable exception to this rule are the early 19th-century diaries of the English landowner **Anne Lister**, which depict an active and conscious lesbian sexuality. Lister has specific vocabulary for sex acts between women, and is well aware that her love for other women is neither pure nor platonic. She refers to her "**Sapphic** love." This may be the first time in English literature that a woman applies such a phrase to herself with this meaning. The late 18th- early 19th-century journals of the Irishwomen Sarah Ponsonby and Eleanor Butler speak of their relationship in almost marital terms but record no evidence of sex (though it is clear that they shared a bed).

In late 19th-century Europe and North America, an increasingly detailed medical/sexual science created complex taxonomies of gender positions and sexual behaviors. Masculinity and femininity, in various case studies, were compared to an ideal of masculinity and femininity that did not necessarily exist in reality. The European empire provided scientists with "strange" or "primitive" objects of study that fed scientific discourses of anthropology and **sexology** with comparisons and examples of wide varieties of gendered and sexual behavior. Much of this information was most likely mythical. It is clear that much of it was gathered coercively. Ideologies of empire were part of the machine through which sexologists like Richard von Kraft-Ebing and Havelock Ellis understood human sexuality. Sexology created ideal types at the same time that it demonstrated the variety of human variance.

At this same period the ideas of sexual identity that were prevalent in 20th-century literature began to develop. Upper-class women began to live in what are often referred to as "**Boston marriages**," live-in life partnerships that were social and economic, and some of which were certainly sexual. The American writer **Sarah Orne Jewett** lived in one such partnership and devoted her fiction to relationships between women, though none of these were sexual. The English aunt and niece who published poetry jointly as **Michael Field** also lived in a similar partnership, as did the socialist-feminist writers **Eva Gore-Booth** and **Esther Roper**. Other significant American 19th-century figures are **Margaret Fuller** and **Emily Dickinson**. In England, **Marie Corelli**, Geraldine Jewsbury and **Christina Rossetti** deserve mention. Edith Simcox, in an unpublished work called *Autobiography of a Shirt Maker*, describes what is believed to be a passion for the George Eliot.

In 1886 Henry James' ***The Bostonians*** described the struggle between a feminist and a man over a young woman. The portrait of feminism here is not kind and the man wins in the resolution of the novel. *The Bostonians* presents evidence again of an established subcultural practice of love between women. One notable collection of 19th-century fiction is Susan Koppelman's edited collection, *Two Friends and Other Nineteenth-Century Lesbian Stories by American Women Writers* (1994). Her use of the term lesbian here is bold, as none of the writers included in the collection would have used it for herself. Koppelman does, however, give a rationalization for its usage. *See also* LADIES OF LLANGOLLEN.

NOVELS. In 1929, when **Virginia Woolf** consolidated a set of lectures on women and fiction into the long essay *A Room of One's Own*, she used many fictional characters based on life. Among these were a thinly disguised version of herself as narrator and a novelist whom she calls Mary Carmichael, clearly based on the birth control reformer Marie Stopes, who had then recently published the novel *Love's Creation*. Woolf's narrator describes reading this novel, which, she says, is not necessarily very good, but is revolutionary in being written from a woman's standpoint about women's lives. Something remarkable, she says happens when a novel is written from this standpoint: "'Chloe liked Olivia' I read. Then it struck me how immense a change was there. Chloe liked Olivia perhaps for the first time in literature." Woolf is arguing that relationships between women, sexual, nonsexual or ambiguous, have been excluded from literature by the heterosexual imperative. It was revolutionary that at the beginning of the 20th century, after more than a century of feminist activism in Europe, women could express feelings for each other and relationships between themselves that had formerly been the province of men. A large portion of women's feelings and desires had been invisible up until this point, according to Woolf.

What Woolf is saying has some truth in it, in the sense that the "women's novel" grew and developed tremendously in response to changing gender roles and the gains made by the **feminist movement**. Yet at the same time, Woolf forgets, for a moment here, the many women who contributed to the development of the novel and who used the new genre of the novel in the 18th and 19th century, to assert and develop possibilities for women's emotional and material lives.

It can be convincingly argued that **Aphra Behn**'s *Orinooko* (1688) was the first novel written in the English language. As the novel developed in French and English in the 18th century, women's sexuality, including lesbianism, revealed itself as a primary preoccupation of the novelistic form. John Cleland's *Fanny Hill, or Memoirs of a Woman of Pleasure* (1749) and **Denis Diderot**'s *La Religieuse* (1760) both use a woman's desire as the driving force of narrative and display a particular fascination with lesbian sexual activity.

During this same historical period women novelists were asserting their own material and romantic questions, needs and desires in the developing genre of the sentimental novel. Charlotte Lennox in both

The Female Quixote: or The Adventures of Arabella (1752) and *Euphemia* (1790) worked to place women at the center of romance narratives as active figures. Though both operate within the framework of heterosexual marriage and the **romance plot**. Female desire and emotional relationships between women are central to these novels. It is important to remember that for upper-class women at this period heterosexuality and marriage were economic and social necessities that did not always correspond to emotional and romantic lives. Lennox's work, while placing women in marriages, describes strong emotional relationships between married women. **Sarah Scott**'s political satire *Millenium Hall* (1762) describes a utopian community in which women can find purpose and fulfillment without marriage. Again the women characters here have strong emotional relationships with each other.

Nineteenth-century European and American women novelists asked important questions about the legal, sexual and social position of women. The concept of novelistic realism, as developed by 19th-century English writers, allowed women novelists room to break away from the stock character types of the sentimental novel and to begin to explore pressing feminist questions. **Charlotte Brontë**, a novelist whom Woolf discusses at length, created, in her character Jane Eyre, a woman who subtly defies the image of women as sexually passive. The title character in her novel *Shirley* (1848) fulfills an economic and social role traditionally reserved for men. Indeed, Shirley might be described as a transgender figure. The novel asks a number of feminist questions about women's intellectual abilities and capacity for leadership. Again, while remaining within the structure of the romance plot, *Shirley* focuses sharply on the emotional relationship between two women. Brontë's *Villette* (1853) describes two young women who like each other very much indeed.

At the turn of the 20th century, novelists such as Edith Wharton and **Willa Cather** began to question the role of women within the traditional structure of the romance plot. Early 20th-century feminism, changing gender roles and the **modernist** movement led to a rich exploration of women's sexuality in the novel. **Nella Larsen, Virginia Woolf, Djuna Barnes, H.D.** (Hilda Doolittle) and **Rosamund Lehmann** all made huge leaps in what Rachel Blau DuPlessis has described as writing their way out of the romance plot. These women made women's desires the central concern of their novels without necessarily focusing those desires on a male hero who would become a husband.

The mid-20th century saw the development of a diversity of forms in the lesbian novel. For the first time a working-class genre of lesbian-written fiction became visible in lesbian **pulp** paperbacks. Writers like **Valerie Taylor**, **Paula Christian** and **Ann Bannon** seized the opportunity that the pulp industry offered in order to explore the ways in which lesbian romance might restructure the novel. **Daphne Du Maurier** opened up the latent lesbian possibilities of the Gothic genre with psychological examinations of woman's same-sex desire. **Patricia Highsmith** (writing as Claire Morgan) achieved widespread recognition for *The Price of Salt* (1952). British Writer **Maureen Duffy**'s *The Microcosm* (1966) again used Gothic devices, this time blended with lesbian bar culture in a landmark novel that influenced many lesbian novelists of the later 20th century. A similar landmark in the United States is Jane Rule's *The Desert of the Heart* (1964). **Isabel Miller** ushered in openly lesbian historical fiction with *Patience and Sarah* in 1969.

The strong presence of a left-leaning **lesbian feminism** in the 1970s and 1980s saw the development of a conscious and directed tradition of lesbian fiction. **Ellen Galford** in Great Britain and **Sarah Schulman** in the United States come out of this tradition and use their lesbian positioning to ask a number of radical questions about the relations between sexuality, racism, nationalism and capitalism. At the turn of the 20th century, the lesbian novel was a strong mainstream publishing category in its own right. First **Jeannette Winterson** and later **Sarah Waters** drew enormous numbers of readers from wide markets. The novels they created draw on the stylistic innovations made by earlier pioneering figures such as Woolf, Barnes and Miller.

– O –

OBJECT-CHOICE. This term, derived from 19th-century sexual psychology refers to the person (or thing) upon which one's desire fixes. A lesbian is often referred to as a woman with a female object-choice, or object-relation. This way of explaining lesbianism does not necessarily depend, then, on the way in which a woman relates to her gender (her **aim**), but simply whom it is that she desires.

O'BRIAN, KATE (1897–1974). The Irish playwright and novelist Kate O'Brian first worked as an editor and journalist. She had her first drama, *The Distinguished Villa*, produced in London in 1926. In 1931 her novel *Without My Cloak* won awards and her career as a writer of historical fiction began. *The Ante-Room* (1934), *The Land of Spices* (1941), *For One Sweet Grape* (1946), *The Lady* (1947), *The Flower of May* (1953) all followed. The 1958 novel *Of Music and Splendour* is perhaps of most interest here, in that it draws clearly lesbian characters. However, many critics find an underlying theme of lesbianism in all of O'Brian's novels. We might therefore place her in a tradition of lesbian novelists, including Mary Renault and Sylvia Townsend Warner, who wrote historical fiction that challenged categories of sexuality, rather than openly lesbian contemporary fiction. O'Brian had a lifelong affinity for Spain, where many of her novels were set. She studied the language and produced several translations, as well as a biography of the Spanish saint and mystic Teresa of Avila (1951). Avila has been a subject for many lesbian writers.

ONE. See HOMOPHILE MOVEMENT; JOURNALISM.

O'NEILL, ROSE (1874–1944). The American artist and author Rose O'Neill is best known as the inventor of the kewpie cartoon characters and the dolls that were based on them. These dolls made O'Neill millions of dollars and allowed her to live a privileged life. She produced four novels: *The Loves of Edwy* (1904), *The Lady in the White Veil* (1909), *Garda* (1929) and *The Goblin Woman* (1930). Critics have remarked on the androgynous nature of both the dolls and O'Neill's fictional characters, but it is chiefly her poetry that interests scholars of lesbian literature. **Jeannette Foster** argues that O'Neill's poetry is far superior to her prose. The fact that so little of something clearly superior exists, and that there is openly lesbian content in the poetry that survives, causes Foster to hint that much of O'Neill's lesbian poetry may have been suppressed or destroyed. Only one volume of poetry was published in O'Neill's lifetime, *The Master-Mistress Poems* (1922). In her **anthology** *The Literature of Lesbianism*, Terry Castle reproduces four poems from this collection, including "A Dream of Sappho" and "Death Shall Not Ease Me of You." The second poem is dedicated "to Kallista."

ON OUR BACKS. *See* PORNOGRAPHY.

ORIENTALISM. The term orientalism was brought into the lexicon of contemporary literary criticism by the late Palestinian scholar and humanist Edward Said. Said's book *Orientalism* (1978) defined the European study of Asia and the Middle East as a major tool for Europe's definition of itself through the creation of a cultural **other**. Ideas of the orient as strange, excessive, decadent, untranslatable, and above all as an object for European study, fed a long and diverse tradition of European literature.

Orientalism is particularly significant here in that European scholars, poets and fiction writers have, for hundreds of years, associated "the East" with sexual deviance and excess. From **Lady Wortley Montague**'s *Embassy Letters* to **Vita Sackville-West**'s remarkably similar productions 200 years later, through the works of Richard Burton (translator of the ***Kama Sutra***) and T. E. Lawrence, the "Orient" has provided an imaginary field for European sexual fantasies. According to Graham Robb, Richard Burton, an orientalist much interested in "pederasty," identified a "'Sotadic Zone' lying between latitudes 30° and 43° in which 'the Vice' was popular and endemic."

European colonial expansion was often justified by the description of colonized people as "uncivilized," and this lack of civilization was often defined through sex and gender practices. So, the heterosexual practice of *sati* (widow burning) in India and of polygyny in the certain parts of the Islamic world were much decried by European feminists and colonists. Fantasies about what happened in the woman-only environments of harems or seraglios were widespread. Lady Wortley Montague's letters are a good example of this. H. Rider Haggard's *She* (1886) is another interesting example of the relations among colonial exploration and excessive female sexuality. Orientalist sexual fantasies still abound in the West, as is evident in specific genres of **pornography** and **erotica** that focus on Asian women.

THE OTHER. This critical term derives from **psychoanalysis**. As articulated by **Sigmund Freud** and later by **Jacques Lacan**, the process of human subjectification (development of the self) centers around the separation of a child from its mother. For Lacan, who articulated this process through the terminology of the science of linguistics, the subject must, in order to be intelligible in syntax, distinguish itself from the object of its utterance. As Juliet Mitchell has said: "His [Lacan's] subject is not an entity with an identity, but a being created in the fissure of a radical split." Following Freud's primal Oedipal drama, the primary object through which a child first identifies is the mother, and then, by extension, all women (the child being implicitly male and heterosexual in the first instance). The idea of defining the self through the other is used by feminist and antiracist theorists to explain the process by which certain groups of people assume centrality by marginalizing ("othering") specific groups of people. Thus some speak of whiteness as central and blackness as other, of Europe as central and Africa or "the East" as other, and of white Europeans as defining themselves as such through the definition of African and Asian peoples as other.

In terms of lesbian and transgendered sexualities this gendered and sexualized process of self and other serves to create invisibility. If two polar opposites called man and woman must be defined in relation to each other in order to conceive of their own existence or enter into meaning, what of those who are neither male nor female, neither masculine nor feminine, or who are both at once? What of those who do not define in relation to an "opposite" sex? Likewise if the self is, in the first instance implicitly male, and the subject (never, as an adult, the object) of desire then what of the woman who actively desires? Lesbian theorists who have answered these questions in interesting ways include **Gloria Anzaldúa** and **Monique Wittig**. *See also* ORIENTALISM.

OUR BODIES, OURSELVES. A book published by the Boston Women's Health Book Collective from 1973, *Our Bodies, Ourselves* contained a wealth of information intended to help women regain control of their own bodies. The radical feminist perspective embodied in this book saw women as having been alienated from their own bodies through the control of a number of misogynist institutions and discourses, including medicine. This project, published in many editions, sought to radicalize women's relationship to their own bodies by freeing them from the disempowerment inherent in the relationship between women and medical science. The book included a section on lesbianism from the start.

– P –

PACKER, VIN. *See* MARIJANE MEAKER.

PASSING. The term passing refers here to people who are able to disguise themselves in an identity other than the one that had been, or would be, ascribed to them from without. Much of the information we have about gender transgressive women before 1900, particularly in the working classes, refers to cases of women who passed for men. Women joined the American Revolutionary War, ran gangs of thieves in 19th-century San Francisco and lived and worked on privateering ships in the Caribbean. One story from the "Newgate Calendar" (tales of criminal cases in England) tells of a woman who was publicly whipped in southwest England for marrying at least three other women while dressed as a man. An extensive **nineteenth-century** literature, particularly in France, uses female characters who pass as men to create novel sexual situations. An article by the San Francisco Lesbian and Gay History Project, "She Even Chewed Tobacco: A Pictorial Narrative of Passing Women in America" gives an overview of the U.S. history of passing women. **Leslie Feinberg**'s 1993 novel *Stone Butch Blues* tells of the central character's experiences as a passing woman. Jackie Kay's 1999 novel *Trumpet* fictionalizes the story of the passing American trumpeter Billy Tipton, and places it in a Scottish context.

PERFORMATIVITY. Theories of performativity derive from work done by the linguist J. L. Austin at Oxford University in the 1950s (published as *How to Do Things wth Words*, 1975). Austin argued that not all speech described action, some speech actually was action, was performative. When a judge bangs her gavel and declares, "I sentence you to five years hard labor," the defendant is sentenced by the act of the judge's speech. Here the verb performs (acts), rather than describing an action. "I sentence you" is a performative speech act, but in order for it to work, it must take place within a social and cultural context. This social and cultural framework is what gives performative utterances their power. The judge speaks within a social structure that makes the judge powerful, condones this form of punishment, marks the defendant as a criminal and backs her words with the physical force of the police and the prison system.

The philosophers Louis Althusser and Jacques Derrida have taken up Austin's notion of performative speech in ways that have been very important for literary and cultural theory. Most significant here, however, is **Judith Butler**'s use of performativity, first articulated in *Gender Trouble* (1990). *Gender Trouble* is an engagement with feminist theory that questions the very category of woman on which **feminism** is based. Gender, Butler argues, is performative rather than **essential**, that is to say that a girl becomes a girl through a series of acts that are reinforced within a social context and not through any predetermined biological destiny. Building on theories of the **social construction** of gender, Butler (in *Gender Trouble*) argues that

> Gender ought not to be conceived merely as the cultural inscription of meaning on a pregiven sex . . . gender must also designate the very apparatus of production whereby the sexes themselves are established.

If then, there is no essential category called woman, which exists prior to its oppression or its liberation, whom does feminism represent? Butler is not arguing for an end to feminism, but rather for the use of feminism to question and disrupt categories of gender and sexuality, rather than to reinforce them. If gender is performance, we need not confine ourselves to two genders, or to one continuous gender throughout our lives. We might choose to perform gender in unexpected and disruptive ways. The idea that one's gender somehow should determine one's object of desire or one's life partner falls apart here. What we ought to do is to question and destabilize the "apparatus" of gender production.

Butler's theory of gender performativity articulates a change in constructions of gender and sexuality that is also present in lesbian fiction after 1990. Writers such as **Shani Mootoo**, **Jeannette Winterson**, Jackie Kay and others present gender and sexuality as performative and fluid. Thus the theory of performativity can be useful for a fuller understanding of their work.

PHILLIPS, KATHERINE FOWLER (1632–1664). The British poet Katherine Fowler Phillips came from a well-to-do family and attended boarding school at a young age. Here, she experienced the first of several **romantic friendships** from which she derived both emotional sustenance and poetic inspiration. Phillips' poetry was very popular in her own lifetime, though she was sometimes satirized in the popular press for trying, as a woman, to engage in the lofty and philosophical practice of poetry. As a figure for lesbian studies, Phillips is a lesson in the historical contingency of sexual identities. Her marriage was long and happy, but not at all romantic. All of the romance in her life was within her "society of friendship," an idealized group that included the women closest to her. In poems to Ann Owen, whom she addresses, according to the custom of the period, by a classical name (Lucasia), she speaks of their love as pure and "Platonick." It is possible that by this she means nonsexual. On the other hand the definition of sex at this period may not have covered the kinds of lesbian contact that it does today. Also, platonic, which today means nonsexual, may then have meant pure and exalted love in the classical sense, a definition that included homosexuality for many writers up until the 19th century. Ultimately, in literary terms, it is unimportant at this historical distance to think about what Phillips did privately. Her writing is deeply significant in that it establishes a rich romantic language for love between women. Though whole collections of her work are no longer in print, she is normally included in anthologies of **early modern** verse.

PIZAN, CHRISTINE DE (c. 1364–c. 1430). The Italian-French writer Christine de Pizan may have been the first woman to earn a living by writing in the modern sense. After the deaths of her father, husband and king, she began writing poems and seeking the patronage of the wealthy as a poet. This activity was highly unusual for a woman in this time and place, but de Pizan is known to have come from a scholarly family. Her father was an Italian academic and medical practitioner. Within the body of de Pizan's work there is a strong thread of feminist argument. This begins with a prolonged criticism of Jean de Meung's *Romance of the Rose* (written about a century earlier). In 1399 de Pizan wrote *Letter to the God of Love*, in 1402 *The Tale of the Rose*, and between 1401 and 1403 *Letters on the Debate of the Romance of the Rose*. She is perhaps best known for *The Book of the City of Ladies* (1405), which depicts a fantastic utopia populated only by women. *City of Ladies* follows the conventions of its time, using sustained allegory and imagining the meeting of both allegorical and historical figures. Its purpose is a consciously feminist one, though de

Pizan would not have used the word **feminism**. She seeks to illustrate the strength, morality and rationality of women, and to undermine misogynist philosophical arguments that she found dominant in the culture at large.

De Pizan's work is highly significant here in the first instance because she enabled women to imagine an economically independent life of writing. Secondly, she imagined a world in which women were culturally central and defined through their relationships with each other, rather than their relationships with men. Her last known work was *Songs in Honor of Joan of Arc* (1429), written while the **transgendered** saint was still alive.

POETRY. Any examination of the history of lesbian poetry must begin with the ancient Greek language poet **Sappho**. Sappho lived, ran a school and wrote poetry in the 7th century B.C.E. on the Mediterranean island of Lesbos. Among her poems were many that were addressed in romantic terms to young women. The prejudice against her independent sexuality began early and the first large-scale burning of her poems took place in the 4th century C.E. Much of what survives of her work is fragmentary. Sappho had a few imitators, but throughout the later Roman period little, if any, lesbian poetry by women survives.

Until relatively recently (the 18th century, perhaps), verse remained the primary medium through which the fanciful, the romantic and the experimental were generally expressed. Prose was retained primarily for theological and philosophical (including scientific) writing. The format of the **romance** narrative was first developed in verse form during the medieval period. Therefore most of what exists of lesbian writing up until the 18th century is in verse form. In the 11th century the Arabic language poet **Walladah bint Al-Mustakfi** continued a strong tradition of Arabic and Persian women's poetry with feminist and lesbian verse. Two love letters from 12th century Germany (written in Latin) express the love of one woman for another in verse form.

During the **early modern** period in Europe, poets such as **Anne Finch**, **Aphra Behn** and **Katherine Phillips** developed a tradition of female to female love verses, which would feed the imaginations of both heterosexuals and lesbian women for centuries. During this same period male writers began experimenting with the subject of **cross-dressing** and lesbianism in erotic and **pornographic** texts. The **nineteenth century** in Europe, paradoxically, saw both a greater repression of female same-sex desire in verse and, eventually, the development of the modern lesbian identity. In the early 19th century the poet **Wu Tsao** gained tremendous popularity in China with her lesbian love poems. In Europe and the United States, however, poets like Christina Rossetti and **Emily Dickinson** expressed a sublimated lesbian desire in the midst of a repressive Protestant culture. Later in the century, the romantic aunt and niece pair who wrote together as **Michael Field** based one of their books on surviving fragments of Sappho's verse. This pair lived in the beginnings of a culture of modern same-sex partnerships. Out of this culture came much of the poetry of **romantic friendship**, which expressed intense sensual desires without necessarily defining them publicly as sexual. In France at the end of the 19th century the American-born poet who wrote as **Renée Vivien** consciously continued the Sapphic tradition in her life and openly lesbian verse. We might consider Vivien the first poet of the fully articulated modern lesbian identity.

A strong 19th-century tradition of male writers playing on lesbian themes has influenced modern lesbian writing. In Great Britain **Algernon Charles Swinburne** is a notable figure writing in this vein. In France **Charles Baudelaire**, **Paul Verlaine** and **Pierre Louÿs** have been influential. This work varies in its view on lesbianism as damning vice, classical purity and innocence, titillating diversion or any combination of the three.

The early 20th century continued with a number of transatlantic lesbian poets who had been part of Vivien's circle. Among these were **Natalie Clifford Barney** and **Gertrude Stein**. In the United States the black lesbian playwright and poet **Angelina Weld Grimké** wrote a body of openly lesbian poetry, much of which remains unpublished to this day.

In the mid-20th century the **second wave of feminism** saw poetry as a tool of testimony and liberation. Modern free verse poetry allows for a nonlinear, highly metaphoric expression and a stress on emotion rather than logic. These qualities—emotion, metaphoric expression and nonlinear thought—were seen to have been traditionally associated with the feminine and thus devalued. They therefore appealed to a movement that sought to celebrate and revalue these qualities. In addition, poetic verse allowed an emotional outlet for experiences of violence and oppression. The movement sought to break the silence around these experiences and therefore poetry readings became an important component of feminist events. Poetry's facility for oral presentation led to its use as a tool for "speaking out" against oppression. Many feminist events included poetry readings in the 1970s and 1980s. In the United States in this period **Audre Lorde, Judy Grahn** and **Adrienne Rich** were all lesbian poets who contributed to the culture of poetry as empowering testimony.

At the end of the 20th century and the beginning of the 21st, lesbian poetry remains a strong and growing field of publishing. **Cherrie Moraga** and **Gloria Anzaldúa** in the United States question the boundaries of genre, sexual identity and linguistic dominance in mixed genre, bilingual productions. In Britain **Carol Ann Duffy** and Jackie Kay continue a second-wave lesbian poetic tradition that questions fixed identity positions and examines the nature of the family, womanhood, sexuality and the authority of the male voice.

POLITICAL LESBIANISM. This term most often refers to the **second wave feminist** idea that there could never be equality in relationships between men and women and the consequent practice of consciously choosing a lesbian social and sexual life. Both American and British novelists of the mid-20th century often depict political lesbian characters. *See also* MANIFESTOS.

POPULAR LITERATURE. The term popular literature is most often used to refer to literary works that gain the widest market distribution and the least critical attention. For a variety of cultural and economic reasons, this category tends to correspond with literature that is consumed by the working classes. **Cross-dressing** women and lesbians have been subjects for popular literature since at least the 18th century. Emma Donoghue cites William King's popular satirical poem *The Toast* (1732) as the first use of the term lesbian in its modern sense. In the 18th and 19th centuries "The Newgate Calendar," a serial publication that gave details of sensational criminal trials in England, featured occasional stories of transgender women, punished for passing as men and entering into marriages with women. So-called Penny Dreadful literature of the 19th century, which enjoyed a large working-class readership, focused on all forms of criminality and deviance, including, very occasionally, lesbianism. In this genre, sexual dissidence of all kinds was set up as a specific kind of criminal act. In France in the same period a genre of **pulp** literature that focused specifically on the lesbian figure began to emerge. These works were exported widely. In 20th-century America, pulp literature that focused on the lesbian achieved the height of its production and distribution. This heralded that shifting of the most visible lesbian identity in culture from that of upper-class **modernist sapphists**, to that of working-class **femme-butch** couples. *See also* CLASS.

PORNOGRAPHY. Representations of sex that are made for sexual uses, the reading or viewing of which is in itself a sexual act, are classed variously as either pornography or **erotica**. Whether a piece of writing is categorized as the former or the latter usually has to do with its social context, implied audience and the kind of sexual arousal it elicits, rather than with the degree of explicitness with which it represents acts of sex. The lesbian has been a central pornographic figure in Western culture for centuries. Critics generally assume that the majority of representations of the lesbian in sexually explicit literature have been constructed for the pleasure of men. Of course, we cannot know with any certainty who actually wrote or read most pornographic texts, let alone who enjoyed them and how. We can know that the majority of producers of pornography until the 20th century were men. It is true, however, that as early as the 18th century, there were establishments for the printing and distribution of pornography in London that were owned and operated by women. From this period, writings about sex and the sexual body were classed as either medical or pornographic, though there was a great deal of overlap between the two. Medical literature seems to have had pornographic uses from the early modern period, and in 1905 Sigmund Freud was still worried that some doctors might read his "Fragment of an Analysis of a Case of Hysteria" (the "Dora" case) as a "roman a clef" designed for sexual pleasure.

By the 19th century, pornography was a huge business in Europe and North America. The **decadent** work of middle-culture writers such as the French novelists **Théophile Gautier** and **Honoré de Balzac** was mirrored in a more widely distributed and less well-regarded form of popular literature that contained more explicit representations of lesbian sex than these writers included in their slightly more well-respected works. Indeed, Balzac himself began as a writer of **pulp** fiction. Graham Robb claims that "In 1892, the U.S. Post Office Department (as it was then called) was destroying French lesbian novels by the ton."

In the post–World War II period a paperback industry based on sensational stories of sex and **crime** enjoyed a huge boom. Within this industry a genre defined roughly as lesbian pulp fiction contained books that ranged from the explicitly sexual to the entirely melodramatic. Again, critics (including early **second-wave feminists**) at first assumed that this literature was produced entirely for the sexual pleasure of men. More recently, however, it has become clear to the academy, as it always has been to many nonacademic lesbians, that this literature sustained and facilitated the lesbian identity throughout the postwar period. Still, this sustenance was formulated as against a pornographic function. That is to say, books were seen as *either* empowering *or* pornographic. This view reflected the second wave feminist idea that pornography was always disempowering for women. A culturally engrained picture of women as sexually passive made it difficult for critics to see women as active consumers of literature designed especially for sexual pleasure.

In the 1980s a set of debates around women, sexual power and pornographic representation took place within the feminist movement. These debates, often referred to as the "**sex wars**," were sparked off at a conference on lesbian sex and power that was held at Barnard College in 1982. Both **Joan Nestle** and **Pat Califia** were outspoken proponents of a lesbian-centered pornography (or erotica) that could both acknowledge the power relations involved in sexual acts and representations and still be psychically safe for all participants. The writings of Nestle and Califia are important examples of pornographic work that places women in active, desiring, consuming positions. The American magazine *On Our Backs* is one English-language example of a specifically lesbian pornography that has emerged since the 1980s.

POSTMODERNISM. The term postmodernism most often refers to a new and self-reflexive understanding of modernity which arose in the late 20th century. In postmodernist literature classic narratives of identity, history and culture are crossed over, complicated, questioned and broken down. A sense of self-reflexivity, parody of traditional styles and forms, disunity, fragmentation and unreliable or unstable narration are all hallmarks of the postmodernist style. In spite of the misleading nature of the name, it is true that most of these experiments were pioneered by the modernist movement in the first half of the 20th century. Postmodernism is, in a sense, an extension of the insights of **modernism**. There is also a close relationship between postmodernism's questioning of unified categories and the critiques of modernity made by many post**colonial** theorists. Lesbian writers who might often be categorized as postmodernist are **Kathy Acker,** Jackie Kay, **Jeannette Winterson** and **Monique Wittig**. Critics of postmodern theory question the political value of dismantling the historical and cultural narratives, and identity positions, through which oppressed people are able to understand and resist their own disempowerment.

POUGY, LIANE DE (1869–1950). Liane de Pougy was the pseudonym of the French music hall star and courtesan Ann-Marie Chassigne. She wrote a best-seller called *Idylle Saphique* in 1901. This confessional, sensational book is said to represent her relationship with Natalie Barney. Chassigne's diaries were published in 1977 as *Mes Cahiers Bleu* (*My Blue Notebooks*). These are of historical and literary significance in that they describe an upper-class lesbian subculture in great detail. Many members of the circle known as the **Academy of Women** are described here.

PSYCHOANALYSIS. The discipline of psychoanalysis is most often associated with **Sigmund Freud**, who popularized its procedures and doctrines in the late 19th and early 20th centuries. Two important influences on Freud, however, were the French neurologist Jean Martin Charcot (1825–1893) and the German psychologist Josef Breuer (1842–1925).

Together the elements drawn from Charcot and Breuer led to some of the basic principles of psychoanalysis: that the human psyche contained conscious and unconscious areas and that painful or traumatic events were often repressed or kept in the unconscious mind, and that these traumatic events caused all manner of symptoms, delusions and dysfunctions that would be relieved by bringing the trauma forward into the consciousness through the talking cure. Equally important to psychoanalysis as Freud developed it was that the primary and most significant trauma in any person's life occurs during the period of childhood when she/he must learn to understand the gender and sexual relationship of her/his parents. Freud fused this primal scene of trauma with the classical myth of Oedipus. Assuming the child to be male, Freud argued that he would experience a rivalry with his father for his mother's affections, which if development was successful would end in him growing up to take his father's place with another woman who would stand in for his mother. The "Oedipal conflict" is perhaps the most highly popularized idea to come out of Freud's work.

It took Freud many years, and much interaction with his female colleagues, to fully articulate a theory of female psychic development. According to him, girl children, like boy children, first experienced an **object-relation** to their mothers. This went along with an early masculine **aim** in girls, characterized by physical activity and clitoral fixations (Freud described the clitoris as an inadequate penis substitute). In order to achieve "normal" psychic development girl children must give up their desire for their mother, their clitoral stimulation and their desire to perform "masculine" functions in the family or the social world. The ability to achieve vaginal orgasm, to fix one's sexuality on the penis, was seen as a requisite for healthy female maturity. Thus many **second-wave feminists** expressed hostility toward Freud and his theories. The primacy of the vaginal orgasm and the idea of the masculine aim were alike decried. It is easy to see that a great deal of what was in reality cultural norms of gender behavior are laid down by Freud as elements of a universal psycho-sexual drama. Freud's *Totem and Taboo* does indeed extend his theories onto peoples in the colonized world in a problematic way.

Nevertheless, psychoanalysis first developed the idea that human sexual development might be a psychic, rather than a physical, matter. This was a revolutionary step for lesbians and other women. In addition it opened a window onto the psycho-sexual life of children that has changed Western culture permanently. Freud's theories became rapidly and widely popular. By the 1920s many psychoanalytic terms were catch phrases throughout Europe and the Americas. These terms, and psychoanalytic ideas, appear frequently in lesbian novels from 1910 onward. Freud trained many psychoanalysts and some of his women students began almost immediately to take up (and take issue with) his ideas regarding the development of women's sexuality. Two of the most significant women in the development of psychoanalysis are Helene Deutsch (1884–1982) and Karen Horney (1885–1952), both German students of Freud who moved to the United States in the early 20th century.

Helene Deutsch was a medical doctor who began working with Freud in 1916. Her life's work focused on the relations between women, mothers and motherhood, thus creating a body of psychoanalytic work that is female centered, though mostly very heterosexually focused. Deutsch published *The Psychology of Women's Sexual Functions*, the first psychoanalytic work devoted entirely to women, in 1925. For the most part Deutsch sees female homosexuality (the **sexological** word "**inversion**" is also often used by Deutsch and her colleagues) as the result of unresolved feelings of the female child toward her mother. Thus, for her, lesbianism is infantile mother/child role play. Teresa de Lauretis argues, however, that there is a great deal of positive material to be derived from Deutsch's work on lesbian relations if her works are read as painstakingly as Freud's often are.

Karen Horney's work concentrated on environmental and social factors in the development of female sexuality. Her *Feminine Psychology* is a collection of essays that she wrote between 1922 and 1937. Included in this collection is the influential "The Problem of Feminine Masochism" in which Horney argues that female subjection to men is a matter of socialization, that women are trained to seek male validation rather than to rely on their own psychic resources. The relationship between Freud and his female colleagues and their development of ideas of female sexuality is narrated in a book by Marie-Christine C. Hamon, translated into English by Susan Fairfield as *Why Do Women Love Men and Not Their Mothers?* (2000).

Other important woman psychoanalysts are Jeanne Lampl-de Groot, who wrote an essay on "The Evolution of the Oedipal Complex in Women," and Joan Riviere, most noted for her "Womanliness as a Masquerade," which prefigures **Judith Butler**'s discussions of performativity.

The psychoanalyst Carl Jung (1875–1961) was a student of Freud who developed the theory of the collective unconscious. Jung applied the techniques of psychoanalysis on a cultural level through the study of myths and folklore. One of Jung's students, M. Esther Harding, has been tremendously influential for the women's movement. Like other early women psychoanalysts, she focused much of her work on marriage and the family. She produced two books, *The Way of All Women* (1933), and *Women's Mysteries: Ancient and Modern* (1933), which discuss cultural mythologies of sex, sexuality and power through a feminine focal point. These works have been important to the women's spirituality movement and have provided a great deal of material for **Dianic Wiccans**.

PSYCHOPATHIA SEXUALIS. *See* SEXOLOGY.

PULP FICTION. This term most often refers to a category of literature that was produced in low-cost paperback form in the United States in the mid-20th century. An area of academic study also focuses on pulp magazines, which contained mainly **crime** and **horror** stories. As regards the lesbian figure, however, it is these midcentury paperbacks that are most significant. A form of cheap paperback fiction (often referred to as dime novels) had existed throughout the 19th century, but changes in the production of paperback books allowed for a cheaper and larger scale process by the 1930s. At the same time, publishing houses that had formerly produced magazines moved into paperbacks. Fawcett Publishing was chief among these. Marketers at these houses hit on the idea of distributing paperback books through channels that had formerly been used only for magazines. Thus from the 1940s paperback sale racks began to appear in corner drugstores, bus stations, Laundromats and cafés.

Jeannette Foster documents a number of pulp productions that appeared prior to World War II. It was after the war, however, that a tremendous boom in paperbacks based on lesbian lives began. They cannot be realistically classed as **novels**, since many posed as either medical studies or nonfiction social inquiries. Though many of these books produced medicalized portraits of lesbians as deviant, and ended with heterosexual plot resolutions, an increasing number of positive portraits of lesbian characters appeared as the 1950s and

1960s wore on. Important pulp writers include **Rea Michaels, Paula Christian, Valerie Taylor** and **Ann Bannon**. During the postwar era and into the era of the **second wave of feminism** many middle-class lesbian critics and activists spoke out against what they saw as damaging representations of lesbians contained in all pulp literature. The depiction of **femme-butch** role-play was the most commonly decried element of pulp narrative. In more recent years, as lesbian theory has formed a more complex view of this practice and of the lesbian reader and the **class** bias of early feminism, a significant body of work has been done on the lesbian paperback.

– Q –

QUEER. The usage of the term "queer" to describe lesbians, transgender people, gay men and bisexuals is derived from its meaning as "strange" or "odd." It was thus first a term applied in a derogatory fashion by heterosexual society. By the early 20th century sexually dissident people had appropriated the word to define themselves. During this period, queer still held both meanings, lending an interesting ambiguity to lines like **Radclyffe Hall**'s "in some queer way she was Jesus," (in her 1928 novel *The Well of Loneliness*). Anglo-lesbian and gay subculture after World War II used the word queer, though it was not a dominant term with which lesbians described themselves. With the **queer movement** in the 1990s, the word queer came into much wider usage as a way to include lesbians, transgender people, gay men and bisexuals under one term. Many people using the term queer seek to blur those more rigidly defined categories that place all sexually dissident people in some relation to heterosexuality. Queer as a term seeks to move beyond a politics of **identity**, though it most often still functions as an identitarian term. This is evidenced by its separate status in the commonly used string of designations lesbian, gay, bisexual, transgendered, queer (lgbtq).

QUEER MOVEMENT. Michele Foucault's *History of Sexuality: Volume One* (first published in French as *La Volonté du Savoir*) describes sexuality not as an identity with which one is born but as a position within a set of social discourses, at various conjunctions of which each individual subject exists. Power, for Foucault, was not necessarily something that existed at the top of the social structure but something that derived from an infinite number of points. Likewise each individual existed as an interlocking network of positions of power and privilege. For example, a middle-class, college-educated, Chicana lesbian is both privileged and oppressed in a variety of ways. The way to liberation therefore lay in recognizing the potential for power and oppression in any given position. This Foucauldian view of power was a tremendous inspiration for gay activists in the 1980s. During the AIDS emergency the AIDS Coalition to Unleash Power (ACT UP) was formed, its name deriving from Foucault's insights.

In the late 1980s and 1990s a **queer** movement growing out of ACT UP carried these same insights into activism around **feminism**, racism, **class** and sexuality. Queer Nation in 1990 and the Lesbian Avengers in 1992 were organizations born out of this movement. Their style of activism heralded a new radicalism, rejecting ideas of assimilation and tolerance, which had characterized some of the most visible lesbian and gay activism of the early 1980s. Queer groups and activists embraced a radical leftist politics that saw the connections between classism, racism, sexism and homophobia. Though the queer movement sometimes characterized itself as something new, in reality it followed a tradition of leftist sexual politics perhaps begun by the late 19th- and early 20th-century German Scientific Humanitarian Committee, some **first-wave feminists**, the communist, antiracist homophiles of the 1940s and 1950s and the Gay Liberation Front activists of the 1970s. *See also* SEXOLOGY.

"THE QUILT." This story (translated into English as "The Quilt" from the original Urdu "*Lihaaf*") published in 1942 by the South Asian feminist writer Ismat Chugtai, caused a scandal by discussing sex between women. The story tells of a young girl who is sent to stay with an aunt and uncle. Through the child's naive narration, the more knowledgeable reader can see first of all that the uncle has relationships with a number of younger boys who attend his artistic salons. We then realize that the child's aunt has a sexual relationship with her maidservant. Not understanding their intimacy, the child is frightened by the shapes they make under the blanket and the noises she hears coming from the two women. Finally, during the maidservant's absence the aunt seeks relief through sexual abuse of the young girl child.

Soon after the story's publication, Chugtai was charged with obscenity by the British Crown, which still controlled India when the story was published. She was acquitted and the trial was widely reported in India. Her autobiography, *Kaghazi Hai Pairahan*, contains a chapter telling of the publication and the sensational trial of *Lihaaf*. This is Chugtai's only treatment of lesbianism, though many of her stories are important feminist landmarks.

– R –

RACHILDE, MARGUÉRITE EMERY VALLETTE (1862–1953). The French writer born Marguérite Emery used the pen name Rachilde throughout her career. She was the most successful woman working in the **decadent** tradition. As a decadent writer, Rachilde positioned herself against what she called "women's" writing (e.g., the romance) and called herself *"un homme de letters"* (a man of letters). At one period she gave herself a boyish haircut to emphasize her identification with the male mind.

Throughout her career Rachilde profited from the popularity of sexually suggestive literature. Her works that are most significant here are *Monsieur Vénus* (1884) and *Madame Adonis* (1886). Like other decadent novels and collections of poetry, *Monsieur Vénus* was first printed in Brussels in order to avoid French censorship. *Madame Adonis* is a **cross-dressing** extravaganza that resembles the works of **Honoré de Balzac** and **Théophile Gautier**. Rachilde wrote literary reviews for *Mercure de France* from 1896 to the 1930s. Here she often reviewed transgender, lesbian and gay narratives. These columns remain a valuable historical and literary resource.

RENAULT, MARY (1905–1983). The novelist known as Mary Renault was born to an English middle-class family as Eileen Mary Challons. She was educated at Oxford and worked as a nurse for much of her life. After World War II she lived for many years in South Africa with her partner Julie Mullard. Renault is best known for a series of historical **novels** set in ancient Greece, and exemplified by *The King Must Die* (1958). The historical pose these novels took, their lack of implication in contemporary identity politics, allowed Renault the freedom to explore complex questions of sexuality. Many of the Greek novels feature male homosexual relationships and Renault's work has been very popular with gay male audiences. She also wrote two novels that were set in the mid-20th century. *The Charioteer* (1953) explores the life of a closeted gay army officer who falls in love with a conscientious objector during the battle of Britain. The kind of anguish and self-loathing expressed here is typical of many novels of the era. The resolution of the novel is troubled. *The Friendly Young Ladies* (1944) is Renault's one novel about a female same-sex relationship. Its two protagonists live a fairly happy bohemian life together until one leaves the other for a man. Renault has said of this novel that it was a reaction against the kind of identitarian plea for acceptance that caused such a stir with *The Well of Loneliness* (1928). She claims that she wanted to do something different, open up new narrative possibilities for the lesbian novel. When it is remembered that *The Well* was still banned in Great Britain when *The Friendly Young Ladies* was published, however, one must wonder if its heterosexual resolution was merely a protection against **censorship**.

RICH, ADRIENNE (1929–). The American poet and essayist Adrienne Rich was born in Baltimore, Maryland, and educated at Radcliffe College. Her first book of poetry, *A Change of World* (1951), was chosen for publication in the prestigious Yale Younger Poets series. It was *Snapshots of a Daughter-in-Law* (1963), however, that brought her recognition and a sense of what her writing might do. This collection was published in the same year as Betty Friedan's *The Feminine Mystique*. It expressed the same kind of dissatisfactions and insights that Friedan said that middle-class housewives around the United States were experiencing at this period. In later writings, which describe her life in the 1950s, Rich reinforces much of what Friedan documented. She became heavily involved in leftist activism in New York in the 1960s and began to devote herself to **second-wave feminism**. Throughout her life, her work has focused on the relations between language and power and the specific way in which voice and silence operate for women in Western culture. Perhaps her most well-known collection of poems, *Diving into the Wreck* (1973), focuses on these concerns.

In 1976 Rich published the nonfiction study *Of Woman Born: Motherhood as Experience and Institution*, which became a feminist classic. Her essays are widely taught and articulate some of the most important developments in **lesbian feminist** theory in the second wave. Two of her most significant essays are "When We Dead Awaken: Writing as Revision" and "Compulsory Heterosexuality and Lesbian Existence." The first of these talks about writing as the means of breaking historical and cultural silences and creating space for liberation in language and culture. The second articulates the concept of the "**lesbian continuum**," which moves beyond the sexual binary lesbian/heterosexual and envisions a world where all relationships between women are valid and empowering. In Rich's view homophobia disempowers all women by stigmatizing any solidarity they might show for each other. She says,

> I mean the term lesbian continuum to include a range through each woman's life and throughout the history of **woman-identified** experience, not simply the fact that a woman has had or consciously desired genital sexual experience with another woman.

These and other important essays are collected in *On Lies, Secrets and Silence* (1979 and *Blood, Bread and Poetry* (1985). Among Rich's more recent collections of poetry is *An Atlas of a Difficult World* (1991).

RICHARDSON, DOROTHY (1882–1957). The English writer Dorothy Richardson is one of the most important of a group of **modernist** writers that includes James Joyce and **Virginia Woolf**. These three novelists made experiments in narrative style and voice that have affected the English **novel** ever since their work first appeared. It was in order to describe Dorothy Richardson's work that the writer May Sinclair coined the term "stream of consciousness," that is now routinely used to describe a form of narrative that follows a character's thoughts through free association. Richardson published the multivolume fiction work *Pilgrimage* between 1915 and 1938. This work drew heavily on autobiographical experience and played freely with narrative style. It is notoriously difficult of access but also an acknowledged masterpiece of modernist writing. The 10th volume, *Dawn's Left Hand* (1931), is most significant here. Like Rosamund Lehmann's *The Weather in the Streets* (1936), it is a kind of antiromance that looks at a marital triangle from the point of view of the other woman. At the same time Miriam, the mistress and the protagonist of *Pilgrimage*, experiences a passionate friendship with another woman. The novel gives this relationship equal space and attention.

RICHARDSON, HENRY HANDEL (1870–1946). The Australian-born writer Ethel Richardson used this pseudonym on her published works. Richardson lived in London as an adult and published her first novel, *Maurice Guest*, there in 1908. *The Fortunes of Richard Murphy* followed in 1930 and Richardson was nominated for the Nobel Prize for Literature in 1932. All of Richardson's work explores female sensuality and sexual power. The short stories contained in the collection *The End of Childhood* (1934) explore female same-sex desire explicitly. After the death of her husband, Richardson spent the rest of her life with partner Olga Roncoroni.

ROMANCE. The meaning of the English word romance has shifted significantly over the last few centuries. At the turn of the 19th century "romantic" still retained some of its original meaning of fanciful, fictional and idealistic, while gaining new connotations of sexual love between two people. Romance once distinguished a type of literature, associated with the novel and with women (or effeminate) readers, which was excluded from the "serious" realm of poetry and philosophical/scientific essay writing.

While we may still associate romance with less serious literature and with the objectification of women, the fact is that the idea of romance, as it evolved in language and literature, was the first through which women made themselves active subjects of desire. *See also* ROMANCE PLOT.

ROMANCE PLOT. The romance plot refers to the development of the story of (primarily heterosexual) love and the structure this story has given to narratives over a period of centuries and across many cultures. In Europe the romance plot first developed in the form of romantic ballads that began in the **medieval period** and survived in both high art and popular oral forms into the **nineteenth century**. With the development and dispersion of the novel form in the 18th and 19th centuries, the romance plot began to dominate storytelling culture. It has moved from the novel into cinema and is a primary structure for narratives in all of the world's major popular film industries.

In its most basic form, the structure of the romance plot consists of the desire of one character for another, or of two characters for each other, the obstacles that come between the desirer(s) and their object, and the eventual union of two characters. Obstacles to the achievement of desire form the suspense, excitement and suspended reading pleasure of the romance. The romance plot is highly significant here for a number of reasons. First, in English throughout the late 18th and 19th centuries, women writers can be said to have dominated the writing of novels, chiefly in the form of the romance. Even novels with other political and social objectives, such as George Eliot's *Middlemarch* (1872), were structured around the romance plot. Secondly, these romance novels tended to focus on women characters, usually young middle-class (and less often upper-class or working-class) women on the verge of adulthood, sexual awareness and marriage. Novels by writers like Jane Austen and the **Brontës**, however different in style and feeling, were all focalized around articulating the sexual and romantic desires of young women. Nineteenth-century slave narratives by authors like Harriet Jacobs highlight the dominance of the romance plot as they try to place even stories about the horrors of slavery within the framework of the romantic or sentimental novel. In using this framework, working with and against it, Jacobs is able to draw upon a whole language available for presenting her particular sexual dilemmas, while she must still struggle with the romance plot's presentation of women as either pure or impure, deserving or undeserving.

The romance plot so dominated women's fiction that Rachel Blau DuPlessis has argued that the history of 20th-century women's writing can be seen as the struggle of women writers to work their way out of the constraints of the romance plot. This struggle has been significant for women in all sexual **identity** positions. Divorce, promiscuity, premarital sex, birth control and abortion, as well as lesbian desire, are all precluded by the traditional framework of the romance plot, in which the woman must remain virgin and pure in order to deserve the love of a man whom she will inevitably marry in conclusion.

Writers of lesbian narratives have responded to the romance plot in two ways. Novels like **Jane Rule**'s *Desert of the Heart* and **Patricia Highsmith**'s *The Price of Salt* merely substitute woman for man as the object of desire. These novels still focus on the desire of one woman who focalizes the narratives, and one object of desire. The women overcome the obstacles in their way and end the book in a moment of union. The structure remains the same. Novels such as **Ann Bannon**'s *Beebo Brinker* series (1957–1963) and **Djuna Barnes**' *Nightwood* (1936) radically disrupt the romance plot. Bannon presents her characters as serial monogamists whose stability is in their community, rather than in any one relationship. Djuna Barnes questions the very nature of romance in a psychoanalytic exploration of lesbian desire and identity. Here both the structure and meaning of the romance plot are consciously undone.

The romance plot is of tremendous historical significance as the first abiding cultural forum within which women readers and writers communicated about their sexuality. Nevertheless, in the past century women writers, and especially sexually dissident women writers, have seen the need to break free of the strictures it imposes on the representation of women's desires. The romance plot is still a powerful influence on the most popular forms of lesbian fiction, as exemplified by writers like **Sarah Waters** and **Jeannette Winterson**.

ROMANTIC FRIENDSHIP. The term romantic friendship most generally refers to a practice common in England and the Americas from perhaps the 17th to the early 20th centuries. Middle-class and upper-class women often experienced, during this period, romantic and sensual feelings for each other, which they expressed in poems, letters and diaries. **Mary Wollstonecraft** used the term to describe her own feelings for Fanny Blood. The first scholarly inquiry into romantic friendship was made by Elizabeth Mavor in her 1971 biographical study of the **Ladies of Llangollen**. This was followed by an American investigation, Carroll Smith Rosenberg's 1975 essay "The Female World of Love and Ritual: Relations between Women in Nineteenth-Century America." Mavor points out that romantic friendships arose among "a cultivated and leisured body of middle and upper-class women in a society in which, with a few notable exceptions, the sexes were traditionally and culturally divided." She argues that English women, through reading and conversation, developed an open, humanistic sensibility a generation before English men. Women therefore "found little cultural reciprocity from the more conservative gentlemen, and as a consequence of this sympathetic discrepancy turned to their own sex."

While the diaries of **Anne Lister** and the trial of Marianne Woods and Jane Pirie in 1811 provide ample evidence of an active, genital lesbian sexual practice by the early 19th century, the public ideal of romantic friendship was nonsexual. It is likely that many women experienced intense emotional attachments while remaining ignorant of physical lesbian sexuality. It is also likely that the definition of what constituted sex was so radically different at this period that much of what would later be called sexual contact took place between women at this period without being regarded as such. It is a documented fact that female romantic friends kissed and embraced openly in public without being defined as lesbian. Finally, it is virtually certain that many women, entirely knowingly, engaged in sexual activity that many thought was impossible under the cover of romantic friendships. Most significantly, romantic friendship was associated with supposed feminine traits of "sensibility" (sensitivity) and emotional excess. As a practice it did not involve any deviation from accepted gender norms. Though many women who enjoyed such friendships were, like **Sarah Scott** and the Ladies of Llangollen, single or separated, romantic friendship was in no way mutually exclusive with heterosexual marriage.

Lillian Faderman in *Surpassing the Love of Men: Romantic Friendship and Love between Women from the Renaissance to the Present* (1985) argues for a continuum of affectionate relationships between women under this umbrella term. She documents the romanticization of same-sex friendships in the 16th and 17th centuries and also follows a strong tradition in France, including figures such as Madamoiselle de Lafayette and Madamoiselle de Sévigné. Both Mavor and Faderman associate romantic friendship in the 18th and 19th centuries with a trend toward sensibility, romanticism and the Gothic.

The 19th-century practice of **Boston marriage** is part of the tradition of romantic friendship among women of the upper-classes, whom independent income often allowed to live together in partnership. The American fiction writer **Sarah Orne Jewett** lived in such a relationship. This practice was already established in England by the 18th century. It continued into the 20th with writers like **Reneé Vivien** and **Natalie Clifford Barney**. This same independence allowed such women to pursue literary careers at historical periods where social conditions made this impossible for less privileged women.

ROPER, ESTHER (1868–1938). The class activist and women's suffragist Esther Roper spent most of her life in the English city of Manchester, where she was born in 1868. She attended what was then the women's department of Manchester University. Roper organized textile workers' and working women's suffrage groups. She was an early influence on the famous suffragist Christabel Pankhurst, though their politics later diverged significantly. Roper remained a committed leftist all her life. Together with her life partner **Eva Gore-Booth**, Roper was a major contributor to the **transgender** journal *Urania*. For further reading see Gifford Lewis' biographical study *Eva Gore-Booth and Esther Roper* (1988).

ROSSETTI, CHRISTINA (1830–1894). The English poet Christina Rossetti grew up in an Italian-English family full of noted artistic and literary figures. The poet's brother, Dante Gabriel Rossetti, was a painter and member of the famous Pre-Raphaelite circle of artists and writers.

Rossetti was involved from her teens in the High Anglican movement, first known in the 1850s as the Oxford movement. This growing sect revived Catholic practices like confession and religious sisterhoods. Jan Marsh in her literary biography of Rossetti argues that the proselytizing of the Oxford movement was aimed specifically at young women. As a young woman, Rossetti struggled between a religious zealotry and her poetic vocation, and throughout her life she produced both "worldly" and devotional verse. Bridging the two concerns in her **poetry** is a tremendous sense of guilt and an almost self-abusive atonement that is often highly sexually charged. As early as 1846, Rossetti was writing

Quickened with a fire
of sublime desire,
She looked up to heaven and cried aloud:
"Death I do entreat thee,
Come! I go to meet thee,
Wrap me in the whiteness of a virgin shroud."

These expressions of an orgasmic, masochistic feminine surrender to the divine are characteristic of Catholic women's mysticism. Though seemingly heterosexual (if we consider God a masculine object choice), they have been most often expressed by women who refuse marriage and heterosexual sex, and quite frequently by women, like Rossetti, who chose to spend much of their lives living and working in female communities. Rossetti suffered a breakdown during her teenage years, which friends, including her doctor, attributed to her religious mania.

Rossetti's juvenile novel *Maude: A Story for Young Girls* (1850), is naively autobiographical but interesting in that it tells of a girl likewise caught between religious devotion and romantic poetic dedication, which were seen as mutually exclusive. In the same year in which *Maude* was written, Rossetti published her first poems (as Ellen Allyn) in a journal called *The Germ*. Early poems of Rossetti's include two on the subject of **Sappho** (Rossetti spells the name Sapho). Though there had been work in English that focused on Sappho's bisexuality, Rossetti focused on the more prevalent trope of suicide, derived from Ovid's story of Sappho's throwing herself off of a cliff for love of a man. The poem "Sapho" focuses yet again on loneliness and a fascination with death. "What Sapho Would Have Said Had Her Leap Cured Instead of Killing Her" dwells on unrequited heterosexual love.

The poem for which Rossetti is perhaps best known, and that is most significant here, is "Goblin Market," the title piece of her first published collection (1862). "Goblin Market" tells, in fairytale fashion, the story of two young sisters who live alone and are tempted by the sin of eating the fruits of "Goblin men." Other girls have fallen before and the sin implied is clearly sexual. We are told of ". . . Jeanie in her grave, / Who should have been a bride; / But who for joys brides hope to have / Fell sick and died." Jan Marsh's biography is significant in that it connects "Goblin Market" to the work that Rossetti did in a home for "fallen women" beginning in 1859. It is possible that the efforts for the Christian salvation of female sex-workers can be said to inform one level of the allegory in "Goblin Market." We are clearly led to see the sin as sexual, might the sickness and death refer to the effects of venereal disease and the spiritual death of "impurity" in which Rossetti certainly believed? In the poem, Laura gives in to temptation and is saved by her sister Lizzie through a set of actions that is highly sensual. As Laura nears death, pining away for the fruit she has once tasted, Lizzie goes to risk contact with the Goblin men. She is made quite deliberately into a female Christ figure here, "White and golden Lizzie stood, / like a lily in a flood / . . . sending up a Golden fire." She manages to resist tasting the fruit forced on her, but through the Goblin's violence she returns covered with the juices of their fruit:

> She cried, "Laura" up the garden,
> "Did you miss me?
> Come and kiss me?
> Never mind my bruises,
> Hug me, kiss me, suck my juices
> Squeezed from goblin fruits for you,
> Goblin pulp and goblin dew.
> Eat me, drink me, love me;
> Laura make much of me;"

Whether or not Rossetti was innocent of the lesbian eroticism here, many people certainly were. The poem, which concludes that "there is no friend like a sister," was sold as a children's nursery book for many years. Only in the late 20th century did scholars begin to read it in another light.

Rossetti published four more collections of verse in her lifetime, *The Princes Progress and Other Poems* (1866), *Sing-Song* (1872), *A Pageant and Other Poems* (1881) and *Verses* (1893). Only *Sing-Song* is without devotional pieces. She also produced two collections of prose, *Commonplace and Other Short Stories* (1870) and *Speaking Likenesses* (1874). *See also* MEDIEVAL WOMEN'S MYSTICISM.

ROYDE-SMITH, NAOMI (1875–1964). Novelist Naomi Royde-Smith lived and wrote in her native England during the early 20th century. She is significant here for her unfriendly intervention in the debates around women's sexuality that took place among the English literary elite in the 1920s. Her novels *Tortoiseshell Cat* (published in 1925, the same year as **Virginia Woolf**'s *Mrs. Dalloway*) and *The Island* (1929) present condemnatory pictures of lesbian characters and relationships. **Jeannette Foster** saw the influence of **Sigmund Freud** on these works as "obvious."

RULE, JANE (1931–). North American novelist Jane Rule was born in the United States but has spent much of her life in Canada. Her novel *Desert of the Heart* (1964) broke new ground as a lesbian **romance**, which allowed its characters the chance of complete fulfillment in its resolution. Life history material shows that many North American lesbians of the postwar generation remember this novel, first titled *Permanent Resident*, fondly as an affirming experience. It was made into the film *Desert Hearts* in 1985.

Rule has also published *Against the Season* (1971), *Lesbian Images* (1975), *Theme for Diverse Instruments* (1976), *Contact with the World* (1980) and *After the Fire* (1989). She taught at the University of British Columbia for many years, beginning in 1958.

RÜLING, ANNA (1880–1953). German lesbian feminist and member of Magnus Hirschfeld's Scientific Humanitarian Committee, Anna Rüling is mostly remembered today for a speech she delivered in Berlin in 1904. This talk was sponsored by Hirschfeld's Committee and entitled "What Interest Does the Women's Movement Have in Solving the Homosexual Problem." It marks Rüling as the first woman who can truly be called a **lesbian feminist**. However Rüling also appears to have been a writer of fiction. **Jeannette Foster** cites her as the writer of a group of three novellas published together under the title *Welcher unter Euch ohne Sünde Ist (Which among You Is without Sin)*. Of the three, one, called "Ratzelhaft," is overtly lesbian but, according to Foster, ends in suicide. These stories were published under the name Theodor Rüling, but it is known that one of Anna's names was Theodor. In *The Second Sex*, **Simone de Beauvoir** cites Rüling regarding homosexuality and prostitution: "According to Anna Rüling, in Germany about twenty or thirty per cent of prostitutes are homosexual." De Beauvoir is apparently citing the same 1904 speech, which actually states that 20 percent of German prostitutes are homosexual. Only one scholarly English-language article on Rüling exists. It is by Hanna Hacker and included in Bonnie Zimmerman's *Lesbian Histories and Cultures: An Encyclopaedia* (2000). The German-language journal *Magnus-Hirschfeld-Gesellschaft* in its December 2003 issue includes an article by Christiane Leidinger that purports to "solve the mystery" of Rüling's identity. Sadly this has not yet been translated into English. It identifies Rüling as Theo Anna Sprüngli, with the birth and death dates given above. *See also* SEXOLOGY.

RUSS, JOANNA (1937–). The writer and academic Joanna Russ is widely credited with sparking the growth of lesbian **science fiction** in the 1970s. Her novel *The Female Man* (1975) tells the story of four women from parallel universes, each of whom experience gender and sexuality in radically different ways. The novel is still widely taught and written about in lesbian fiction and women's studies courses in the English-speaking world.

Russ began her publishing career in the *Magazine of Fantasy and Science Fiction* in 1959 with the short story "Nor Custom State." Other science fiction works include *The Adventures of Alyx* (1976), *We Who Are About To* (1977), *The Two of Them* (1978), *Extra (ordinary) People* (1984) and *The Hidden Side of the Moon* (1987). All of these works experiment with the position of female characters in narrative and focus to some degree on the unstable nature of gender and sexuality. She has said that she chose the science fiction genre early in her writing career in order to be able to use the techniques of literary realism to present ways of being that had not yet been imagined. In 1980 Russ published her only nonfiction short novel, *On Strike Against God*, a **coming-out story**.

Russ is also a respected writer on feminism and women's writing and a professor at the University of Washington. She has published three important works of feminist theory and criticism: *How to Suppress Women's Writing* (1983), *To Write Like a Woman: Essays in Feminism and Science Fiction* (1995) and *What Are We Fighting For?: Sex, Race, Class and the Future of Feminism* (1998). She has won the two most prestigious awards in American science fiction, the Hugo and Nebula prizes, once each and been nominated for each more than once.

– S –

SACKVILLE-WEST, VITA (1892–1962). As a young woman the English writer Victoria Sackville-West fell passionately in love with another wealthy debutante, Violet Trefussis. The two eloped a number of times and Sackville-West's first novel *Dragon in Shallow Waters* (1921) is dedicated to "L," the initial for Lushka, her pet-name for Trefussis. Her second novel *Challenge* (1923) tells of the relationship between the two and was suppressed in Great Britain by both Vita and Violet's parents. The author was obliged to publish first in the United States.

Sackville-West married the career diplomat Harold Nicolson and the two had a long open marriage during which each had affairs with a variety of partners of both sexes. Traveling with Nicolson to diplomatic posts, Sackville-West's journals and letters form an interesting body of British imperialist travel literature. This includes an orientalist sexual tourism that may be interesting to students of colonial literature and theory.

In all, Sackville-West produced 13 novels and 12 poetry collections. *The Edwardians* (1930) has been West's most successful novel, in terms of sales. *All Passion Spent* (1932) is perhaps her best. She produced six biographies, of which the most notable here are ***Aphra Behn: The Incomparable Astra*** (1927) on the sexually adventurous 17th-century writer and *Saint Joan of Arc* (1936), on the **cross-dressing** 16th-century saint.

Sackville-West is probably best known for her relationship with the great modernist writer **Virginia Woolf** whom she met after her affair with Trefussis had cooled. Woolf's *Orlando* (1928) is a fanciful portrait of Sackville-West as a long-lived transsexual hero/ine. The original edition was illustrated with portraits of several generations of Sackville-West's family. In later life, Sackville-West was a popular writer on gardening, making many contributions to the mainstream press. Three volumes of her correspondence have been published since her death in 1962, including letters between her and Virginia Woolf. *See also* ORIENTALISM.

SAHELI. Hindi word for an idealized romantic friendship between two women. This term is analogous to the more widely written and talked about concept of *yaari* (for an idealized male friendship and as the slang term *yaar* analogous to the American-English "brother"). The term *saheli* has a long history in literature and culture and has recently been reclaimed by feminist activists in South Asia and the South Asian diaspora. It may be said to decenter the heterosexual definition of women by emphasizing their relationships with each other.

SAKHI. This South Asian word for female companion, denoting either friend or lover, has been claimed by **Giti Thadani** and other lesbian activists in South Asia and the South Asian diaspora. An organization of lesbians and an archive project based in Delhi are called *Sakhi*.

SAND, GEORGE (1804–1876). French writer and personality born Amandine Aurore Lucile Dupin, later Baronet Dudevant by marriage. George Sand was quickly dissatisfied with married life. At a young age she left the country seat of her husband and moved to Paris where she quickly became famous for her independent lifestyle, cross-dressing and numerous sexual affairs. She first wrote journalism for *Le Figaro* and other papers, also coediting the *Revue Indépendente*. Her novels *Valentine* (1832) and *Lelia* (1833) announced her lifelong advocacy of free love and unconventional marriage arrangements that would give women greater power and freedom.

Sand's one well-documented affair with a woman was with the actress Marie Dorval and correspondence between the two is preserved. Graham Robb notes that she reacted with disgust when presented with the idea of sex between two men. In later life Sand became and remained a committed socialist and, after her retirement to the countryside, her later novels focus on peasant life. In all, Sand produced 80 novels and 20 plays. Editions of "complete works" have been published in French since the mid-19th century.

SAPPHIC ODE. This common poetic form refers to poetry composed of quatrains containing three 11-syllable and one five-syllable lines. It has been used by writers (like Algernon Charles Swinburne) who seem to wish specifically to raise the titillating suggestion of lesbian desire and by those (such as Ezra Pound) who may not. Nineteenth- and early 20th-century poets writing in French, such as **Renée Vivien** and **Paul Verlaine**, used a line of 13 syllables referred to as *vers sapphique*.

SAPPHIST. This term was applied to women who loved other women (openly or by reputation) from at least the 18th century. It was used frequently in French (*saphiste*, *saphisme*) and other European languages as well as English. The term implies "follower of **Sappho**," referring to the poet's expressed erotic desires for other women. It was probably also applied, however, to **cross-dressing** women who may or may not have experienced same-sex desires.

SAPPHO (c. 630 B.C.E.–?). Sappho was an aristocratic Greek poet who wrote in the Aeolian dialect and lived on the Mediterranean island of Lesbos. Married to a man, she had numerous romantic and sexual affairs with other women, which are documented in what survives of her work. Though historical facts are scarce, it seems that she held a school or gathering place where wealthy young women made music and **poetry**. Many of the surviving pieces of her poems are fragments of lyric love poems addressed to the young women whom she mentored in this way. The relationships that are visible through this work, together with the extensive literature of male same-sex love from **classical Greece**, illustrate a society in which sexual relationships are constructed as separate from heterosexual marriage, and in which same-sex love, among the upper classes, was idealized.

Sappho was highly respected by other classical scholars. Plato famously referred to her as the "tenth muse." Before the burning of the library at Alexandria, nine collections of her poems existed there. With the rise of patriarchal monotheism Sappho's poetry was increasingly viewed as dangerous and sinful, in its implicit threat to male sexual, familial and social sovereignty. Saint Gregory of Nazianzus first ordered the burning of her work in 380 A.D. and Pope Gregory the VII again ordered that her work be publicly burned in 1073. From 1073 until the 18th century the only fragments of her work that survived were preserved in quotes from other scholars, some of whom changed the gender of the poems' addressees in order to make the female speaker appear heterosexual. The changes were obviated by fragments of printed poems found on strips of paper used as wrappings on mummified bodies in Egypt. The existence of these widely distributed printed versions of her poems testify to Sappho's once tremendous popularity in the ancient Mediterranean world.

Sappho is enormously significant in her own right, having made innovations in poetic meter and form that influenced writers into the early 20th century. These survive as the Sapphic meter and the **Sapphic ode**. She is also significant, however, in that her life and surviving work formed the model for sexually dissident women writers from her own lifetime until the 21st century. The term lesbian, for women who form sexual attachments with other women, is derived from Lesbos, the name of the island on which Sappho lived. From the 17th to the early 20th centuries "Sapphic" referred to any act of, or inclination to, sex between women, and also to any literature that depicted or suggested the same. The focus of European scholars on classical life and literature from the early modern period forward enabled sexually dissident writers to make use of Greco-Roman constructions of sex and sexuality, which allowed them room for the expression of same-sex desires. For lesbians and bisexual women, Sappho is the embodiment of this opportunity. Her historical figure provides a sense of the stability and inevitability of lesbian desires.

SAPPHO WAS A RIGHT-ON WOMAN. In 1972 Sydney Abbot and Barbara Love wrote and published *Sappho Was a Right-On Woman: A Liberated View of Lesbianism*. The cover of the first edition proclaimed it "the first account written by lesbians about themselves and their struggle." The words "liberated" and "struggle" place this book within the context of 1960s and 1970s American liberation movements. This work had a clear purpose as an intervention in early 1970s **feminist** debates. Abbot and Love were members of the group Radicalesbians, which challenged the homophobia inherent in the "mainstream" women's movement. The content of this work dated rapidly as the lesbian-feminist movement developed greater understandings of gender, sexuality, race and history, yet it remains significant as the first major American work to articulate the relationship between lesbianism and feminism.

SARTON, MAY (1912–1995). Belgian-American writer May Sarton first published a group of sonnets that appeared in *Poetry* magazine in 1930. She had lived in both the United States and Europe up until that time, developing an important attachment to her mentor Marie Closset, (founder of the Institut Belge de Culture Française who wrote as Jean Dominique). Her travels brought her into contact with **Hilda Doolittle**, **Bryher**, **Virginia Woolf**, and other important 20th-century literary figures. Her first novel, *The Single Hound*, was published in 1938.

Sarton's 1965 novel *Mrs. Stevens Hears the Mermaids Singing* was perceived to announce her lesbianism to the world. It drew immediate attention from lesbian and other feminists and brought Sarton her most widespread recognition up until that point. Biographical scholarship shows her to have been ambivalent about the reaction to *Mrs. Stevens*. While she was glad of literary attention she saw the "universal" nature of her literary vision as undermined by her categorization as a lesbian writer.

During her lifetime Sarton produced 19 novels, 17 **poetry** collections and a number of nonfiction works, including several memoirs and two children's books. Significant works are *A Shower of Summer Days* (1952), which details, among other things, the desire of an adolescent girl for her kind and passionate aunt, *Plant Dreaming Deep* (1968), a memoir that presents an important defense of the creative abilities of independent single women, the novel *Kinds of Love* (1970), which details the many unrecognized ways in which the members of a small community love each other, and *Journal of a Solitude* (1973), an autobiographical work that is widely taught on women's literature courses. Other autobiographical works that obscurely detail Sarton's lesbian relationships are *The House by the Sea* (1977) and *Recovering* (1980). Some critics believe her most important collection of poetry to be *In Time Like Air* (1958). Susan Sherman has edited the letters that detail one of the most lasting romantic attachments of Sarton's life in the volume *Dear Juliette: Letters of May Sarton to Juliette Huxley*.

SCHOOLS. In 1870 the German **sexologist** Carl Westphal published in his journal a study of a female patient who had a sexual attraction to the students at a girl's boarding school, attaching, in a nonfiction context an identity (medical definition) to a girl whose situation was already a common theme in literature. The sexologist Havelock Ellis believed that sex segregated environments led to the greater expression of same-sex desires. It is certainly true that middle-class women's literature before the mid-20th century expressed romantic and sexual attachments between women most often in the girl's boarding school or women's college setting.

Virginia Woolf's *A Room of One's Own* presents the organization and hardship experienced by those who established the women's colleges at Oxford and Cambridge as an important contribution to the women's movement. These colleges, and others like them, functioned as an important arena for communications and organizing between women, but also as a context for homosocial and homosexual bonding. They also nurtured many great women writers. Historical documentation shows that 19th- and early 20th-century women's schools had a complex set of subcultural practices for expressing various levels of desire between women. Slang terms like "smash" and "rave" were commonly used to talk about these feelings. Both **Charlotte** and **Emily Brontë** seem to have experienced such attachments. Early 20th-century American women's colleges and boarding schools regularly employed female teachers, deans and headmistresses who lived together in same-sex partnerships. The Marxist feminist scholar Dorothy Wolff-Douglas and her partner Katherine Du Pre Lumpkin, who lived and worked at Smith College in the first half of the 20th century, were one such couple.

The paranoia about female relationships depicted in Lillian Hellman's *The Children's Hour* (1939) must be read in the context of this widespread acceptance of female couples at girl's schools and women's colleges. Many novels, such as Mary Patton-Waldron's *Dance on the Tortoise* (1930) and Mary Lapsley's *Parable of the Virgins* (1931), express this kind of fear of the all-female environments of women's schools breeding "unhealthy desires." Other novels, such as **Antonia White**'s *Frost in May* (1933) and **Christa Winsloe**'s *The Child Manuela* (1933) use the girl's school setting as a background for the expression of discontent with gender norms and the heterosexual imperative. **Katherine Tynan**'s autobiography (1919) describes the shining moments of the Irish poet's young life at a convent boarding school as being her physical love for other young women. In 1960s Great Britain, **Brigid Brophy** continued the tradition of the lesbian school girl's novel with *The Finishing Touch* (1963).

SCHULMAN, SARAH (1958–). American journalist, novelist, playwright and AIDS activist. Schulman's first novel was *The Sophie*

Horowitz Story (1984). *Rat Bohemia* (1995) is perhaps the best representation of the body of her work. She works regularly as a journalist in the mainstream press and has produced seven novels and two nonfiction works. One of the latter is the significant *My Gay American History: Lesbian and Gay Life during the Reagan/Bush Years* (1994). As a tool of her AIDS activism, Schulman's work concentrates nearly as much on representations of gay men as on representations of lesbians, and the gay community she presents is unified, though not unproblematic. Schulman lives and works on the Lower East Side of Manhattan and her work is instrumental in the development of the late 20th- and early 21st-century idea of lesbian and gay identity as urban and multicultural.

SCHWABE, TONI (1877–1952). Toni Schwabe was a German poet, feminist and member of Magnus Hirschfield's Scientific Humanitarian Committee. Her 1909 collection *Kom, Kühle Nacht* (*Come, Cool Night*) has some lesbian content and borrows formal and narrative elements from the work of **Pierre Louÿs**. *See also* SEXOLOGY.

SCOTT, SARAH (1723–1795). The English novelist Sarah Scott was a committed intellectual from childhood. At the age of 28 she married, but the marriage lasted barely a year before Scott separated from her husband and set up house on her own. She enjoyed a close, and possibly romantic, friendship with Barbara Montague for many years. Scott's first novel was *History of Cornelia* (1751), written in the year she married. Her sister was the well-known **bluestocking** Elizabeth Montague, and Scott herself had clearly feminist sentiments. These are expressed in *A Journey through Every Stage of Life* (1754) and *The Test of Filial Duty*, in a series of letters (1757). She is best known and most relevant here for *Millenium Hall* (1762), which depicts a microcosmic female utopia. The book is written as a travel narrative from the point of view of a man who happens upon the idyllic all-woman community of Millenium Hall. In it women are portrayed in independent loving partnerships. Scott makes a direct comment on the gender politics of the **romance** novel here, saying that women can have happy endings without marriage.

SCIENCE FICTION. Lesbian science fiction writing in English must date itself from Charlotte Perkins Gilman's 1915 utopian novel *Herland*. Though it does not explicitly depict lesbian sex or romance, *Herland* presents an all female society that has developed from a group of lost colonists after all its men have died. The stranded women develop a facility for parthenogenesis and thus live on through several generations and evolve into a pacifist agricultural society, which is misunderstood by the male explorers who eventually discover it. Though this novel lacks any overt lesbian content, its radical feminist presentation of the sexual and biological freedom available to women exempted from the need to reproduce heterosexually hugely influenced the development of lesbian science fiction.

As a genre, lesbian science fiction (in terms of both prolific lesbian authors and overt lesbian content) emerged in the 1960s and gained momentum in the 1970s. It's most significant event is clearly the publication of **Joanna Russ**'s *The Female Man* in 1975. In using the classic devices of parallel universes and time travel to present lessons about the contingent and constructed nature of gendered and sexualized roles, Russ paved the way for this subgenre, which combined the intellectual pleasures of science fiction with the political goals of **lesbian-feminism**.

Another trajectory in the representation of lesbians in science fiction texts is exemplified by the lesbian **pulp** novel *World without Men* published under the name of Charles Eric Maine in 1958. This novel again presents a female only world (this time futuristic) but emphasizes the biological imperative toward heterosexual sex through the dissatisfaction of its heroine and an eventual heterosexual plot resolution. Thus, in these novels, the dystopic future reinforces a heterosexual worldview. There is, of course, an overlap between pulp fiction and lesbian-authored science fiction.

The feminist writer Marge Piercy is significant for her *Woman on the Edge of Time* (1976), which presents a radical feminist utopia in which, again, childbirth is removed from biological relation and gender difference has become less polarized. As much as this picture seems prolesbian, her homophobic portrait of a **butch** lesbian villain in *He, She and It* (1991, also published as *Body of Glass*) shows Piercy in a less than sympathetic light.

Some important lesbian science fiction writers who have emerged in English since Russ are **Jewelle Gomez**, Elizabeth A. Lynn, writing from the 1970s, and, in the 1980s, Melissa Scott. Jessica Amanda

Salmonson edited the collections *Amazons* (1979) and *Amazons II* (1982), which are important early landmarks.

SECOND-WAVE FEMINISM. This term generally refers to the reemergence of a widely popular feminist movement after World War II. The publication of Betty Friedan's *The Feminine Mystique* in 1963 is generally marked as the beginning of the American Second Wave. In many ways, this conception that **feminism** experienced a lull between the 1930s and the 1960s erases important political and cultural moves made by lesbians and other women in the 1940s and 1950s. Freidan's feminist analysis in *The Feminine Mystique* rests upon a virulently homophobic view of gay men and a feigned ignorance of lesbianism, which is clearly contrary to her own knowledge and life experience as a student and activist in the 1940s. This kind of erasure of the contribution of lesbians to feminist and other political arenas caused an almost immediate rupture within the mainstream movement of the 1960s and early 1970s. Splinter groups like Radicalesbians were formed by 1970 and developed into a vibrant lesbian-feminist movement in their own right.

For the lesbian movement and lesbian literature, the most important innovation of the feminist second wave was that it popularized the idea that biological sex did not determine gender roles, which were in fact culturally and socially constructed. This separation of sex from gender had been explored in **sexology** and lesbian literature throughout the 20th century, but now gained a clear articulation and fairly widespread acceptance.

Literary works associated with the second wave that are of particular significance here are: *Sexual Politics* (1968), a literary study of canonical male writers by the bisexual **Kate Millet**, *The Dialectic of Sex* (1970) by the sexually dissident Shulamith Firestone, which asserted the radical feminist desire to remove the burden of childbirth from women's bodies, and the beginning in 1970 of the publication by the Boston Women's Health Book Collective of many editions of the hugely influential ***Our Bodies, Ourselves***, which included a chapter on lesbianism that sought to make lesbianism a feminist, rather than a medical, issue. Second-wave feminists were also widely influenced by **Simone de Beauvoir**'s 1949 *The Second Sex*, which contains a forthright, though now very dated, chapter on lesbianism.

SENSATION NOVELS. This term is commonly applied to a group of popular, middle-culture works published in England in the 1860s and dealing with crime and intrigue. These novels were clearly influenced by French **decadent** fiction. Sensation novels were not always detective stories, though they contained many elements of what developed into **crime fiction**. The most widely read authors of sensation fiction are Wilkie Collins, Ellen Wood and Mary Elizabeth Braddon. Collins was a good friend of the hugely popular Charles Dickens. Mary Elizabeth Braddon lived with and later married the publisher John Maxwell. Sensation novels are significant here in the first instance in that they dealt, in a less explicit way, with some of the same salacious material treated in penny dreadfuls of the same period. Their plots often include suggestions of incest, bigamy, sexual slavery and "**oriental**" excess that may be associated with homosexuality, though they achieved a recognition somewhat more respectable than novels that were more explicit in their treatment of these themes.

Secondly, sensation novels are particularly concerned with questions of **identity**. Their plots often involve characters masquerading under assumed names, hiding or being kept from the knowledge of marriages or births, looking uncannily like each other, being falsely imprisoned under mistaken identities, etc. These anxieties about identity come at a period just prior to 1870 when the idea of individual identity begins to form around a particularly visible sexual component. In the decade following the 1860s heterosexual and homosexual will be used to apply to individuals for the first time. Sensation fiction highlights a concern with shifting social roles and imminent increases in the legal and economic autonomy of women. Thus the eponymous (anti)heroine of Mary Elizabeth Braddon's *Lady Audley's Secret* embodies both the thrill and the fear of feminine excess. Wilkie Collins' *Armadale*, as Jenny Bourne Taylor demonstrates, contains hints of the policing of female sexual transgression. In some sense, sensation fiction heralds the opening of a space in the popular novel that would be quickly occupied by the lesbian.

SEXOLOGY. The science of human sexuality, which developed from the mid-19th century. Early sexology was most active in Germany where a number of medical researchers dedicated themselves to the study of human "sexual aberrations" from the 1860s. It is from this science that the words heterosexual, homosexual and bisexual derive. Sexology created a language in which women and men could talk about same-sex desires and gender transgressions, but it simultaneously cemented the idea of natural categories from which these desires and transgressions deviated. The English sexologist Havelock Ellis, for example, divided women who desired other women into a number of categories based on their deviation from an accepted ideal of femininity. This idea of same-sex desire as a deviation from femininity assumes that gender and sexual desire are tied to each other — e.g., that **aim** and **object-choice** were at least partially equivalent.

Later historians of gender and sexuality differ in their views of sexology as either a liberating discourse or a damaging medicalization, which had the effect of pathologizing same-sex desires and transgender personalities. In reality sexology did both of these things. As a science it was tremendously influential and, by the 1920s, very widespread in its acceptance as a scientific discipline. Various sexologists aligned themselves and their theories to various political positions, from the socialist views of Edward Carpenter, to the civil rights style activism of Magnus Hirschfeld and his colleagues and the eugenics of Otto Weininger, whose theories found favor with the Nazi regime.

Important German figures in the sexology movement were Karl Westphal (1833–1890), Karl Heinrich Ulrichs (1825–1895), Richard Krafft-Ebing (1840–1902) and Iwan Bloch (1886–1931). Most significant, in terms of both sexology itself and of its relationship to literature, is Magnus Hirschfeld (1868–1935). Hirschfeld was himself a Jewish gay man whose first book, published in 1896, was entitled *Sappho und Sokrates*. (Note the use of **classical Greek** names to signify same-sex desire here). In 1914 Hirschfeld published *Die Homosexualität des Mannes und des Weibes* (*The Homosexuality of Males and Females*). In 1899 he founded the Scientific Humanitarian Committee, with which both **Toni Schwabe** and **Anna Rüling** were involved, along with other writers and feminists who may have been lesbian. In 1919 Hirschfeld formed the Institute for Sexual Sciences. The Institute remained opened and built an extensive archive until 1933, when it was destroyed by a band of Nazi youths. A reported 40,000 items, including 20,000 written documents were lost in this destruction and many reproductions of a photograph showing the Nazis burning books actually depict the burning of the Institute's materials. The sexologist Otto Weininger was more acceptable from a fascist standpoint, as his theories of gender continuity showed non-European cultures as weakened by an excessive femininity. Magnus Hirschfeld is most important here for his journal *Jahrbuch fur sexuelle Zwischenstufen*, published from 1899 until 1923. The 23 volumes of this journal included a regular survey of sexually dissident literature that had been published each year. As such the *Jahrbuch* remains an important historical document for researchers of lesbian literature.

An important Italian figure is Paola Montegazza (1831–1910), who documented many cross-cultural examples of same-sex love while condemning such practices on moral grounds. Two important English figures are Edward Carpenter (1844–1929) and Havelock Ellis (1859–1939). Edward Carpenter was a committed socialist, humanitarian and poet, who published *Homogenic Love and Its Place in a Free Society* in 1895 and *The Intermediate Sex* in 1908. Like Weininger and other German sexologists, Carpenter argued for the existence of an intermediate sex that was gendered between masculinity and femininity. Havelock Ellis published his *Studies in the Psychology of Sex* between 1897 and 1910. Ellis' 1896 *Sexual Inversion*, including the chapter "Sexual Inversion in Women" was published first in German. The book was the object of **censorship** proceedings in England. In his work Ellis popularized the idea of sexual **inversion**, which influenced lesbian literature for decades. The theory of sexual inversion posits that those who desire people of the same sex do so because they are in reality more closely aligned with a sex not corresponding to their body, that is to say that women desire other women because they are psychologically and sometimes physically more like men than they are like "normal women." He explained same-sex desire as what would later be called transgendered or transsexual states of being. The Journal **Urania**, published privately in Great Britain, engaged with many of the same issues raised by sexologists during the same period.

From the outset sexology had a close relation to literature. Many sexologists in the 19th and early 20th centuries cited as many case histories from literary (even fictional) works as they did from patients or respondents. Havelock Ellis's chapter on "Sexual Inversion in Women" refers to several novels and literary biographies and

Hirschfeld's relationship to literature has already been mentioned. From the late 19th century, fiction in French, German and English was being influenced by sensational sexological "discoveries" and theories. Jeannette Foster argues that as early as 1870, Westphal's report on a lesbian woman influenced Adolphe Belot's novel *Mademoiselle Giraud, ma femme*, serialized that same year. Likewise, once sexology gained widespread attention women writers began to use its theories and ideas to define sexually dissident characters. **Radclyffe Hall**'s *The Well of Loneliness* famously used Ellis and Kraft-Ebing's theories of sexual inversion and the writer convinced Havelock Ellis (with some difficulty) to write a preface for the work. **Djuna Barnes**'s *Nightwood* likewise makes use of sexological, as well as **psychoanalytic**, pictures of inversion and same-sex desire. As late as the 1960s, sexologically, as well as more psychoanalytically, derived lesbian character types were used in popular literature.

Sigmund Freud was influenced much more by sexology than is commonly recognized. In his case studies of homosexual and bisexual patients he often refers the reader to Ellis and Krafft-Ebing and a letter to a pained mother about her homosexual son. He assures her that her son is not sick and recommends that she read Havelock Ellis. Essays like "Some Psychical Consequences of the Anatomical Distinction Between the Sexes" and "Psychogenesis of a Case of Homosexuality in A Woman" draw heavily on sexology in their depiction of sexual development and lesbian desire. Though later scholars tend to pit Freud and the sexologists against each other, arguing that sexology saw homosexuality as congenital and psychoanalysts saw it as a developmental issue, each of the two approaches contains elements of both of these explanations. Thus, the sexologically influenced *The Well of Loneliness* depicts its heroine Stephen Gordon as born in an abnormal body, but also as a girl child whose parents wanted a son and often treated her like one.

From the turn of the 20th century, sexology was an active discipline in North America. In 1941 George Henry published his *Sex Variants: A Study of Homosexual Patterns*, which contains 80 life histories of lesbian and bisexual women living in and around New York City. These are of tremendous historical interest and significance. Sexology's most widely known American practitioner was Alfred Kinsey, who published *Sexual Behavior in the Human Female* in

1953. In a public already prepared by the notoriety of *Sexual Behavior in the Human Male* (1948), the response to this study was immediate. Editorials in the popular press decried Kinsey for ignoring "the role of emotion" in female sexuality, though this problem was not raised in response to the male study. This report again had immediate effect on lesbian literature. It is mentioned by Ann Aldrich (**Marijane Meaker**) in *We Walk Alone* (1954) and by one of **Valerie Taylor**'s characters in *Return to Lesbos* (1963).

Sexology most certainly has had a lasting and worldwide influence. In the 1930s Magnus Hirschfeld was heard and well received in India. The Kinsey Institute for the study of human sexuality was established in 1948 and continues into the 21st century, as do centers for sexological research in China. It will be evident that sexology, like other branches of medical/psychological science, has been dominated by male practitioners. However some significant studies were published by women researchers. The German **lesbian feminist** writer Elisabeth Dauthenday wrote the pamphlet *The Uranian Question and Women* in 1906. In 1929 the American researcher Katherine Bement Davis published *Factors in the Sex Life of Twenty-Two Hundred Women*. Two of *Urania*'s most important contributors and editors were feminist life partners **Eva Gore-Booth** and **Esther Roper**. The lesbian scholar **Jeannette Foster** served as a librarian for Alfred Kinsey's projects in the 1940s.

As scientific research, sexological texts were able to talk frankly about any number of sex acts while maintaining a socially acceptable position that sometimes, though not always, protected them from censorship. Much **erotic** literature, from the 17th century onward, posed as medical. The French sexological writer Jacobus X certainly treads the line between science and **pornography**. In the famous "Dora Case," Sigmund Freud states that he knows that some doctors "in this very city" (Vienna) are reading sexual case histories for their own enjoyment. By the 1920s both psychoanalysis and sexology were linked to dissident sexual practices in the public imagination. A thriving **pulp** fiction industry exploited these connections and published many works that posed as medical nonfiction, also reproducing sexological texts in inexpensive paperback form.

However damaging and conservative sexological texts may appear to later readers, it is true that many, though not all, sexologists saw their work as part of a liberal humanitarian mission. Both Havelock Ellis and George Henry argued for tolerance of lesbians, gay men and bisexual people in the prefaces of their work. Magnus Hirschfeld was reportedly so zealous in his pursuit of legal freedoms for homosexuals that he was willing to blackmail other gay men in order to gain their support. Sexology gave lesbian writers of the 20th century a language with which to draw characters and a framework with which to begin to challenge the heterosexual imperative. By the turn of the 21st century the majority of lesbian writers had outgrown the need for this framework.

SEXUAL DISSIDENCE. The term sexual dissidence evolved out of the work of Alan Sinfield and Jonathan Dollimore at the University of Sussex in the 1980s. Its most accessible articulation is in Dollimore's *Sexual Dissidence: Augustine to Wild, Freud to Foucault* (1991). The benefit of this term is that it is historically and culturally flexible, referring to resistance to dominant norms of gender and sexuality, rather than to **identity** positions that may change with time and context.

"SEX WARS." The term "sex wars" refers to a debate around the nature of sexual power and sexual exploitation that took place between American **feminists** during the 1980s. At the same period these issues were debated around the globe in different forms. In 1980 the American group National Organization for Women (NOW) passed a resolution condemning pornography and sado-masochistic (SM) practices. At the same time, many lesbian writers were exploring the nature of sexual power from a position of agency, rather than one of victimization. That is to say, that writers such as **Joan Nestle** and **Pat Califia** were thinking about the ways in which women could empower themselves through a conscious play with sexual positions of power. The **second-wave feminist** view that **pornography** was always disempowering for women was challenged by an emerging lesbian pornography mini-industry, which created images and narratives for consumption by women.

In 1982 the Barnard College (New York) conference series The Scholar and the Feminist held its ninth annual conference, entitled "Towards a Politics of Sexuality." Some of the scheduled papers talked about the subversive and empowering nature of SM practices and **femme-butch** role play. A group of feminists protested, complaining formally to the college and picketing the conference. The issue became one of **censorship** and feminists divided themselves between procensorship and anticensorship camps. The former is best represented by Andrea Dworkin and Catherine MacKinnon, the latter by Nestle and Califia. The debates that followed over the next decade changed the nature of feminism and shifted its focus from the victimization of women to the possibility for female agency and power.

SJÖÖ, MONICA (1938–). Lesbian author, visual artist, radical lesbian activist and proponent of **Goddess** spirituality, Monica Sjöö was born in Sweden but has spent most of her life residing in Great Britain. She is widely known among a generation of lesbian feminists for her book, coauthored with Barbara Mor, *The Great Cosmic Mother: Rediscovering the Religion of the Earth* (1987). She has also written *Return of the Dark, Light Mother* and *The Norse Goddess*. Sjöö's works have been important to the evolution of **Dianic Wicca**.

SMITH, BARBARA (1946–). American activist and race/gender theorist. Barbara Smith has been instrumental in creating a critical and political language for American lesbians of color. Her article "Toward a Black Feminist Criticism" theorizes the relationships among racism, homophobia and sexism. In 1974 she was one of the founding members of the **Combahee River Collective**. She was also a cofounder of Kitchen Table Women of Color Press, which published a large number of highly significant works by black and Latina lesbians. Among these works is the classic, coedited by Smith with Patricia Bell Scott and **Gloria T. Hull**, *All the Women Are White, All the Blacks Are Men, but Some of Us Are Brave* (1981). Smith also edited the collection *Homegirls: A Black Feminist Anthology* (1983) and published a collection of essays entitled *The Truth That Never Hurts: Writings on Race Gender and Freedom* (1998). With Lorraine Bethel she coedited a special issue of the journal *Conditions, Conditions 5: The Black Women's Issue*.

Barbara Smith's politics are antiracist, feminist and socialist. She is well known for her particular definition of **feminism**, in the essay "The Race for Theory":

Feminism is the political theory and practice that struggles to free all women: women of color, working-class women, poor women, disabled women, lesbians, old women—as well as white, economically privileged, heterosexual women. Anything else is not feminism, but merely female self-aggrandizement.

Smith is a fellow at the W. E. B. DuBois Institute for African-American Research at Harvard University.

SOCIAL CONSTRUCTION. The set of sociological theories that come under the heading social constructionist refer to anything from attitudes toward work and marriage to criminal behavior. These theories share the idea that human behavior is determined, shaped and defined by socialization that occurs after birth. In terms of sexual identity then, social construction theory argues that lesbian, bisexual and heterosexual women understand themselves, and are understood as such due to a complicated interaction of learned ideas and behaviors. Social construction then, contradicts the **essentialist** notion that identity is fixed immutably at birth. The most influential theorists in the lesbian and gay studies movement, such as Michel Foucault and **Judith Butler**, share, in the most basic sense, a grounding in a social constructionist position on sexuality.

SÖDERGRAN, EDITH (1892–1923). The poet Edith Södergran was born in Russia to a Swedish-speaking family that also had Finnish connections. Her first poems were written in German but she later wrote exclusively in Swedish. Her first published collection was *Dikter* (1916). Later collections included *Septemberlyran* (*The September Lyre*, 1918), *Rosenaltaret* (*The Rose Altar*, 1919), *Framitidens Skugga* (*Shadow of the Future*, 1920). A volume entitled *Landet Som Icke Ar* was published posthumously in 1925.

SOMERVILLE, EDITH (1858–1949). The Anglo-Irish writer and suffragist Edith Somerville is well known for a number of books published together with her life partner Violet Martin. The meeting and relationship between the two women is described in a memoir by Somerville, *Irish Memories* (1917), written after Martin's death. In their collaborative writings the two women used the male pseudonyms Martin Ross (Martin) and Guilles Herring (Somerville).

Among their published works is the novel *The Real Charlotte* (1894) and the collection of short stories *Some Experiences in the Life of An Irish R. M.* (1899). After Martin's death, Somerville continued to sign her partner's name to her writing, claiming that they collaborated through the medium of automatic writing.

SOR JUANA INÉS DE LA CRUZ (1648–1695). Mexican colonial poet, intellectual and nun born Juana Ramírez de Asbaje. Juana Asbaje was born to a slave-owning family in what is now rural Mexico and sent to Mexico City to live with relatives at a young age. There she was introduced at the court of the colonial viceroy and later took vows at the Carmelite convent of San Jeronimo. She was a precocious child who apparently astonished her elders with her facility for Latin and rhetoric. Once at San Jeronimo she became a respected intellectual and well-published author of plays, treatises and poems, studying mathematics, philosophy and natural science. As Sor Juana Inés de la Cruz, she is notable here for her love poems, written to Maria Luisa, condesa de Paredes in the 1680s. Addressed as "Phyllis," "Lysi" and "Lisida" in the poems, Maria Luisa was the wife of the colonial viceroy and seems to have returned Sor Juan's affections. Sor Juan Inés de la Cruz remains a Latin American feminist icon best known for the open letter titled "Repuesta a Sor Filetea" (1691). This letter was a reply to an open criticism against her made by an unsympathetic bishop writing under the female pseudonym "Sor Filotea." It articulates a humanist defense of the intellectual rights of women and a personal defense of Sor Juan's involvement in "worldly affairs" in spite of her Carmelite vows.

SOUTH ASIAN LITERATURE. Though largely unrecognized both inside and outside of South Asia, a vibrant tradition of female same-sex desire exists in ancient South Asian literature and in contemporary literature of South Asia and the South Asian diaspora. **Giti Thadani** documents the covering of ancient stories of female same-sex desire with later myths and stories. Her work seeks to create a tradition of what might be called lesbian desire and identity stretching back thousands of years. Like Charlene Spretnak's *Lost Goddesses of Early Greece* (1992), Thadani's *Sakhiyani* (1996) argues that an earlier mythology of a "gynofocal cosmos" was overtaken by an invading culture with patriarchal gods. Her work presents evidence of this earlier worldview within surviving myth structures and in ancient artifacts, and documents the imposition of patriarchal heterosexuality. In the earliest of the ancient Vedic texts, the *Rig Veda* (1500 B.C.E.), Thadani argues for a cover-up of nonheterosexual relations between women and of a feminine, nonprocreative sexuality.

South Asia's ancient Laws of Manu (*Manavdharamshastra*), codified between 400 B.C.E. and 300 A.C.E., differ from Middle Eastern (including biblical) texts of the same period in that they show a clear recognition of lesbian sexual practices. The *Manavdharamshastra* names two sets of punishments for what it sees as the unnatural vice of sex between two women. Punishment is more severe if sex takes place between women from different social classes (castes). The great Sanskrit text, the *Mahabharata*, presents **cross-dressing** and transgender female characters, such as Amba whose marriage prospects are ruined by an abduction. After a great deal of prayerful devotion Amba is reincarnated as a female to male transgender person who, in male form can have his revenge on her abductor Bishma. This story is consciously echoed in **Bankim Chandra Chatterji**'s revolutionary novel *Anandamath* (1882) with its cross-dressing warrior heroine.

The 11th-century story of *Kalingasena,* reproduced by Vanita and Kidwai in *Same-Sex Love in India* (2000), tells of a young girl who is courted by a married female celestial being. The two women can only carry on their affair while Kalingasena remains unmarried. Their sad parting before her wedding is the climax of the tale. The original of this story exists in a compendium called *Kathasaritsagara* and is attributed to one Samadeva Bhatta.

In the 20th century the scandal surrounding the Urdu woman writer Ismat Chugtai's story **"The Quilt"** is a notable event. A number of stories of girl's **school** romances, published throughout the 20th century, parallel traditions in other parts of the world. A Hindi story of romantic friendship called "*Sharadi*" ("Farewell") was published in May 1938 in the *Kanya Mahavidyalaya* college paper at Jalandar. Vanita notes the strong woman-centered feminist influence evident in the paper and the many unmarried women who worked there in the early 20th century. Shobana Siddique's midcentury Hindi story "Full to the Brim" and the Malayalam male author V. T. Nandakumar's novel *Two Girls* (1974) are also notable examples of lesbian school romances. *Two Girls* achieved instant notoriety. In 1970 the Punjabi woman writer Kewal Sood published the novel *The Hen Coop*. The extended allegory of a group (or groups) of hens who live without a cock and produce sterile eggs forms the moral background for this tale of predatory lesbian seduction. A woman called Sheela is seduced into lesbian life by an older woman, who manages her student hostel. She in turn seduces her servant in later life. At the climax of the novel, Sheela murders her original seducer.

In the preface to her *Facing the Mirror*, **Ashwini Sukthankar** pointedly distances herself from Thadani's historical project. Sukthankar argues that lesbians in South Asia and in South Asian communities must use all available energy to focus on present realities and difficulties. She then presents a vibrant and diverse collection of contemporary lesbian writing from India. In the 21st century several newsletters are produced within South Asia and South Asian diasporic communities. *Shamakami* is published on the subcontinent, as is *Freedom*. The *Trikone* (triangle) organization, based in San Francisco, publishes a newsletter addressing South Asian lesbians and gay men worldwide. *See also* DE, SHOBHA; KAMA SUTRA; KAMANI, GINU; MOOTOO, SHANI; NAMJOSHI, SUNITI.

SOUTHERN GOTHIC. The term Southern Gothic generally applies to fiction and plays produced by writers from the southern United States from the 1930s. William Faulkner and Eudora Welty are among the most well-known writers in the genre. The term borrows from European Gothic fiction a sense of the horrific and the grotesque. Southern Gothic fiction often shares a sense of painful and traumatic history with "classic" European Gothic fiction. Most often, however, critics who use the term Southern Gothic use it to denote fiction that contains "freakish" characters and a sense of, as Eve Kosofsky Sedgwick has said, the Gothic more generally, "being massively cut off from the self."

Within the wider tradition of Southern Gothic, a number of white lesbian and gay male writers developed a specifically **queer** style of narration that presented a particular view of southern race/gender hierarchies. Their characters are often "freakish" and alienated due to an inability to conform properly to their assigned gender roles. Writers like Flannery O'Connor and **Carson McCullers** present female characters who refuse to conform to the feminine roles assigned to them. Considering that southern racial violence often rested upon the false idea of the need to protect "pure," feminine and helpless white women, we might see the refusal on the part of these writers to present these kinds of women as a specific protest against racial violence. Thus southern Gothic fiction marries **sexual dissidence** in women to the struggle for racial freedom.

STEIN, GERTRUDE (1874–1946). American writer of prose and poetry famous for her influence on the modernist movement. Gertrude Stein was born in Pennsylvania but spent her later life in Paris with her lifelong partner **Alice B. Toklas** with whom she set up house around 1910. The Stein family was wealthy and well traveled and the death of their parents left Gertrude and her brothers and sisters independent when she was still an adolescent. Stein briefly attended Radcliffe College before enrolling at Johns Hopkins University as a medical student and researcher. While at Johns Hopkins she associated with a circle of feminists who attended Bryn Mawr and Smith Colleges for women.

Between World War I and World War II, Stein and Toklas set up a house in Paris where many writers and artists congregated and shared ideas. Stein (along with her brother Leo) was an important collector of modern art and many critics discuss the relationship between Cubist techniques in visual art and Stein's literary innovations, particularly in *Three Lives* (1909) and *Tender Buttons* (1911). She anticipated late 20th-century philosophical innovations with her exploration of the way in which language signifies meaning. The work that Stein produced in the middle period of her writing life pursues this question of language and signification and thus often unhooks sound from meaning. This has given Stein a reputation for difficulty of access as a writer.

The lesbian content of Stein's work is most obvious in the novel *Things as They Are* (first published in 1951). This largely autobiographical work details Stein's early relationship with May Bookstaver. It was originally written in 1903 as *QED* but kept from publication until after the writer's death. "Melanctha," one of three stories in the volume *Three Lives* is said to translate the story of Stein's affair with another woman into the love affair between two heterosexual black Americans. Stein thus, from a white perspective, transferred the difference of lesbian desire onto racial difference. *The Autobiography of Alice B. Toklas* (1932) is in reality Stein's autobiography, though the title bears her partner's name and uses Toklas as a fictionalized narrator. Naiad press posthumously published a collection of Stein's poems entitled *Lifting Belly*, which contains **erotica** addressed to Toklas. Also notable is the libretto that Stein wrote for an Opera called *The Mother of Us All* (1947), based on the life of the American feminist (and, some say, lesbian) Susan B. Anthony.

STRACHEY, DOROTHY (1865–1960). The English writer Dorothy Strachey was born into a talented, intellectual family. Her brothers were the writer and member of the **Bloomsbury Group**, Lytton Strachey, and James Strachey, the first English translator of **Sigmund Freud**. Her sister Joan Strachey was an academic who became principal of Newnham College Cambridge. Dorothy Strachey is significant here for her novel *Olivia*, which was first published in 1949, but was written much earlier. *Olivia* fictionalized the author's schoolgirl love for her headmistress, Marie Souvestre. Souvestre ran a fashionable French boarding school, which Eleanor Roosevelt also attended. *Olivia* was adapted for the screen by **Colette** in 1951, and remains an important historical example of postwar French cinema and of the history of lesbian desire on the screen. The novel is one of a handful of lesbian novels that many English-speaking lesbians remember reading in the postwar period.

STRINDBERG, AUGUST (1849–1912). Swedish playwright, novelist and notorious misogynist. August Strindberg is well respected as a literary figure both in and outside of Sweden, despite his virulently antifeminist views. His first marriage to Siri von Essen broke up after numerous affairs including one that von Essen had with a woman called Marie Caroline David. After this break-up Strindberg vented his anger in the 1887–1888 novel *Confessions of a Fool*. The later play *Fröken Julie* (*Miss Julie*) also treated women who upset the "natural" order of male and female gender roles. The novel and play are significant in being an early misogynist view that directly equated female emancipation with lesbian "vice."

SUKHTHANKAR, ASHWINI (1974–). The Indian editor and journalist Ashwini Sukthankar was born in Mumbai (Bombay), but has lived throughout the South Asian diaspora. In 1999 she broke ground with her edited collection *Facing the Mirror: Lesbian Writing in India*. Sukthankar has also published articles on South Asian lesbian identity and the South Asian lesbian rights movement in *The New Internationalist* and other journals.

SWENSON, MAY (1919–1989). American poet May Swenson taught poetry at a number of U.S. colleges and universities, beginning with Bryn Mawr women's college. After a period of publishing in magazines she brought out her first collection of poems, *Another Animal*, in 1954. In all there exist 11 collections of her work, of which three are posthumous. Throughout her life she wrote many explicitly lesbian erotic poems. This theme is combined with a deep sense of communion with the natural world. The final collection published during her lifetime was *In Other Words* (1987). Swenson served as chancellor of the Academy of American Poets from 1980 until 1989.

SWINBURNE, ALGERNON CHARLES (1837–1909). English **decadent** poet. Swinburne is associated with the Pre-Raphaelite movement and well known for the sado-masochistic fantasies depicted in his **poetry**. His controversial collection *Poems and Ballads* (1886) contained a number of poems that depicted lesbian desire. One poem, "Anactoria," is narrated in the voice of **Sappho**. In it the poet addresses her female lover and describes a series of erotic fantasies. Swinburne was greatly influenced by the French poet **Charles Baudelaire**, and displays a similar Gothic decadence. He is less well known for an unfinished, untitled novel usually referred to as *Lesbia Brandon*, after the name of its main character, a cross-dressing **sapphist**. An addition of this incomplete manuscript, with commentary, was edited by Randolph Hughes and published by Falcon Press in 1952.

– T –

TAYLOR, VALERIE (1913–1997). American writer born Velma Young. Valerie Taylor was a prolific writer of popular fiction and a woman active in creating support networks for American lesbian writers. She published poetry as Nacella Young, lesbian fiction as Valerie Taylor and Gothic romances as Frances Davenport. Taylor cofounded Mattachine Society's Midwestern branch in 1965 and the **Lesbian Writers' Conference** in Chicago in 1974.

As Valerie Taylor, Young produced a number of **lesbian pulp** classics for Fawcett publications. These novels are remarkable in their broadly socialist, feminist and antiracist agenda. Taylor placed the lesbian in the greater context of the social tapestry of the postwar United States. Her works show the clear influence of, or solidarity with, the radical leftist politics of early founding members of the Mattachine Society.

Among the best known of her lesbian novels are *The Girls in 3-B* (1959) and *Stranger on Lesbos* (1960). Three of her novels—*A World without Men*, *Journey to Fullfillment* and *Return to Lesbos*—were reprinted by Naiad press in the early 1980s. A collection of Taylor's papers, covering the years from 1923 to 1997, is housed at Cornell University in Ithaca, New York. *See also* HOMOPHILE MOVEMENT.

TEASDALE, SARA (1884–1933). American poet Sara Teasdale wrote poems to express romantic desire for women throughout her life. She carried on romantic friendships with Marion Cummings Stanley and Margaret Conklin, as well as one 15-year marriage.

As a young woman Teasdale founded a group calling itself the Potter's Circle with other women poets in St. Louis. They published a journal for a brief period. Her first volume of poetry, *Sonnets to Duse and Other Poems* (1907) contained a number of sonnets addressed to the actress Eleonora Duse (1858–1924). She later moved to Chicago where she became involved with the editors of *Poetry* magazine. Many of her later poems were addressed pseudonymously to other women.

Among Teasdale's collections of **poetry** are *Rivers to the Sea* (1915), *Flame and Shadow* (1920) and *Dark of the Moon* (1926). She won a number of prizes including the Columbia University Poetry Society Prize (1918), which would later become the Pulitzer Prize for poetry. She suffered from depression throughout her life and died of an overdose of prescription drugs in 1933.

TEY, JOSEPHINE (1896–1952). Scottish **crime** writer born Elizabeth Mackintosh set her 1946 mystery *Miss Pym Disposes* in a girl's **school**. The culture of "crushes" and "raves" (same-sex romantic attachments) is well documented here. The cover-up of accidental murder in this book is the result of one woman's love for another. The protagonist of *To Love and Be Wise* (1950) appears to be a gay man but turns out to be a transgendered woman in love with her female cousin.

THADANI, GITI. Indian activist, educator and writer Giti Thadani is the author of *Sakhiyani: Lesbian Desire in Ancient and Modern India* (1996) and founder of Sakhi, a Delhi lesbian collective. *Sakhiyani* (Hindi for girlfriends) is based on Thadani's extensive traveling research throughout India. Her work aims to identify, preserve and share knowledge of ancient visual art (mainly of a sacred nature) which represents sexual love between women. She has described herself as a scholar of "liminal sexualities," thus both identifying a set of sexual practices that are situated in relation to a dual system of sexuality and creating more complexity than a simple appropriation of the term lesbian would. Thadani identifies a relationship between the erasure of historical desire between women and a contemporary culture of misogyny that affects women of all sexual identities. Her involvement in local education programs throughout India focuses on this connection.

THE TOAST. *See* EARLY MODERN PERIOD.

TOKLAS, ALICE B. (1877–1967). American hostess of a modernist salon in Paris in the 1920s and 1930s. Alice B. Toklas is best known for **Gertrude Stein**'s 1933 work *The Autobiography of Alice B. Toklas*, which presents events in Stein's life using Toklas as a fictional narrator. Toklas was born to a Jewish family in San Francisco and moved to Paris after the turn of the century. There she met Stein and quickly established their salon. They played hostess to, and influenced, many of the most noted writers of the **modernist** movement.

Toklas published the celebrated volume *The Alice B. Toklas Cookbook*, containing autobiographical material as well as recipes, in 1954. In 1963 she published a memoir *What Is Remembered*. She lived closely with Stein from the time they met until Stein's death, so that little extended correspondence exists. Their domestic notes to each other have been edited and published by Kaye Turner. These, together with Stein's erotic poetry, published by Naiad as *Lifting Belly*, reveal a full and complex lesbian relationship in which Stein and Toklas thought of (and referred to) each other as husband and wife, respectively.

TORRES, TORESKA. French-born writer Toreska Torres, daughter of the sculptor Mazek Szwarc, is best known for her novel *Women's Barracks* (1950). Torres herself served with the Free French Forces at the age of 18 and the novel details a variety of lesbian relationships which take place in the women's army. Its eventual resolution is heterosexual and its horrified focus is largely on a predatory and "perverse" older bisexual woman. Some lesbian and gay literature resources claim Torres as a lesbian. There is no evidence for this and the novel does not provide evidence of any real familiarity with the lesbian subject-position or with 1940s lesbian subculture. She was, however, married to the playwright Myer Levin, to whom she is said to have introduced *The Diary of Anne Frank* in French translation. Thus Torres might be indirectly credited with the diary's entry into English.

Women's Barracks was a best-seller for Fawcett Publishing's Gold Medal line and this led to the expansion of its interests in producing **lesbian pulp** fiction. It was also the subject of censorship efforts by the so-called "Gathings Committee," a U.S. congressional committee that was set up at the end of 1952 to investigate "obscenity" in the mass-market publishing industry. For these reasons the novel stands out in the historical record and it has received attention from historians of lesbian literature in the late 20th century.

TRAGEDY. Tragedy is a mode of narrative first highly developed in **classical Greek** drama in which a serious theme and an unhappy ending are intended to elevate the sensibilities of an audience. It is a commonplace assertion that lesbian and gay narratives exist in the tragic mode more often than in any other. While gay male writers of the 20th and 21st centuries sometimes reiterate the tragic mode with ironic camp inflection, lesbian drama and fiction does not often make this move.

There are two reasons for this equation of lesbian literature with tragedy, representing two different, but related, authorial positions. First, the tragic mode evokes the emotion of sympathy more than any other. When **Radclyffe Hall** wrote *The Well of Loneliness* she intended it as a plea for the acceptance of "inverted" women. She felt the need, in her quest for sympathy, to have her hero, the congenitally inverted Stephen Gordon, end the novel tragically alone, having given up her "less inverted" lover to a man. This in spite of the fact that Hall's own life experience, and that of many of her friends, showed this sacrifice to be unnecessary. The sympathy engendered by the tragic mode has served a political purpose for lesbian writers.

Secondly, the tragic endings of so many lesbian narratives serve to punish lesbian and bisexual characters for their "immoral" transgressions. Traditionally the most basic and popular of narrative structures reward "good" characters and punish "bad" ones. Thus, in the 19th and early 20th centuries, lesbian sex was more acceptable, and could sometimes escape censorship, if it took place in the middle of the narratives between characters who were punished at the end. So the heroines of both **Patricia Highsmith**'s *The Price of Salt* and **Ann Bannon**'s *Journey to a Woman*, must give up any hope of ever seeing their children again in order to lead lesbian lives. Bannon's character Vega Purvis, from *Journey to a Woman* is a classic tragic lesbian figure. Unable to control her desires, her marriage or her alcoholism, she possesses a horribly scarred body and a criminally insane mind. Bannon's innovation is to center her novel not on Purvis, but on a lesbian character who escapes Purvis and manages to establish a lesbian life for herself beyond the end of the novel.

Heather K. Love suggests that lesbian tragedy is not merely a form of internalized homophobic punishment. She argues that the tragic mode in its lesbian form enables writers to express "the exclusionary regimes of the modern," in other words that the figure of the tragic lesbian is a powerful figure that exemplifies the alienation at the core of the modern condition.

TRANSGENDER. In the late 20th century the term transgender came into use among activists and (less often) medical/psychological professionals to refer to individuals who did not conform to the accepted norms of male or female roles that they had been assigned at birth. The idea that biological sex should automatically determine a person's gender **identity** has been challenged by a growing transgender movement. The female-to-male transgender movement, in 19th- and early 20th-century literary figures like **George Sand** and **Radclyffe Hall**, was associated with both **feminism** and lesbianism. After the advent of the transgender movement a more complex analysis of the relationships among gender, sex and sexuality has separated these transgressive positions theoretically, though in individuals and in political strategy they exist in any number of combinations. Kate Bornstein's important book *Gender Outlaw* has been tremendously influential in the transgender movement. Authors such as **Leslie Feinberg** articulate a transgender history that is intertwined with **femme-butch** lesbian culture of the mid-20th century.

TRANSSEXUAL. In the 19th century, terms like "sexual intermediate" referred to what early 20th-century people would call lesbians and gay men. The word transsexual, from the late 20th century, is used to refer to people whose bodies, either by choice or by birth, do not conform to a strict female/male binary. The term intersex is also sometimes used to distinguish people whose biological sex at birth is neither male nor female. The American-British writer Del LaGrace Volcano has been instrumental in articulating a female-to-male transsexual identity in both academic and popular literature.

TRANSVESTITE. In 19th-century literature this term referred to **cross-dressing** people (people who wear clothing normally associated with the "opposite" sex) who were also assumed to experience same-sex desires. In later 20th-century English, the term, among theorists and activists at least, has been largely replaced by the terms cross-dresser and transgender. In Italian, Portuguese, French and Spanish the term *travesti* still persists, usually to describe male-to-female transgender people.

TREFUSIS, VIOLET (1886–1968). Violet Trefusis is best known for her affair with the writer **Vita-Sackville West**. She was an upper-class English debutante whose family traveled in the same circles as the Sackville-Wests and both before and after their marriages the two women eloped together. Sackville-West wrote a novel, *Challenge*, detailing their relationship. **Virginia Woolf** acknowledged in correspondence that her novel *Orlando* was in part based on the Trefusis/Sackville-West relationship. Critics identify the Sasha episode in the novel, during which the transgender heroine is a man, as referring specifically to Sackville-West's affair with Trefusis.

Trefusis' letters to Vita reveal her to have been unhappy in her marriage and deeply in love with Vita. These letters detail only Violet's side of the correspondence, as her family burned Vita's letters in an attempt to quash the history of the affair. Trefusis' letters are collected and published as *Violet to Vita: The Letters of Violet Trefusis to Vita Sackville-West* (1989), edited by Mitchel A. Leaska and John Phillips.

TRIBADE. Noun for a woman who loves other women sexually. The English word tribade is attributed by the *Oxford English Dictionary* to two distinct Greek and Latin roots. The first is the verb *to rub*, which denotes the marking of lesbian sex as sex in the absence of the phallus. The second is a noun for *lewd woman*. Tribade was used more frequently than **sapphist** in the late 17th and 18th centuries to denote women who might be called lesbian today. It appears in literature until the mid-20th century, when it begins to appear more frequently as the verbal noun tribadism, which denotes a particular sexual practice, rather than the **identity** position it referred to in earlier centuries.

TROUBRIDGE, UNA (1887–1963). Born Una Elena Taylor, Troubridge is best known as the dynamic and influential life partner of the writer **Radclyffe Hall**, with whom she spent the last 28 years of Hall's life. Lesbian-**femme** critics argue that she is less visible to history than Hall because of her femme position in their relationship. She was working as a sculptor before her marriage and had a tremendous social presence in upper-class London, where she was known for her beauty and intelligence. Una Troubridge is of literary importance in her own right. She was the driving force behind Hall's literary career, developing and maintaining crucial contacts and herself making the ultimate decision to publish the novel for which Hall is most famous, *The Well of Loneliness*. She was also the first person to translate the works of **Colette** into English. Troubridge published *The Life and Death of Radclyffe Hall* (1961) after her partner's death. The couple's papers, saved by Troubridge, are now housed largely at the University of Texas at Austin. Included in this collection are Troubridge's day books and diaries, which describe the life of the two writers in minute detail.

TYNAN, KATHERINE (1861–1931). Irish nationalist poet and novelist Katherine Tynan is now best remembered for her friendship with the poet W. B. Yeats, and sadly ignored in her own right. Though the majority of her work contains little if any lesbian content, her autobiography (1919) describes intense and passionate same-sex attachments that Tynan and her classmates formed in their convent **school**. These relationships are painted by Tynan in a favorable, even an idealized, light. It may be that she never conceived of them as sexual.

– U –

URANIA. The classically derived term Urania denotes heaven and heavenly inspiration. The **early modern** poet Milton famously invokes Urania as his muse in *Paradise Lost*. **Uranian** was the term used in Plato's *Symposium* to denote a pure and heavenly same-sex (trans-generational) love, which was opposed to earthly and sullied heterosexual love.

For this and other reasons, *Urania* was the name taken by a transgender journal published in England between 1915 and 1940. The journal was edited and often largely written by the male-to-female transgendered writer Thomas Baty (1869–1954), who generally identified herself as Irene Clyde in print. Two other important contributors were the feminists and life-partners **Eva Gore-Booth** and **Esther Roper**. The mission of *Urania* was a gender free society, which its editors believed was both a natural and desirable outcome of the evolutionary process. Alison Oram quotes the mission statement printed in each issue:

> *Urania* denotes the company of those who are firmly determined to ignore the dual organization of humanity [i.e., maleness and femaleness] in all its manifestations. They are convinced that this duality has resulted in the formation of two warped and imperfect types. They are further convinced that in order to get rid of this state of things no measures of "emancipation" and "equality" will suffice, which do not begin by a complete refusal to recognize or tolerate the duality itself.

The journal features a number of articles and stories on female same-sex desire as evidence that gender roles were not biologically determined and were, in any case, naturally breaking down.

Oram argues that the editors and contributors to *Urania* were consciously opposed to the science of **sexology**, which was becoming increasingly popular during the decades of its publication. While it is true that *Urania*'s gender politics were more radical than those of scientific writers like Havelock Ellis, they probably ought to be viewed more as part of a complex debate in which each of the voices enabled and enriched the other, whether through concord or through opposition. It seems unlikely that the title *Urania* did not draw, at least partially, upon the increasingly popular term **Uranian** for same-sex (mostly male) desire coined by Karl Heinrich Ulrichs, a sexologist.

URANIAN. This term was coined by the gay male **sexological** writer Karl Heinrich Ulrichs (1825–1895), who wrote largely about male same-sex desire, which he viewed as pure and elevated in the **classical Greek** sense. The German word that Ulrichs used was *Urning*, which crossed over into English as Uranian. The name was also applied to what would now be called lesbian or bisexual women, as articles in Magnus Hirschfeld's *Jahrbuch fur sexuelle Zwischenstufen* show. The term remained in use sporadically until the mid-20th century.

– V –

VAID, URVASHI (b. 1958). Indian-American lawyer, activist and writer. Urvashi Vaid has been active in the antiwar and prisoner's rights movements as well as being a driving force behind the United States Lesbian and Gay political lobby. She cofounded the Boston Lesbian/Gay Political Alliance and worked with the National Lesbian and Gay Task Force from 1985, holding the executive directorship from 1989. Her book *Virtual Equality: The Mainstreaming of Gay and Lesbian Liberation* (1995) examines the problems inherent in a liberal politics of Lesbian and Gay liberation and argues for a broad-based movement with an awareness of issues of race, **class** and gender. Her liberal analysis is summed up in her assertion that, regarding legitimization and liberation, "the former makes it possible to imagine the latter."

VAMPIRE FICTION. The first representation of a lesbian vampire in English fiction is generally agreed to be that of the Irish writer Sheridan Le Fanu's (1814–1873) *Carmilla*. This story was first published in 1872. The story is set in Eastern Europe and follows the tradition of Eastern European settings and folkloric sources for the vampire narrative. Its heroine and narrator is a young girl of 19, who is plagued by the eponymous vampire. Carmilla's advances are both sinister and erotic. One scene between Carmilla and the narrator runs thus:

> How beautiful she looked in the moonlight!
> Shy and strange was the look with which she quickly hid her face in my neck and hair, with tumultuous sighs, that seemed almost to sob, and pressed in mine a hand that trembled.
> Her soft cheek was glowing against mine. "Darling, darling," she murmured, "I live in you; and you would die for me, I love you so."

Sue-Ellen Case argues that the relation between gay people and monstrous entities, especially vampires, derives from the view that heterosexual sex is procreative—life-giving—and same-sex activity is by opposition associated with death. In addition, the vampire's mouth is an orifice with teeth and seen by many as a kind of *vagina dentata*, therefore representing the threat of the phallic woman in much the same way that the lesbian does.

Jewelle Gomez's novel *The Gilda Stories* (1991) reverses the association of lesbians and vampires with horror and death. Her story presents lesbian vampires who do not kill their victims but simply put them into a kind of trance and drink their blood, leaving pleasant dreams and visions in exchange. *Minimax* (1992), an interesting example by Ann Olivia, uses **Natalie Clifford Barney** and **Renée Vivien** as lesbian vampire characters. One thing that the figure of the long-lived vampire allows the writer to do is to celebrate a sense of lesbian literary history by bringing historical figures back from the dead. With the late 20th-century advent of powerful and active Gothic heroines, lesbian vampire fiction became a thriving subgenre of the Gothic, enjoying a modest publishing success.

VAUDÈRE, JANE DE LA. This is possibly the pseudonym of a woman called Mademoiselle Crapez. In any case, throughout the 1890s and the first decade of the 1900s a number of sensational novels in French were published under the name Jane de La Vaudère. These novels cover the gamut of popular sensational topics from **orientalism** through sexual deviance. Her novels, many of which are described as *"romans passionels,"* include *Le Harem de Syta* (1895), *Le*

Mystère de Kama (1901) and *La Cité des Sourires* (1907). Most relevant here are the 1897 novel *Les Demi-Sexes* and *Les Androgynes* (1902). **Rachilde** reviewed *Les Demi-Sexes* in *Mercure de France*, decrying its false medical pose. This review highlights the growing relationship between sexology and lesbian fiction, both sensational and "serious."

VENARD, CÉLESTE, COMTESSE DE CHABRILLAN (1824–1909). Céleste Venard lived and worked as a courtesan in 19th-century Paris. She published memoirs of her life as a courtesan in 1854 and again in 1858. Recently these memoirs have been translated into English and published as *The French Consul's Wife: Memoirs of Céleste de Chabrillan in Gold Rush Australia* (1998) and *Memoirs of a Courtesan in Nineteenth-Century Paris* (2003). According to **Jeannette Foster**, a woman using this name wrote something called *Le Sappho*. Foster's source is Lewanowski in *Das Sexual Probleme* in 1858.

VERLAINE, PAUL (1844–1896). The 19th-century French poet Paul Verlaine followed the **decadent** tradition that figured lesbians as figures of fascinating and sinful excess. Verlaine was himself the lover of the poet Arthur Rimbaud, whom he spent time in prison for wounding with a gun. He is significant here for the collection published in France in 1884 as *Parallèlment*, which pursues a lesbian theme. Like other French authors fearing censorship, Verlaine first had these poems printed in Brussels, where they appeared in 1867 as *Scènes d'amour saphique*.

VERS SAPHIQUE. See SAPPHIC ODE.

VICE VERSA. See BEN, LISA; JOURNALISM.

VIVIEN, RENÉE (1877–1909). The writer known as Renée Vivien was born Pauline Tarn to an American mother and an English father. Vivien spent most of her childhood in France and returned there from England when she came of age after her father's death. Independent wealth allowed Vivien to pursue a life as an avowed sapphist who wrote openly about her love for women. She lived in Paris from 1898 until the end of her life but also maintained other homes, including one on the island of Lesbos.

Renée Vivien's mother made an attempt to have her declared insane when Vivien was still under age. It is not clear whether this had anything to do with the young woman's feelings for other women. Most biographer's see it as an attempt to gain control of her inheritance. Vivien did have a romantic relationship with Violet Shillito as a young woman. Her most celebrated relationship is with the American writer **Natalie Clifford Barney**. By all accounts this was a very difficult and passionate partnership and in one of its cessuras Vivien had an affair with a member of the Rothschild family named Baroness Hélène Zuylon de Nyevelt, with whom she collaborated on a number of works under the pseudonym Paule Riversdale. There also exists a passionate correspondence with a Turkish woman, then living in Istanbul, called Kérimé Turkhan-Pacha. Barney and Vivien founded a salon for women writers often called "**The Academy of Women**," which Barney carried on after Vivien's death and which included at various times **Colette**, **Gertrude Stein**, Romaine Brooks, **Djuna Barnes**, **Lucie Delaru-Mardrus**, **Rachilde** and **Elisabeth de Gramont**.

Vivien is best known for her symbolist **poetry**. Early on in her life her style was in tune with the poetic innovations of her day. She continued to work in the symbolist mode after other poets had moved on to new innovations and for this reason, and for an increasing openness about her gender and her sexuality, she was less respected as time went on. Early collections of her work were published under the name R. Vivien, and later as Rene Vivien (the masculine form of her name) disguising her identity as a female poet. By the time she began signing her work as Renée Vivien, thus announcing her gender, she was already a celebrated poet. Among her many collections of poems are *Études and préludes* (1901), *Brumes de fjords* (1902), *Cendres et poussières* (1902), *Évocations* (1903), *Du vert au Violet* (1903), *Les Vénus des aveugles* (1904) and *A l'heure de mains jointes* (1906).

Vivien constructed her own sexual identity after the model of **Sappho** (whom she referred to, according to the classically correct form, as Psappha). On a trip to the United States she and Natalie Barney began the study of classical Greek at Bryn Mawr College for women, and they continued with a private classical tutor after their return to

Paris. In 1903 Vivien translated Sappho into modern French and also presented her own adaptations of the poems, using the volume to recreate the school that Sappho led at Mytelene. Both Vivien's house at Lesbos and the Academy of Women in Paris were attempts to recreate this woman-centered space where romantic and sexual love between women was open and valued. In 1904 Vivien published her modern French translations of eight Greek women poets as *Les Kitarèdes*. She expressed her ideas about gender and sexuality through the idea of the "gynandromorph," which she saw as a kind of feminine, but sexless, idealized being. Vivien was a pioneer of the idea that women needed to reclaim figures from cultural history in order to create stronger mythical structures through which to imagine themselves and their lives. In various writings she rewrote the traditional stories of the apocryphal figure of Lilith and the biblical Vashti, both of whom she presents as defiant women who refuse to submit to the control of powerful male figures.

Vivien published fiction, biography and criticism as well as poetry. She made multiple contributions to the feminist journal *La Fronde*, edited by Marguerit Durand. In 1904 she published the novel *Une femme m'apparut* (*A Woman Appeared to Me*), which drew extensively on her own life. This was translated into English by **Jeanette Foster** and published by Naiad Press in 1976. Just before her death in 1909, Vivien published a biography of Ann Boleyn.

In 1906, after the publication of *A l'heure des mains jointes*, Vivien suffered increasing public scrutiny. Her health suffered and she became more and more reclusive. Many friends told stories of her drawn curtains and dark rooms, as well as her increasing dependence on alcohol and her refusal to eat. She had suffered from depression throughout her life and had attempted suicide more than once. She died of alcoholism and anorexia in 1909. Vivien's character and life are depicted by her contemporary and acquaintance Colette, in *The Pure and the Impure* (1932).

– W –

WALKER, ALICE (1944–). The bisexual black American writer and activist Alice Walker was born into a sharecropping family in the southern states. She attended Spelman College (a historically black college for women) from 1961 and later Sarah Lawrence College (then also for women) in New York, where she was mentored by Muriel Ruykeyser. Walker was active in the Civil Rights movement of the 1960s, and some of her experiences with antiracist work in the American south are reflected in her novel *Meridian* (1976). Her first novel was *The Third Life of Grange Copeland* (1970). Most significant here are *The Color Purple* (1982) and *Possessing the Secret of Joy* (1992). *The Color Purple* is an epistolary **bildungsroman** in which the main character, Celie, is a southern black woman with a history of sexual and violent abuse. Part of Celie's journey toward empowerment and a stable sense of self is her relationship with the sexually emancipated blues singer, Shug Avery. The novel won Walker the Pulitzer Prize, but was also heavily criticized within the black and white communities for a variety of reasons. Hayward, California, public schools refused to purchase it, and it was banned in at least two other states. Critics claimed, among other things, that its colloquial southern black dialogue was disempowering to black Americans. Critics also objected to the novel's depiction of child sexual abuse. *Possessing the Secret of Joy* was written as a protest against the practice of female circumcision, in both Africa and the Western world. This novel includes a celebration of the idea of an ancient pan-sexuality that includes the sensual love of nature and the love of women for each other. Walker continues her work as an activist. Among many collections of her essays is *Anything We Love Can Be Saved: A Writer's Activism* (1997). She is important as a literary critic for her "rediscovery" of the work of the American anthropologist and novelist Zora Neale Hurston.

WALLADAH BINT AL-MUSTAKFI (1001–1080). The Arabic-language poet Walldah Bint Al-Mustakfi, lived most of her life in Andalusia, where her father was a colonial governor. She held an influential literary salon and wrote verse that drew on a strong women's tradition in Arabic. Much of the sentiment she expresses would be called feminist today. Al-Mustakfi has been referred to by Western **orientalists** as "the Arab **Sappho**," because she addressed many poems to her lover Muhjah, a woman. Most of these have been lost due to reticence in reproducing them because of their lesbian content.

WARNER, SYLVIA TOWNSEND (1893–1978). The English writer and political activist Sylvia Townsend Warner was born in London and lived her later life in Dorset. Her collections of poetry include *The Espalier* (1925) and *Time Importuned* (1928). She published the novel *Lolly Willowes*, a fantasy about a witch, in 1926. This was followed by *Mr. Fortune's Maggot* (1927) and *The True Heart* (1928). Her 1936 novel *Summer Will Show* describes a romantic relationship between two women during the 1848 revolution in France. Her acknowledged masterpiece is the novel *The Corner That Held Them* (1948), a historical novel about a group of 14th-century nuns. Later collections of short stories include *The Innocent and the Guilty* (1971) and *Kingdoms of Elfin* (1977). In 1930 Warner met and fell in love with the writer **Valentine Ackland**, and the two lived together until Ackland's death in 1969. Together Warner and Ackland published the poetry collection *Whether a Dove or a Seagull* in 1933. This collection is significant in that it refused to espouse what some critics see as the patriarchal notion of individual authorship. The first edition did not make it clear who had authored which poems, though critics (perhaps fairly) declared Ackland the inferior poet and claimed to be able to distinguish the two writers' work.

Warner was a committed leftist who joined the communist party in 1935. In 1937, during the Spanish Civil War, she attended the International Conference of Writers in Defence of Culture in Barcelona. Both she and Ackland were active in the fight against the rise of fascism in Europe in the 1930s. The papers of both Warner and Ackland are held in a special room of the Dorchester Public Library in Dorset.

WATERS, SARAH (1966–). British lesbian writer of historical novels. Sarah Waters published her first novel *Tipping the Velvet* in 1998 and achieved almost immediate popular success. *Affinity* (1999) and *Fingersmith* (2002) followed. These first three novels make use of popular 19th-century novelistic forms—the **bildungsroman**, the Gothic novel and the **sensation novel** respectively—for the articulation of a **postmodern** concept of lesbian identity. Waters' technique involves intensive historical research into the period in which the novels are set as well as the history of lesbian identifications and representations in English culture.

WEIMAR REPUBLIC. Germany declared its first republican government in the final days of World War I, after the resignation of the Kaiser. During this period the country was experiencing terrible economic hardship and social unrest. Berlin was considered unsafe for the new government, which removed to the city of Weimar, thus gaining the name the Weimar Republic. The period generally referred to as Weimar Germany lasted from 1918 until the Nazis began to gain power in 1930.

In 1918 and 1919 several cities in Germany were taken over by disillusioned returning soldiers and worker's councils and the Social Democratic Party controlled the republican government. The Weimar constitution was adopted in the summer of 1919 and an atmosphere of political leftism and relative tolerance prevailed throughout the 1920s. Due to the economic instability that was the legacy of the Kaiser's rule and the war debt imposed on the republic by the victors of WWI, the republic never managed to stabilize the economy or gain entire social control. This left the field open for the rise of the extreme right in the 1930s.

The era of the Weimar Republic is significant here in that it represents the first forum in which a recognizably modern lesbian identity gained mass visibility and a reasonable level of acceptance. German women had been allowed political participation since 1908 and a strong women's movement had existed since the mid-19th century. Magnus Hirschfeld's Scientific Humanitarian Committee had included women among its members for decades and this political and cultural support led to a strong lesbian community that was often conscious of the need for political organization. Thus many lesbian bars in Weimar Berlin carried a stamp of approval from Hirschfeld's committee and the several national lesbian magazines, which flourished during the era and encouraged women to patronize only these bars.

One must be careful not to assume that expressions of lesbianism in this era were entirely empowering and positive in the way we might think of today. The science of **sexology** largely informed popular ideas of lesbianism and transgender identities, as held by heterosexuals and lesbians alike. Therefore many lesbians and transgender women saw themselves as biologically different, almost as freaks of nature. At this time the idea of biologically determined sexual identity was empowering for many women, as it allowed a claim to human rights and tolerance. A hundred years later, however, some of the fiction and poetry produced then may seem overly tragic and disempowering.

Alongside a flourishing club culture and a film industry that began to seriously address lesbians for the first time, a number of writers, such as **Anna Elisabeth Weirauch**, published openly lesbian works. National magazines such as *Die Freundin* included poetry and fiction in each of their issues. Conservatives who decried this openness about sexuality saw the links between feminism, political leftism and the increased opportunities for lesbian expression and visibility.

Due to its existence as a period of tremendous sexual experimentation and openness and its abundance of mass cultural production, Weimar Germany is a popular object of study among scholars of gender and sexuality. Beginning in 1980 with Lillian Fadermann and Brigitte Eriksson's *Lesbians in Germany: 1890s–1920s*, a number of excellent books on the subject have been produced. Anke Gelber's *The Art of Taking a Walk: Flanerie, Literature and Film in Weimar Germany* (1999) presents a good overview of the popular culture of the period. In 1996 Allison Brown translated the German scholar Claudia Schoppmann's *Days of Masquerade: Life Stories of Lesbians during the Third Reich* into English. This work focuses on many women who lived through both the Weimar period and World War II. In 1933 a group of Nazi youth destroyed the archives of the Scientific Humanitarian Committee in Berlin. This marked the beginning of the Nazi persecution of many homosexual men and lesbians. Gay and lesbian literary and film production stopped almost completely. Within three years of a period of openness and tolerance, the rise of the extreme right crushed a vibrant subculture almost completely. *See also* JOURNALISM.

WEIRAUCH, ANNA ELISABETH (1887–1970). The Romanian-born writer Anna Elisabeth Weirauch spent most of her life in Germany. She spent her early career as a playwright but is most significant here for her novel *The Scorpion*. This was published in Germany in three volumes (standard for that time) beginning in 1919. *The Scorpion* tells the story of the suppression and eventual liberation of someone who is "different"—i.e., lesbian. It is an early example of the **coming-out** novel in that sense. Like **Edna St. Vincent Millay**

and **Virginia Woolf**, Weirauch eschews sexological and psychoanalytic explanations for her character's difference, focusing instead on the fact of difference itself. *The Scorpion* was republished as a **pulp** paperback under the title *Of Love Forbidden* by Fawcett's Crest line in 1958.

THE WELL OF LONELINESS. This novel was first published by **Radclyffe Hall** in 1928. *The Well of Loneliness* is famous primarily for its sensational **censorship** trials in both the United States and Great Britain. Through these trials it achieved a degree of notoriety and a lasting popularity it might never have achieved on its own.

The *Well* is not nearly as well written as Hall's earlier novel *The Unlit Lamp* (1924), which deals less openly with love between women. From the outset Hall set out in *The Well* to expose the "problem" of the female "invert." As her terminology shows, the work was heavily influenced by **sexological** discourse, in particular Havelock Ellis, whom she eventually convinced to write a preface. As a classic picture of **inversion** the book reads in many ways like a case history. Its main character Stephen Gordon is born with unusual bodily traits: "a strong little figure, narrow-hipped and wide-shouldered; her flanks as wiry and thin as a greyhound's." This description precisely echoes sexological "observations" about the bodily morphology of inverts. At the same time the narrator tells us that Stephen's parents greatly desired a boy and that she is in many ways treated like one. This leaves the reader with the question, is inversion a matter of nature or nurture? Is it an essential state of being or a socially constructed relationship to gender? In any event, it is clear throughout the novel that Stephen's desire for women is a product of her gender, which is masculine. She desires women because she ought to have been a man. Jay Prosser has argued convincingly that *The Well* is not a lesbian work but a transgender one. This explanation of the lesbian as the woman gendered masculine who desires feminine women, leaves us with the question, why do feminine women desire Stephen back? The novel attempts to answer this in a number of unsuccessful ways. Ultimately Stephen nobly sacrifices her partner Mary for a man who can make her "truly happy." Thus, the book erases the desire of feminine women for other women and it has been much criticized for this.

Radclyffe Hall preferred to describe women who loved women through the idea of inversion because inversion was seen as congenital. In arguing for the human rights of inverts Hall wanted to assert that they "were born that way" and "couldn't help it," therefore they did not deserve to be discriminated against. The issue of sexual freedom here is based, not on a critique of social structures of sexual control, but on the idea of human rights for those who are inescapably different. Hall saw the novel very much as an argument for the liberation of inverted women. The book's final sentences are "Acknowledge us, oh God, before the whole world. Give us also the right to our existence!" Its heavy-handed use of sexology and overly determined sense of **tragedy** leave Hall little room for narrative subtlety and good prose. It was this that led **Virginia Woolf** to describe the book as decidedly "dull." Nevertheless, Woolf and other **Bloomsbury** writers did attempt a defense of the book once it came under fire from the Home Office.

An upcoming general election certainly led to Conservative condemnation of the book, which was eventually printed in Paris. There was a trial in England that led to the book's banning. This ban was not lifted until 1948, though the book was read by those who purchased it from abroad. By the 1950s *The Well* was a common item in British lending libraries, where lesbians report having borrowed and read it. In 1929 the book was questioned and brought to trial in the United States. It sold thousands of copies while the Society for the Suppression of Vice tried every legal expedient to have it banned and the papers grew fascinated with the figure of Radclyffe Hall. The lawyer Morris Ernst, who also defended *Forever Amber* and *Ulysses*, achieved a victory in his defense of *The Well*.

The Well has never been out of print in the US and during the 1950s and 1960s it was issued in a number of mass-market paperback reprints. In countless life history accounts, lesbians of several generations mention this as the novel that influenced their lives more than any other.

WHITE, ANTONIA (1899–1980). The English novelist Eirene Botting published using this pseudonym throughout her life. She is most significant here for *Frost in May* (1933), which tells a story of girl's **school** romance and Catholic mysticism. Her characters, students at a girl's boarding school, persist in both religious and romantic excesses in spite of attempts to control them. The story does not end well, but nevertheless has been popular with lesbian audiences. White/Botting's other novels include *The Sugar House* (1952) and *Strangers* (1954).

WILHELM, GALE (1908–1991). The American novelist Gale Wilhelm spent most of her adult life living and writing in Berkley, California. Her 1935 novel *We Too Are Drifting* has become an American lesbian classic. Its plot, on the surface, appears very similar to **Radclyffe Hall**'s *The Well of Loneliness*. The novel features a lesbian protagonist who first has an unhappy affair with a bisexual woman and then a second affair with a young and innocent woman. Eventually she loses this partner to a man. Wilhelm's style, however, is more modernist than Hall's and her character portraits feel more internal and subjective. A second novel, *Torchlight to Valhalla* (1938), has also been very popular with lesbian audiences. Both of these works were reprinted by the lesbian Naiad Press in the 1980s. Wilhelm's novel *The Strange Path* appeared in **pulp** paperback form in 1961.

WINSLOE, CHRISTA (1888–1944). The German playwright and novelist Christa Winsloe is best known for the film adaptation of her play *The Child Manuela*. This appeared as *Mädchen in Uniform* in 1932. After the success (and censorship) of the film, Winsloe produced a novelistic version in 1933. The story tells of a defiant young schoolgirl's love for her female teacher. Interestingly, Nazi objections to the film seem to focus on it as an antiauthoritarian work, rather than as a lesbian one. English translations of the original play were already available in 1932, and this gives some idea of its popularity. Winsloe wrote an earlier novel that is significant here. It was titled *Men Return Home* (c.1920) and featured a young rape survivor. Set during World War I, the novel follows this woman as she passes for a man for the duration of the war. **Jeannette Foster** also documents another novel, translated in 1936 as *Girl Alone*, which includes a peripheral lesbian character who is hopelessly in love with the heroine. *See also* SCHOOLS.

WINTERSON, JEANETTE (1961–). The English novelist Jeannette Winterson was born in a working-class northern village and educated at Oxford University. Her first novel, *Oranges Are Not the Only Fruit*

(1985), is a semiautobiographical account of her fundamentalist Christian upbringing and first experiences of love. The novel was very successful and Winterson gained widespread recognition when it was adapted for television by the BBC. *Oranges* begins a set of experiments with magic realist style that is further pursued in the historical novels *The Passion* (1987) and *Sexing the Cherry* (1989). These two are perhaps Winterson's best works. While *Oranges* is productive of **identity** in the manner of the **coming-out** novel, *The Passion* and *Sexing the Cherry* allow room for lesbians and transgender characters to do things in novels other than become who they are. These novels, like *Oranges*, interrogate the idea of history and the process of storytelling itself. After *Sexing the Cherry*, Winterson's novels became increasingly self-conscious and less popular, though she maintains a devoted fan base. She is often held up as an example of the **postmodern** novelist, though her narrative experiments differ little, if at all, from those made by **modernist** writers such as **Virginia Woolf** and **Djuna Barnes**. *Gut Symmetries* (1997), is an example of this later work. Winterson's most recent novel to date is *Lighthousekeeping* (2004).

WITTIG, MONIQUE (1935–2003). The French novelist and critic Monique Wittig was a key figure in the lesbian feminist movement of the later 20th century. Her theory, exemplified by the collection *The Straight Mind and Other Essays* (1992), is a concise interrogation of the social history of feminine and lesbian subjects since the Enlightenment. She looks at these subjects as products both of the symbolic order expressed through language and of material structures of power. Her theory is thus important as a bridge between, or blending of, two very separate strands of thought about gender, the symbolic and the material. Wittig made an important early intervention in **cultural feminism** when she published, together with Sande Zeig, *Lesbian Peoples: Materials for a Dictionary* (1973).

Wittig's novels weave myth together with her political and philosophical inquiries. The first of these was *The Opoponax* (1964). *Les Guérillières* (1969) is an epic narrative that imagines a war between patriarchal and **amazon** warriors. Like many of Wittig's works it draws upon **classical** myth and culture. *The Lesbian Body* (1973) seeks to challenge the idea of a unified individual subject, expressed through the pronoun "I" (which Wittig writes in French as "j/e"). This novel dissects the human body (site of the subject) in prose to such an extent that its English translation required a medical professional. *Across the Acheron* (1987) plays upon the mythical Greek idea of the river between life and afterlife. Its French title, *Virgile, non*, makes clear Wittig's play on Virgil's *Aeneid* and Dante's *Divine Comedy*. Unlike these two travelers in the underworld, Wittig follows a female guide. Wittig lived and worked as an academic in the United States until her death in 2003.

WOLLSTONECRAFT, MARY (1759–1797). The political philosopher, novelist and critic Mary Wollstonecraft was associated with the English Jacobin movement of the 18th century. As such, her early thinking followed the French philosopher Jean-Jacques Rousseau, and saw the human individual as a product of social forces, rather than as an essential self, or product of divine intervention. Wollstonecraft is best known for her extended feminist political essay, *A Vindication of the Rights of Woman* (1792) and for *The Wrongs of Woman: or, Maria* (1798), which illustrated the same arguments through the fictional story of one woman's life. As Wollstonecraft is often pigeonholed as a "woman" writer, separate from the political movement exemplified by the men around her, it is often forgotten that these two works were preceded by *A Vindication of the Rights of Men* (1790). Wollstonecraft is significant here for her earliest fictional work, the semiautobiographical *Mary: A Fiction* (1788), which details one of several intense romantic friendships with other women that Wollstonecraft experienced throughout her life. In fictionalizing her own life, she did not intend to hide the facts of her biography. Rather, she was following a tradition begun by Rousseau and carried on by her contemporaries of imbuing fiction with social truth by drawing on the biographical details of the writer's own life. All of Wollstonecraft's other works are also highly significant here, however, for redefining the nature of women's role in the social arena and questioning long established social institutions such as marriage.

"WOMAN-IDENTIFIED-WOMAN" MANIFESTO. *See* MANIFESTOS.

WOOLF, VIRGINIA (1882–1941). The English critic and novelist born Virginia Stephen was raised in London, where she would have preferred to spend her life. A series of emotional breakdowns often led to long stays in the suburbs or the country for "rest." As a young woman she established, with her sister Vanessa, a house in the Bloomsbury neighborhood of London where a kind of salon or gathering place existed for a group of writers, visual artists, critics and composers who came to be known as the **Bloomsbury Group**. They advocated free love, leftist politics and the aesthetic principles of "modern" art. In 1910 she married Leonard Woolf, with whom she spent the rest of her life in a platonic partnership. The aristocratic writer **Vita Sackville-West** is said to have been the only person ever to arouse Woolf's passion. The two had a brief affair and a longer friendship.

It is important, though not always remembered, that when discussing Virginia Woolf a distinction should be made between her own experiences of same-sex desire and romantic attachment and her literary portraits of bisexual and **inverted** characters. Woolf's work is of incalculable importance to the development of literature in English overall and to lesbian literature specifically. Her character portraits are carefully painted and evidence her conscious refusal to portray same-sex desire or transgender movement through the lenses of **sexology** and **psychoanalysis**, which dominated sexually dissident literature at this period. Within the **modernist** movement, Woolf was the most consummate master of the new narrative techniques that allowed new constructions of human subjectivity. Her astonishing skill led to immediate popularity and critical respect within her own lifetime. Woolf published her first novel, *The Voyage Out*, in 1915. *Jacob's Room* (1922) and *To the Lighthouse* (1927) followed, the latter being a semi-autobiographical family portrait. *Mrs. Dalloway* (1925) is Woolf's most popular and influential novel. This contains a poignant memory of the lost opportunity for a lesbian relationship. Mrs. Dalloway remembers, years later, the one time she ever kissed a woman as the most perfect moment of her life. Most significant here may be the **transgender** historical fantasy *Orlando* (1925), which is based upon the family history of Sackville-West and dedicated to her. Woolf's most experimental novel is *The Waves* (1931) in which she takes her narrative experiments to their furthest point.

A Room of One's Own, Woolf's most famous essay, is a fictionalization of two lectures on women and fiction, which she gave at Oxford and Cambridge in 1928. The essay, which first appeared in 1929, is significant as both a feminist statement and a stylistic masterpiece. It has had a tremendous influence on feminist literary studies. The extended essay *Three Guineas* (1938) again uses a combination of fictional techniques and rhetoric to present a political argument, this time against fascism and patriarchal, militaristic regimes. With her husband Leonard, Woolf established the Hogarth Press, which printed a number of important modernist works, as well as the first English translations of the work of **Sigmund Freud**, made by Bloomsbury member James Strachey.

WU TSAO (c. 1800–?). The Chinese poet Wu Tsao was born into the 19th-century merchant class and worked within a strong female poetic tradition. She had an unhappy marriage and sought solace with a number of female courtesans, to whom she addressed her love poetry. Late in her life, she retired as a Taoist priestess. Some of her poems are translated into English and included in the anthology, *Orchid Boat: Woman Poets of China* (Kenneth Rexroth and Ling Chung, editors and translators, 1973).

– Y –

YOURÇENAR, MARGUERITE (1903–1987). Belgian-French writer, born Marguerite Crayencour. Yourçenar was born into a wealthy French family in Belgium and emigrated to the United States early in World War II. Mainly a writer of historical fiction, Yourçenar lived a lesbian life (for a long time with partner Grace Frick) but for the most part did not treat lesbianism or sexual relationships between women in her writing. Exceptions are a "Sonnet to Hermaphroditus" in an early collection of poetry and a tale from the 1936 collection *Feux*. *Feux* (Fires) is a collection of tales focused on **classical Greek** figures, interspersed with autobiographical material. The final one of these tales is "**Sappho**, ou le suicide." She is best known for the 1950 novel translated into English as *Memoirs of Hadrian*. Other novels include *Denier Du Rêve* (1934) and *Coup de Grâce* (1957). In 1980 she published a biographical study of the gay male writer Yukio Mishima, *Mishima: A Vision of the Void*. Here, she said, she tried to focus on the "universal" nature of Mishima's vision and tragedy, as opposed to his homosexuality. This exemplifies the stance of many writers of Yourçenar's generation, including **May Sarton**, who saw the specific **identity** lesbian as detracting from what they perceived as the all-important universal position of great literature. Yourçenar was made the first ever female member of the *Académie Française* in 1980. Her birthplace, at Bailleul near Lille, is now the *Musée de Marguerite Yourçenar*.

– Z –

ZOLA, EMILE (1840–1902). The French novelist Emile Zola began his career as a journalist. He published his first collection of short stories in 1864. Overall his work represents a tradition of 19th-century realism that paralleled the movement in Great Britain, and ran counter to the stylistics of the **decadent** works produced by **Honoré de Balzac** and **Théophile Gautier**. Like Balzac, Zola wrote a number of interlinked novels. *La Curée* (1874), *Nana* (1880) and *Potbouille* (1883) all include characters that can be read as **sapphic**. Most significant here is *Nana*, which details the life of a tremendously successful courtesan. The eponymous Nana is a horribly decadent figure and her excessive sexuality is fantastically connected with the imminent downfall of Parisian civilization itself. Through Nana, as through a rupture in the social fabric, the resources of the nation are drained. In the course of her increasing addiction to sexual excess, Nana begins a lesbian relationship with a young woman named Satin. This episode introduces us to what may perhaps be the first lesbian bar scene in literature, in the Café Laure. Zola clearly represents a subculture made up of what we might call **butch** and **femme** types here. The portrait overall is highly unfriendly. Nana's bisexuality is the ultimate sign of her immoral sexual excess and she dies tragically, after bringing the nation to the brink of ruin.

Bibliography

CONTENTS

Introduction	221
Works Quoted in the Dictionary	224
Archives and Special Collections	226
Scholarly Journals	227
Literary and Historical Criticism	227
Philosophical and Psychoanalytic Theory	230
Autobiography and Author Studies	231
Correspondence	237
Anthologies of Lesbian Literature	238

INTRODUCTION

As an area of study, lesbian literature is relatively new. In English at least, we must date its advent from the publication of Jeannette Foster's groundbreaking *Sex Variant Women in Literature* in 1957. Prior to this, no critical literary study had focused on the presentation of female same-sex desire in any genre of writing. It would be wrong, however, to assume that a body of lesbian literature existed unrecognized for centuries before Foster came along. Her study follows by less than 100 years the widespread recognition of lesbian as a category of female identity. Scholars of the early modern period such as Emma Donoghue and Valerie Traub, whose studies are included below, document both the use of the word lesbian and other related terms, as well as a growing body of erotic literature depicting female same-sex desire from at least the 18th century. Yet it was only with more recent changes in economic and social organization, and the consequent arrival of sexology and psychoanalysis in Western culture at large, that the category lesbian became a prominent means of organizing individual lives in our society. At the same time, literary criticism that focuses on the relation between literature and its social context, thus highlighting the relevance of questions of identity and sexuality to the production of literature, is also fairly new. Until the mid-20th century, literary criticism rested on ideas of artistic unity and a universally acknowledged "greatness" (or lack thereof) in the works under scrutiny.

The works of some German and English sexologists quote heavily from literature that depicts female same-sex love and sexual desire, as well as female-to-male transgender movement. Thus we might count men like Richard Von Kraft Ebing and Havelock Ellis as the earliest of critics of lesbian literature. Their motives, however, were in establishing the boundaries of social and medical identities, rather than the boundaries of literary genre. For the earliest exhaustive study one should turn to Jeanette Foster, whose work is not only still useful but now historically significant in its own right.

Foster's study focuses on the representation of female same-sex desire, rather than on the identity of the authors who may have created the works she studies. In this way she is able to trace the evolution of female same-sex desire as a literary trope, even in historical periods where the concept of the lesbian did not exist. For a brief period in the 20th century, during the 1960s, 1970s and 1980s, many critics, editors and authors became concerned with a fixed notion of lesbian identity as exclusive, rather than inclusive. This is reflected in anthologies and critical studies from this period. Terry Castle's recent anthology, *The Literature of Lesbian: A Historical Anthology from Ariosto to Stonewall* (2003), brings us back to the notion of tracing the idea of the lesbian in culture. Castle acknowledges her debt to Foster, but also brings us into a post-Foucauldian frame where we can study literature as one of the primary arenas in which what she calls "the idea of the lesbian" developed in our culture. So, lesbian literary criticism is as unstable and contingent as the idea of the lesbian herself. The texts listed in this bibliography are intended both to give an understanding of the broad and changing field of lesbian literary studies and a view of this historically changeable identity in literature itself.

Under the heading "Works Quoted in the Dictionary" I have included all of the editions from which my citations in the dictionary itself are drawn. These are intended to enable the interested researcher to follow my trail back for deeper inquiry.

Under the heading "Archives and Special Collections" I have included the largest and most historically significant collections of material relating to lesbians and lesbian literature. While the James C. Hormel Gay and Lesbian Centre in San Francisco is probably the largest and best-funded collection of material, the Lesbian Herstory Archives in Brooklyn, New York, is the most historically significant in the United States. The Magnus Hirschfeld Archive in Berlin has been revived since the destruction of Hirschfeld's original archive by fascists in 1933. It contains a wealth of material relating to the discipline of sexology, the early dissemination of the modern lesbian identity and the history of lesbian literature and activism in Germany.

The "Scholarly Journals" listed under that heading are the most widely distributed and well-respected academic periodicals that regularly publish lesbian studies material. Though a number of feminist and women's studies journals also frequently include lesbian material, they are omitted here in the interests of brevity.

Under the heading "Literary and Historical Criticism" I have included broad studies in lesbian literature, as well as those that focus on particular genres, historical periods or cultural spaces. As discussed above, Jeanette Foster's work is the best starting point for both beginning and advanced scholars, due to both her painstaking scholarship and the historical significance of her work. Lillian Faderman's *Surpassing the Love of Men* (1985) gives a good historical overview of the development of the lesbian identity in English-language culture and thus makes a good basic background for literary study. Though it is difficult to single out one critical volume, Paulina Palmer's *Contemporary Lesbian Writing* (1993) gives a good overview of contemporary critical ground, while *New Lesbian Criticism: Literary and Cultural Readings* (1992), edited by Sally Munt, gives a good background to relevant critical debates around lesbian writing and the lesbian identity. Kenneth Plummer's *Telling Sexual Stories* (1994) is an important study for anyone wanting to understand the relationship between literary narrative and the formation of sexual identities.

Under the heading "Philosophical and Psychoanalytic Theory," I have included both historically significant works, such as those of Sigmund Freud, and the most influential contemporary philosophical inquiries, such as those of Gloria Anzaldúa and Judith Butler. The particular essays by Freud that are included here are the most significant in terms of the development of psychoanalytic ideas of lesbian identity and are most often mentioned in studies of lesbian literature.

The section headed "Autobiography and Author Studies" contains memoirs and other autobiographical writings, as well as single-author studies on some of the most significant writers covered in the dictionary entries. The biographies of Colette and Radclyffe Hall are perhaps the most historically significant in terms of tracing both these two particular authors and, more broadly, the social settings that were instrumental in the development of the modern lesbian identity. The works on Angelina Weld Grimké, Lorraine Hansberry and Alice Dunbar Nelson begin to redress the Eurocentric bias of much American lesbian historiography and literary criticism.

The section on "Correspondence" contains several volumes of letters that detail lesbian affairs involving significant 19th- and 20th-century literary figures. The correspondence of Vita Sackville-West with both Violet Trefusis and Virginia Woolf have been particularly influential and are often referred to in literary studies of Woolf and West.

Under "Anthologies of Lesbian Literature" I have included a number of collections produced from the mid-20th century to the present day. Terry Castle's *The Literature of Lesbianism: A Historical Anthology from Ariosto to Stonewall* (2003) is the most exhaustive and reflects the most current scholarship. This work is best complimented by the historically significant *This Bridge Called My Back: Writings by Radical Women of Color* (1981), edited by Cherríe Moraga and Gloria Anzaldúa, which begins to redraw the landscape of American feminist and lesbian criticism through the eyes of African-American and Latina women. Sharon Lim-Hing's *The Very Inside* (1994) and Ashwini Sukthankar's *Facing the Mirror* (1999) present contemporary lesbian writing from East Asia and South Asia, respectively. Sarah Hoagland and Julia Penelope's *For Lesbians Only: A Separatist Anthology* (1992) presents a justification for an exclusive definition of lesbian literature that is interesting from a historical and critical standpoint.

WORKS QUOTED IN THE DICTIONARY

Acker, Kathy. *Don Quixote*. London: Paladin, 1986.
Anonymous. "Hic Mulier; or the Man Woman." In Barbara J. Baines (ed.), *Three Pamphlets on the Jacobean Feminist Controversy*. Delmar, N.Y.: Scholar's Facsimiles and Reprints, 1978.
Baudelaire, Charles. "Les femmes damnées." (Richard Howard, trans.) Quoted in Terry Castle (ed.), *The Literature of Lesbianism: A Historical Anthology from Ariosto to Stonewall*. New York: Columbia University, 2003.
Butler, Judith. *Gender Trouble: Feminism and the Subversion of Identity*. London: Routledge, 1990.
———. *Bodies That Matter: On the Discursive Limits of Sex*. London: Routledge, 1993.
Castle, Terry (ed.). *The Literature of Lesbianism: A Historical Anthology from Ariosto to Stonewall*. New York: Columbia University Press, 2003.
Chugtai, Ismat. *"The Quilt" and Other Stories*. (Tahira Naqvi and Syeda S. Hameed, trans.) Riverdale-on-Hudson, N.Y.: The Sheep Meadow Press, 1994.
De Gouges, Olympe. *The Rights of Woman*. (Val Stevenson, trans.) London: Pythia, 1989.

Fielding, Henry. *The Female Husband, or the surprising story of Mrs. Mart, alias Mr. George Hamilton.* Liverpool: Liverpool University Press, 1960.
Foster, Jeannette. *Sex Variant Women in Literature.* Tallahassee, Fla.: Naiad Press, 1985.
Freeman, Jo. "The Bitch Manifesto." Pittsburgh, Pa.: Know Inc., 1971.
Gay Liberation Front. "Gay Liberation Front Manifesto." London: Gay Liberation Front, 1979. (Housed in The British Library.)
Grahn, Judy. "The Confessions of Edward the Dyke." In *The Work of a Common Woman.* London: Onlywomen, 1985 (pp. 26–30).
Hall, Radclyffe. *The Well of Loneliness.* London: Virago, 1982.
Hamilton, Eliza Mary. "A Young Woman Seen in Church." In Terry Castle (ed.), *The Literature of Lesbianism: An Anthology From Ariosto to Stonewall.* New York: Columbia University Press, 2003 (pp. 424–25).
Lalita, K., and Susie Tharu (eds.). *Women Writing in India: 600 B.C. to the Twentieth Century.* New York: Feminist Press, 1991.
LeFanu, Sheridan. *Carmilla.* Mountain Ash, Wales: Sarob Press, 1998.
Love, Heather K. *Failure as a Way of Life: Ambivalence, Abjection and the Making of the Modern Lesbian Identity.* Doctoral Dissertation, University of Virginia, 2001.
MacLane, Mary. *The Story of Mary MacLane, by Herself.* London: Grant Richards, 1902.
Mansfield, Katherine. "Bliss." In *Short Stories.* London: Everyman Press, 1983.
Mavor, Elizabeth. *The Ladies of Llangollen: A Study in Romantic Friendship.* Harmondsworth, England: Penguin, 1971.
Mistral, Gabriela. "Give Me Your Hand." In *Selected Poems of Gabriela Mistral.* (Ursula K. LeGuin trans.) Santa Fe: Museum of New Mexico Press, 2003.
Mitchell, Juliet, and Jacqueline Rose. *Feminine Sexuality: Jacques Lacan and the École Freudienne.* New York: W. W. Norton, 1983.
Montague, Mary Wortley. *The Turkish Embassy Letters.* London: Virago, 1994.
Oram, Alison. "Sex Is an Accident: Feminism, Science and the Radical Theory of *Urania.*" In Laura Doan and Lucy Bland (eds.), *Sexology in Culture: Labelling Bodies and Desires.* Cambridge, UK: Polity Press, 1998.
Radicalesbians. "The Woman-Identified-Woman Manifesto." Pittsburgh, Pa.: Know Inc., 1970. (Housed at the Lesbian, Gay, Bisexual and Transgendered Collection at Duke University Library.)
Rich, Adrienne. "Compulosry Heterosexuality and Lesbian Existence." In *On Lies Secrets and Silence.* New York: W. W. Norton, 1980.
Robb, Graham. *Strangers: Homosexual Love in the Nineteenth Century.* London: Picador, 2003.
Rossetti, Christina. "The World." In *A Choice of Christina Rossetti's Verse.* London: Faber and Faber, 1970.

———. "Goblin Market." In Sandra Gilbert and Susan Gubar (eds.), *The Norton Anthology of Literature by Women: The Traditions in English*. New York: W. W. Norton, 1985.

Rowson, Everett K., and J. W. Wright Jr. *Homoeroticism in Classical Arabic Literature*. New York: Columbia University Press, 1997.

Sedgewick, Eve Kosofsky. *The Cohorence of Gothic Conventions*. London: Routledge, 1986.

Smith, Barbara. "The Race for Theory." In Gloria Anzaldúa (ed.), *Haciendo Caras/Making Face, Making Soul: Creative and Critical Perspectives by Feminists of Color*. San Francisco: Aunt Lute, 1990 (pp. 35–45).

Solanis, Valerie. *SCUM Manifesto*. New York: Verso, 2004.

Stanton, Elizabeth Cady (ed.). *The Women's Bible*. Boston: Northeastern University Press, 1993.

———. "Declaration of Sentiments." In E. C. Stanton, *A History of Woman Suffrage*. Rochester, N.Y.: Fowler and Wells, 1889.

White, Patricia. "Female Spectator, Lesbian Specter: *The Haunting*." In Diana Fuss (ed.), *Inside/Out: Lesbian Theories, Gay Theories*. London: Routledge, 1992 (pp. 142–172).

Wollstonecraft, Mary. *A Vindication of the Rights of Women*. London: Penguin, 1992.

Woolf, Virginia. *A Room of One's Own and Three Guineas*. Oxford: Oxford University Press, 1992.

ARCHIVES AND SPECIAL COLLECTIONS

Canadian Lesbian and Gay Archives, 56 Temperance Street, Suite 201, Toronto Canada (correspondence address: P.O. Box 639, Station A, Toronto, Ontario, M5W 1G2, Canada)

The Hall-Carpenter Archives, BM Archives, London, WC1N 3XX, England

The Human Sexuality Collection, Division of Rare and Manuscript Collections, 2B Karl Kroch Library, Cornell University, Ithaca, New York, 14853, USA

James C. Hormel Gay and Lesbian Center, San Francisco Public Library, 100 Larkin Street, San Francisco, California, 94102 USA

Lesbian Archives and Information Centre, The Glasgow Women's Library, 109 Trongate Street, Glasgow, G1 5HD, Scotland

Lesbian, Gay, Bisexual and Transgender Collection, Perkins Library, Duke University, Durham, North Carolina, 27708, USA

The Lesbian Herstory Archives, P.O. Box 1258, New York, New York, 10116, USA

Magnus Hirschfeld Archive for Sexology, Humboldt-Universität zu Berlin, Prenzlauer Promenade 149-152, D-131189, Berlin, Germany

Sakhi Collective Delhi, Jami Project Archives, P.O. Box 3526 Lajpat Nagar, New Delhi, India (or P.O. box 7032, Srinawas Puri, New Delhi, 110 065, India)

SCHOLARLY JOURNALS

GLQ: A Journal of Lesbian and Gay Studies, Duke University Press
Journal of Homosexuality, Haworth Press
Journal of Lesbian Studies, Haworth Press
Journal of Women's History, Indiana University Press
Woman: A Cultural Review, Routledge Publications
Sexualities, Sage Publications

LITERARY AND HISTORICAL CRITICISM

Abel, Elizabeth. *Writing and Sexual Difference*. Chicago: Chicago University Press, 1982.

Abelove, Henry, Michèle Aina Barale, and David M. Halperin. *The Lesbian and Gay Studies Reader*. New York and London: Routledge, 1993.

Abraham, Julie. *Are Girls Necessary?: Lesbian Writings and Modern Histories*. London: Routledge, 2002.

Abukhalil, As'ad. "A Note on the Study of Homosexuality in Arab/Islamic Civilization." *Arab Studies Journal* 1(2), pp. 32–34.

Aidoo, Ama Ata. "Literature Feminism and the African Women Today." In Delia Jarrett-Macauley (ed.), *Reconstructing Womanhood, Reconstructing Feminism: Writings on Black Women*. London: Routledge, 1996 (pp. 156–174).

Allen, Carolyn. *Following Djuna: Women Lovers and the Erotics of Loss*. Bloomington: Indiana University Press, 1996.

Allen, Paula Gunn. *The Sacred Hoop: Recovering the Feminine in American Indian Traditions*. Boston: Beacon Press, 1986.

Andreadis, Harriette. *Sappho in Early Modern England: Female Same-Sex Literary Erotics, 1550–1714*. Chicago: University of Chicago Press, 2001.

Anzaldúa, Gloria. *Borderlands/La Frontera: The New Mestiza*. San Francisco: Aunt Lute Books, 1987.

——— (ed.). *Haciendo Caras/Making Face, Making Soul: Creative and Critical Perspectives by Women of Color*. San Francisco: Aunt Lute Books, 1990.

Beauvoir, Simone de. *The Second Sex* (H. M. Parshley, ed. and trans.) London: Penguin, 1987 (first published as *Le Deuxième Sexe*, 1949).

Collecott, Diana. *H.D. and Sapphic Moderism, 1910–1950.* Cambridge, UK: Cambridge University Press, 1999.

Davis, Madeline, and Elizabeth Lapovsky Kennedy. *Boots of Leather, Slippers of Gold: The History of a Lesbian Community.* New York: Routledge, 1993.

Doan, Laura (ed.). *The Lesbian Postmodern.* New York: Columbia University Press, 1994.

———. *Fashioning Sapphism: The Origins of a Modern English Lesbian Culture.* New York: Columbia University Press, 2001.

Doan, Laura, and Jay Prosser (eds.). *Palatable Poison: Critical Perspectives on the Well of Loneliness.* Chichester, N.Y.: Columbia University Press, 2001.

Donoghue, Emma. *Passions between Women: British Lesbian Culture 1668–1801.* London: Scarlet Press, 1993.

Duberman, Martin B., Martha Vicinus, et al. (eds.). *Hidden from History: Reclaiming the Gay and Lesbian Past.* New York: New American Library, 1989.

DuPlessis, Rachel Blau. *Writing Beyond the Ending: Narrative Strategies of Twentieth-Century Women Writers.* Bloomington: Indiana University Press, 1985.

Faderman, Lillian. *Surpassing the Love of Men: Romantic Friendship and Love between Women from the Renaissance to the Present.* London: The Women's Press, 1985.

———. *Odd Girls and Twilight Lovers.* Harmondsworth, England: Penguin, 1991.

Foster, Jeannette. *Sex Variant Women in Literature.* Tallahassee, Fla.: Naiad Press, 1985 (first published by Vantage Press in 1956).

Freedman, Estelle, et al. (eds.). *The Lesbian Issue: Essays from Signs.* Chicago University Press, 1985.

Galvin, Mary E. *Queer Poetics: Five Modernist Women Writers.* Westport, Conn.: Greenwood Press, 1999.

Grahn, Judy. *Another Mother Tongue: Gay Words, Gay Worlds.* Boston: Beacon Press, 1984.

———. *The Highest Apple: Sappho and the Lesbian Poetic Tradition.* San Francisco: Spinster's Ink, 1985.

Grier, Barbara. *The Lesbian in Literature: A Bibliography.* Tallahassee, Fla., Naiad Press, 1981.

Griffin, Gabriele (ed.). *Outwrite: Lesbianism and Popular Culture.* London: Pluto Press, 1993.

Hallet, Nicky. *Lesbian Lives: Identity and Auto/biography in the Twentieth Century.* London: Pluto Press, 1999.

Hull, Gloria T. *Color, Sex and Poetry: Three Women Writers of the Harlem Renaissance.* Bloomington: Indiana University Press, 1987.

Jay, Karla, and JoAnne Glasgow (eds.). *Lesbian Texts and Contexts: Radical Revisions.* London: Onlywomen Press, 1992.

Jones, Sonya (ed.). *Gay and Lesbian Literature since World War II: History and Memory*. New York: Harrington Park Press, 1998.

Keller, Yvonne. "Pulp Politics: Strategies of Vision in Pro-Lesbian Pulp Novels, 1955–1965. In Patricia Juliana Smith (ed.), *The Queer Sixties*. London: Routledge, 1999 (pp. 1–25).

deLauretis, Teresa. *Technologies of Gender: Essays on Film, Theory and Fiction*. Bloomington: Indiana University Press, 1987.

McRuer, Robert. *The Queer Renaissance: Contemporary American Literature and the Reinvention of Lesbian and Gay Identities*. New York University Press, 1997.

Marcus, Eric. *Making History: The Struggle for Gay and Lesbian Rights: 1945–1990*. New York: Harper Collins,1992.

Marks, Elaine, and George Stambolian (eds.). *Homosexualities and French Literature*. Ithaca, N.Y.: Cornell University Press, 1979.

Meese, Elizabeth. *Sem(erotics): Theorizing Lesbian Writing*. New York University Press, 1992.

Munt, Sally (ed.). *New Lesbian Criticism: Literary and Cultural Readings*. Hemel Hempstead, England: Harvester Wheatsheaf, 1992.

Murray, Stephen O., and Will Roscoe. *Islamic Homosexualities: Culture, History and Literature*. New York University Press, 1997.

Palmer, Paulina. *Contemporary Lesbian Writing*. Milton Keynes, England: Open University Press, 1993.

Plummer, Kenneth. *Telling Sexual Stories: Power, Change and Social Worlds*. London: Routledge, 1994.

Prosser, Jay. *Second Skins: The Body Narratives of Transsexuality*. New York: Columbia University Press, 1998.

Radstone, Sussanah (ed.). *Sweet Dreams: Sexuality, Gender and Popular Fiction*. London: Lawrence and Wishart, 1998.

Raitt, Suzanne (ed.). *Volcanoes and Pearl Divers: Lesbian Feminist Studies*. London: Onlywomen Press, 1993

Ratti, Rakesh (ed.). *A Lotus of Another Color: An Unfolding of the South Asian Lesbian and Gay Experience*. Boston: Alyson, 1993.

Robb, Graham. *Strangers: Homosexual Love in the Nineteenth Century*. London: Picador, 2003.

Rosenberg, Caroll Smith. "The Female World of Love and Ritual: Relations between Women in Nineteenth-Century America." *Signs* 1 (1975), pp. 1–29.

Rowson, Everett K., and J. W. Rowson. *Homoeoticism in Classical Arabic Literature*. New York: Columbia University Press, 1987.

Scott, Bonnie Kime (ed.). *The Gender of Modernism: A Critical Anthology*. Bloomington: Indiana University Press, 1990.

Sedgwick, Eve Kosofsky. *Epistemology of the Closet*. London: Penguin, 1990.

Sinfield, Allen. *Out on Stage: Lesbian and Gay Theatre in the Twentieth Century*. New Haven, Conn.: Yale University Press, 1999.
Stein, Arlene. *Sex and Sensibility: Stories of a Lesbian Generation*. Berkeley: University of California Press, 1997.
Thadani, Giti. *Sakhiyani: Lesbian Desire in Ancient and Modern India*. London: Cassell, 1996.
Traub, Valerie. *The Renaissance of Lesbianism in Early Modern England*. Cambridge, UK: Cambridge University Press, 2002.
Vanita, Ruth, and Saleem Kidwai (eds.). *Same-Sex Love in India: Readings from Literature and History*. London: Macmillan, 2000.
Waelti-Walters, Jennifer. *Damned Women: Lesbians in French Novels, 1796–1996*. Montreal: McGill-Queen's University Press, 2000.
Wahl, Elizabeth Susan. *Invisible Relations: Representations of Female Intimacy in the Age of Enlightenment*. Stanford, Calif.: Stanford University Press, 1999.
Warner, Michael (ed.). *Fear of a Queer Planet: Queer Politics and Social Theory*. Minneapolis: University of Minnesota Press, 1994.
Winkel, Laurie. "The 'Sweet Assasin' and the Performative Politics of the *SCUM Manifesto*." In Patricia Juliana Smith (ed.), *The Queer Sixties*. London, Routledge, 1999, pp. 62–85.
Zimmerman, Bonnie. *Lesbian Histories and Cultures: An Encyclopaedia*. New York: Garland, 2000.
Zimmerman, Bonnie, and George E. Haggerty (eds). *Professions of Desire: Lesbian and Gay Studies in Literature*. New York: Modern Language Association, 1995.

PHILOSOPHICAL AND PSYCHOANALYTIC THEORY

Anzaldúa, Gloria. *Borderlands/La Frontera: The New Mestiza*. San Francisco: Aunt Lute Books, 1987.
Butler, Judith. *Gender Trouble: Feminism and the Subversion of Identity*. London: Routledge, 1990.
———. *Bodies That Matter: On the Discursive Limits of Sex*. London: Routledge, 1993.
———. *The Psychic Life of Power*. Stanford, Calif.: Stanford University Press, 1997.
Daly, Mary. *Beyond God the Father: Toward a Philosophy of Women's Liberation*. Boston: Beacon Press, 1973.
Freud, Sigmund. "Femininity." In *The Standard Edition of the Complete Psychological Works of Sigmund Freud, Volume XXII*. London: Hogarth Press, 1964 (original essay, 1933).

———. "Psychogenesis of a Case of Homosexuality in a Woman." In *The Standard Edition of the Complete Psychological Works of Sigmund Freud, Volume XVII*. London: Hogarth Press, 1955 (original essay, 1920).

———. "Fragment of an Analysis of a Case of Hysteria." In *The Standard Edition of the Complete Psychological Works of Sigmund Freud, Volume VII*. London: Hogarth Press, 1953 (original essay, 1905).

———. "Some Psychical Consequences of the Anotomical Distinction between the Sexes." In *The Standard Edition of the Complete Psychological Works of Sigmund Freud, Volume XIX*. London: Hogarth Press, 1961 (original essay, 1925).

Fuss, Diana. *Essentially Speaking*. London: Routledge, 1989.

———. *Inside/Out: Lesbian and Gay Theories*. London: Routledge, 1991.

Kristeva, Julia. *Powers of Horror: An Essay on Abjection*. New York: Columbia University Press, 1982.

Lacan, Jacques. *Écrits: A Selection*. (Bruce Fink et al., trans.) New York: W. W. Norton: 2002.

Mitchell, Juliet, and Jacqueline Rose (eds.). *Feminine Sexuality: Jacques Lacan and the École Freudienne*. London: Macmillan, 1982.

Roof, Judith. *A Lure of Knowledge: Lesbian Sexuality and Theory*. New York: Columbia University Press, 1991.

AUTOBIOGRAPHY AND AUTHOR STUDIES

Valentine Ackland

Ackland, Valentine. *For Sylvia: An Honest Account*. London: Chatto and Windus, 1985.

Mulford, Wendy. *This Narrow Place: Sylvia Townsend Warner and Valentine Ackland: Life, Letters and Politics*. London: Rivers Oram, 1988.

Djuna Barnes

Field, Andrew. *Djuna: The Life and Times of Djuna Barnes*. New York: Putnam, 1983.

Parsons, Deborah. *Djuna Barnes* (Writers and Their Work Series). Plymouth, England: Northcote House, 2003.

Natalie Clifford Barney

Jay, Karla. *The Amazon and the Page: Natalie Clifford Barney and Renée Vivien*. Bloomington: Indiana University Press, 1988.

Rodriguez, Suzanne. *Wild Heart: A Life: Natalie Clifford Barney and the Decadence of Literary Paris*. New York: Ecco, 2003.
Souhami, Diana. *Wild Girls: Natalie Barney and Romaine Brooks*. London: Weidenfield and Nicolson, 2004.

Sylvia Beach

Beach, Sylvia. *Shakespeare and Company*. London: Faber and Faber, 1960.
Fitch, Noel Riley. *Sylvia Beach and the Lost Generation*. Harmondsworth, England: Penguin, 1985.

Aphra Behn

Todd, Janet. *The Secret Life of Aphra Behn*. London: Pandora, 1999.
——— (ed.). *Aphra Behn Studies*. Cambridge, UK: Cambridge University Press, 1996.
———, and Derek Hughes (eds.). *The Cambridge Companion to Aphra Behn*. Cambridge, UK: Cambridge University Press, 2004.

Eva Gore-Booth and Esther Roper

Lewis, Gifford. *Eva Gore-Booth and Esther Roper: A Biography*. London: Pandora, 1988.

Eleanor Butler and Sara Ponsonby

Butler, Eleanor. *Ladies of Llangollen: Letters and Journals of Lady Eleanor Butler and Sarah Ponsonby*. Marlborough, England: Adam Matthew, 1997.
Gordon, Mary Louisa. *Chase of the Wild Goose: The Story of Lady Eleanor Butler and Miss Sarah Ponsonby, Known as the Ladies of Llangollen*. London: L. and V. Woolf, 1936.
Mavor, Elizabeth. *The Ladies of Llangollen: A Study in Romantic Friendship*. Harmondsworth, England: Penguin, 1973.
Pritchard, John. *An Account of the Ladies of Llangollen*. Llangollen, Wales: H. Jones, 1880.

Willa Cather

Bloom, Harold (ed.). *Willa Cather* (Modern Critical Views). Langhorne, Pa.: Chelsea House, 1991.

Stout, Janis P. *Willa Cather: The Writer and Her World*. Charlottesville and London: University Press of Virginia, 2000.

Colette

Hinde, Joan Stewart. *Colette*. Boston: Twayne, 1983.
Thurman, Judith. *Secrets of the Flesh: A Life of Colette*. London: Bloomsbury, 1999.

Daphne Du Maurier

Aurbach, Nina. *Daphne Du Maurier: Haunted Heiress*. Philadelphia: University of Pennsylvania Press, 2002.
Du Maurier, Daphne. *The Rebecca Notebook and Other Memories*. London: Virago, 2005.
Foster, Margaret. *Daphne Du Maurier*. Pittsfield, Mass.: Arrow, 1994.

Michael Field

Donoghue, Emma. *We Are Michael Field*. Bath, England: Absolute, 1998.
Sturgeon, Mary. *Michael Field*. London: G. G. Harrap, 1922.
Thain, Marion (ed.). *Michael Field and Fin-de-Siècle Culture and Society: The Journals, 1868–1914*. Marlborough, England: Adam Mattew, 2003.

Emma Goldman

Falk, Candace. *Love, Anarchy and Emma Goldman*. New Brunswick, N.J.: Rutgers University Press, 1990.
Moritz, Theresa. *The World's Most Dangerous Woman: A New Biography of Emma Goldman*. Vancouver, BC: Subway, 2001.

Angelina Weld Grimké

Hull, Gloria T. *Color, Sex and Poetry: Three Women Writers of the Harlem Renaissance*. Bloomington: Indiana University Press, 1987.
Miller, Erika M. *The Other Reconstruction: Where Violence and Womanhood Meet in the Writing of Ida B. Wells-Barnett, Angelina Weld Grimké and Nella Larsen*. New York: Garland, 1999.

Radclyffe Hall

Baker, Michael. *Our Three Selves: A Life of Radclyffe Hall*. London: Hamilton, 1985.

Souhami, Diana. *The Trials of Radclyffe Hall*. London: Virago, 1999.
Troubridge, Una. *The Life and Death of Radclyffe Hall*. London: Hammond, 1961.

Loraine Hansberry

Cheney, Anne. *Lorraine Hansberry*. Boston: Twayne, 1984.
Nemiroff, Robert (ed.). *To Be Young, Gifted and Black: Lorraine Hansberry in Her Own Words*. New York: Prentice Hall, 1969.

Lorena Hickock

Faber, Doris. *Life of Lorena Hickock: E.R.'s Friend*. New York: William Morrow, 1980.

Sarah Orne Jewett

Donovan, Josephine. "The Unpublished Love Poems of Sarah Orne Jewett." *Frontiers: A Journal of Women's Studies*. 4.3 (1979), pp. 26–31.
———. *Sarah Orne Jewett*. New York: Unger, 1980.

Anne Lister

Liddington, Jill. *Presenting the Past: Anne Lister of Halifax*. Hebden Bridge, England: Pennine Pens, 1994.
Whitbread, Helena (ed.). *I Know My Own Heart: The Diaries of Anne Lister*. London: Virago, 1988.

Carson McCullers

Gleeson-White, Sarah. *Strange Bodies: Gender and Identity in the Work of Carson McCullers*. Tuscaloosa: University of Alabama Press, 2003.
Savigneau, Josyanne. *Carson McCullers: A Life*. London: The Women's Press, 2001.

Katherine Mansfield

Kaplan, Sydney Janet. *Katherine Mansfield and the Origins of Modernist Fiction*. Ithaca, N.Y.: Cornell University Press, 1991.
Smith, Angela. *Katherine Mansfield. A Literary Life*. Basingstoke, England: Palgrave, 2000.

Gabriela Mistral

Fiol-Matta, Lucia. *A Queer Mother for the Nation: The State and Gabriela Mistral*. Minneapolis: University of Minnesota Press, 2002.

Mary Wortley Montague

Halsband, Robert. *The Life of Lady Mary Wortley Montague*. Oxford University Press, 1960.

Alice Dunbar Nelson

Hull, Gloria T. (ed.). *Give Us Each Day: The Diary of Alice Dunbar Nelson*. New York: W. W. Norton, 1984.

Anaïs Nin

Tookey, Helen. *Anaïs Nin, Fictionality and Femininity: Playing a Thousand Roles*. Oxford: Clarendon, 2003.

Richard-Allerdyce, Diane. *Anaïs Nin and the Remaking of Self: Gender, Modernism and Narrative Identity*. Dekalb: Northern Illinois University Press, 1998.

Mary Renault

Zilboorg, Caroline. *The Masks of Mary Renault: A Literary Biography*. Columbia: University of Missouri Press, 2001.

Dorothy Richardson

Bronfen, Elisabeth. *Dorothy Richardson's Art of Memory: Space, Identity, Text*. England: Manchester University Press, 1999.

Winning, JoAnne. *The Pilgrimage of Dorothy Richardson*. Madison: University of Wisconsin Press, 2000.

Christina Rossetti

Marsh, Jan. *Christina Rossetti: A Literary Biography*. London: Cape, 1994.

Vita Sackville-West

Glendenning, Victoria. *Vita: The Life of Vita Sackville-West*. London: Wiedenfield and Nicolson, 1983.

George Sand

Jack, Belinda Elizabeth. *George Sand: A Woman's Life Writ Large*. London: Chatto and Windus, 1999.

Sappho

Snyder, Jane McIntosh. *Lesbian Desire in the Lyrics of Sappho*. New York: Columbia University Press, 1997.

May Sarton

Fulk, Mark K. *Understanding May Sarton*. Columbia: University of South Carolina Press, 2001.
Peters, Margot. *May Sarton: A Biography*. New York: Knopf, 1997.

Gertrude Stein

Souhami, Diana. *Gertrude and Alice: Gertrude Stein and Alice B. Toklas*. London: Wiedenfield and Nicolson, 2000.
Walker, Jayne L. *The Making of a Modernist: Gertrude Stein from Three Lives to Tender Buttons*. Amherst: University of Massachusetts Press, 1984.

Una Troubridge

Ormrod, Richard. *Una Troubridge: The Friend of Radclyffe Hall*. London: Cape, 1984.

Renée Vivien

Jay, Karla. *The Amazon and the Page: Natalie Clifford Barney and Renée Vivien*. Bloomington: Indiana University Press, 1988.
Perrin, Marie. *Renée Vivien, le corps exsangue: de l'anorexie mentale à la creation littéraire*. Paris: Harmattan, 2003.

Sylvia Townsend Warner

Harman Claire. *Sylvia Townsend Warner: A Biography*. London: Chatto and Windus, 1989.
────── (ed.). *The Diaries of Sylvia Townsend Warner*. London: Virago, 1995.
Mulford, Wendy. *This Narrow Place: Sylvia Townsend Warner and Valentine Ackland: Life, Letters and Politics*. London: Rivers Oram, 1988.

Mary Wollstonecraft

Johnson, Claudia L. *The Cambridge Companion to Mary Wollstonecraft*. Cambridge, UK: Cambridge University Press, 2002.
Taylor, Barbara. *Mary Wollstonecraft and the Feminist Imagination*. Cambridge, UK: Cambridge University Press, 2003.

Virginia Woolf

Bell, Quentin. *Virginia Woolf: A Biography*. London: Pimlico, 1996.
Perry, Michèle. *"This Loose, Drifting Material of Life": A Reading of Virginia Woolf's Diaries*. Oxford University Press, 2003.
Snaith, Anna. *Virginia Woolf: Public and Private Negotiations*. New York: St. Martin's Press, 2000.

CORRESPONDENCE

DeSalvo, Louise (ed.). *The Letters of Vita Sackville-West to Virginia Woolf*. London: Virago, 1984.
Dillon, Millicent (ed.). *Out in the World: Selected Letters of Jane Bowles, 1935–1970*. Santa Barbara, Calif.: Black Sparrow Press, 1985.
Fields, Annie (ed.). *Letters of Sarah Orne Jewett*. New York: Houghton Mifflin, 1911.
Leaska, Mitchel A. and John Phillips (eds). *Violet to Vita: The Letters of Violet Trefusis to Vita Sackville-West*. London: Mandarin, 1989.
Pinney, Sussanah (ed.). *I'll Stand by You: The Letters of Sylvia Townsend Warner and Valentine Ackland*. London: Pimlico, 1998.
Sherman Susan (ed.). *Dear Juliette: Letters of May Sarton to Juliette Huxley*. New York: W. W. Norton, 1999.
Streitmatter, Rodger (ed.). *Empty without You: The Intimate Letters of Eleanor Roosevelt and Lorena Hickok*. New York: Simon and Schuster, 1998.

ANTHOLOGIES OF LESBIAN LITERATURE

Anzaldúa, Gloria. (ed.) *Haciendo Caras/Making Face, Making Soul: Creative and Critical Perspectives by Feminists of Color.* San Francisco: Aunt Lute Books, 1990.
Anzaldúa, Gloria, and Cherrie Moraga (eds.). *This Bridge Called My Back: Writings by Radical Women of Color.* Watertown, Mass.: Persephone Press, 1981.
Barber, Karen (ed.). *Bushfire: Stories of Lesbian Desire.* Boston: Lace Publications, 1991.
Castle, Terry (ed.). *The Literature of Lesbianism: A Historical Anthology from Ariosto to Stonewall.* New York: Columbia University Press, 2003.
Coote, Stephen (ed.). *The Penguin Book of Homosexual Verse.* London: Penguin, 1983.
Donaghue, Emma (ed.). *Poems between Women: Four Centuries of Love, Romantic Friendship and Desire.* New York: Columbia University Press, 1997.
Fadermann, Lillian (ed.). *Chloe Plus Olivia: An Anthology of Lesbian Literature from the Seventeenth Century to the Present.* London: Penguin, 1994.
Gomez, Alma, and Cherrie Moraga. *Cuentos: Stories by Latinas.* New York: Kitchen Table/Women of Color Press, 1983.
Hoagland, Sarah, and Julia Penelope (eds). *For Lesbians Only: A Separatist Anthology.* London: Onlywomen Press, 1992.
Joyce, Delaney L., and Catherine E. McKinley (eds.). *Does Your Mama Know?: An Anthology of Black Lesbian Coming Out Stories.* Redbone Press, 1998.
Keesey, Pam (ed.). *Dark Angels: Lesbian Vampire Stories.* Cleis Press, 1995.
Koppelman, Susan (ed.). *Two Friends and Other Nineteenth-Century Lesbian Stories by American Women.* Norman: Oklahoma University Press, 1991.
Lim-Hing, Sharon (ed.). *The Very Inside: An Anthology of Writing by Asian and Pacific Islander Lesbian and Bisexual Women.* Toronto, Ont.: Sister Vision Press, 1994.
Ramos, Juanita (ed.). *Compañeras: Latina Lesbians.* London: Routledge, 1994.
Sukthankar, Ashwini. *Facing the Mirror: Lesbian Writing from India*, Delhi: Penguin Books, 1999.

About the Author

Meredith Miller was born on Long Island, in New York. She lived for many years in New Orleans. There she gained a bachelor's degree in a general studies program entitled Women's Culture as World Literature from the University of New Orleans in 1993. At the same time she learned to eat fire with other Lesbian Avengers. In 1996 she earned a master's in English and comparative literature from Columbia University. That year, on her birthday, Manhattan was covered with six feet of snow in one day. In 1997 Meredith moved to Sussex, England, to begin a Ph.D. in English literature, which she completed in 2001. She lived with her daughter on the campus of the University of Sussex for three years. She now lives in Plymouth, England, just under Dartmoor. She teaches English and creative writing at the College of St. Mark and St. John, affiliated with Exeter University. Her published articles include "Secret Agents and Public Victims: The Implied Lesbian Reader" (*Journal of Popular Culture* 35.1, Summer, 2001) and "*The Feminine Mystique*: Sexual Excess and the Pre-Political Housewife" (*Woman a Cultural Review* 16.1, Spring, 2005).